S0-BBJ-280

®

References for the Rest of Us! ®

COMPUTER BOOK SERIES FROM IDG

Are you intimidated and confused by computers? Do you find that traditional manuals are overloaded with technical details you'll never use? Do your friends and family always call you to fix simple problems on their PCs? Then the *...For Dummies®* computer book series from IDG Books Worldwide is for you.

...For Dummies books are written for those frustrated computer users who know they aren't really dumb but find that PC hardware, software, and indeed the unique vocabulary of computing make them feel helpless. *...For Dummies* books use a lighthearted approach, a down-to-earth style, and even cartoons and humorous icons to diffuse computer novices' fears and build their confidence. Lighthearted but not lightweight, these books are a perfect survival guide for anyone forced to use a computer.

> *"I like my copy so much I told friends; now they bought copies."*
>
> **Irene C., Orwell, Ohio**

> *"Quick, concise, nontechnical, and humorous."*
>
> **Jay A., Elburn, Illinois**

> *"Thanks, I needed this book. Now I can sleep at night."*
>
> **Robin F., British Columbia, Canada**

Already, hundreds of thousands of satisfied readers agree. They have made *...For Dummies* books the #1 introductory level computer book series and have written asking for more. So, if you're looking for the most fun and easy way to learn about computers, look to *...For Dummies* books to give you a helping hand.

™

IDG BOOKS WORLDWIDE

7/96r

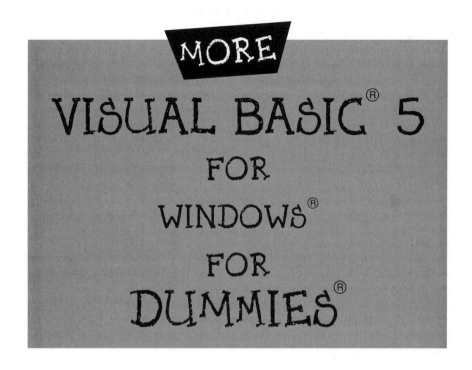

MORE
VISUAL BASIC® 5
FOR
WINDOWS®
FOR
DUMMIES®

by Wallace Wang

Author of *Visual Basic® 5 For Windows® For Dummies®*

IDG Books Worldwide, Inc.
An International Data Group Company

Foster City, CA ✦ Chicago, IL ✦ Indianapolis, IN ✦ Southlake, TX

MORE Visual Basic® 5 For Windows® For Dummies®

Published by
IDG Books Worldwide, Inc.
An International Data Group Company
919 E. Hillsdale Blvd.
Suite 400
Foster City, CA 94404
http://www.idgbooks.com (IDG Books Worldwide Web Site)
http://www.dummies.com (Dummies Press Web Site)

Copyright © 1997 IDG Books Worldwide, Inc. All rights reserved. No part of this book, including interior design, cover design, and icons, may be reproduced or transmitted in any form, by any means (electronic, photocopying, recording, or otherwise) without the prior written permission of the publisher.

Library of Congress Catalog Card No.: 97-70736

ISBN: 0-7645-0133-X

Printed in the United States of America

10 9 8 7 6 5 4 3 2 1

1B/RV/QV/ZX/IN

Distributed in the United States by IDG Books Worldwide, Inc.

Distributed by Macmillan Canada for Canada; by Transworld Publishers Limited in the United Kingdom and Europe; by WoodsLane Pty. Ltd. for Australia; by WoodsLane Enterprises Ltd. for New Zealand; by Longman Singapore Publishers Ltd. for Singapore, Malaysia, Thailand, and Indonesia; by Simron Pty. Ltd. for South Africa; by Toppan Company Ltd. for Japan; by Distribuidora Cuspide for Argentina; by Livraria Cultura for Brazil; by Ediciencia S.A. for Ecuador; by Addison-Wesley Publishing Company for Korea; by Ediciones ZETA S.C.R. Ltda. for Peru; by WS Computer Publishing Company, Inc., for the Philippines; by Unalis Corporation for Taiwan; by Contemporanea de Ediciones for Venezuela. Authorized Sales Agent: Anthony Rudkin Associates for the Middle East and North Africa.

For general information on IDG Books Worldwide's books in the U.S., please call our Consumer Customer Service department at 800-762-2974. For reseller information, including discounts and premium sales, please call our Reseller Customer Service department at 800-434-3422.

For information on where to purchase IDG Books Worldwide's books outside the U.S., please contact our International Sales department at 415-655-3023 or fax 415-655-3299.

For information on foreign language translations, please contact our Foreign & Subsidiary Rights department at 415-655-3021 or fax 415-655-3281.

For sales inquiries and special prices for bulk quantities, please contact our Sales department at 415-655-3200 or write to the address above.

For information on using IDG Books Worldwide's books in the classroom or for ordering examination copies, please contact our Educational Sales department at 800-434-2086 or fax 817-251-8174.

For press review copies, author interviews, or other publicity information, please contact our Public Relations department at 415-655-3000 or fax 415-655-3299.

For authorization to photocopy items for corporate, personal, or educational use, please contact Copyright Clearance Center, 222 Rosewood Drive, Danvers, MA 01923, or fax 508-750-4470.

LIMIT OF LIABILITY/DISCLAIMER OF WARRANTY: AUTHOR AND PUBLISHER HAVE USED THEIR BEST EFFORTS IN PREPARING THIS BOOK. IDG BOOKS WORLDWIDE, INC., AND AUTHOR MAKE NO REPRESENTATIONS OR WARRANTIES WITH RESPECT TO THE ACCURACY OR COMPLETENESS OF THE CONTENTS OF THIS BOOK AND SPECIFICALLY DISCLAIM ANY IMPLIED WARRANTIES OF MERCHANTABILITY OR FITNESS FOR A PARTICULAR PURPOSE. THERE ARE NO WARRANTIES WHICH EXTEND BEYOND THE DESCRIPTIONS CONTAINED IN THIS PARAGRAPH. NO WARRANTY MAY BE CREATED OR EXTENDED BY SALES REPRESENTATIVES OR WRITTEN SALES MATERIALS. THE ACCURACY AND COMPLETENESS OF THE INFORMATION PROVIDED HEREIN AND THE OPINIONS STATED HEREIN ARE NOT GUARANTEED OR WARRANTED TO PRODUCE ANY PARTICULAR RESULTS, AND THE ADVICE AND STRATEGIES CONTAINED HEREIN MAY NOT BE SUITABLE FOR EVERY INDIVIDUAL. NEITHER IDG BOOKS WORLDWIDE, INC., NOR AUTHOR SHALL BE LIABLE FOR ANY LOSS OF PROFIT OR ANY OTHER COMMERCIAL DAMAGES, INCLUDING BUT NOT LIMITED TO SPECIAL, INCIDENTAL, CONSEQUENTIAL, OR OTHER DAMAGES.

Trademarks: All brand names and product names used in this book are trade names, service marks, trademarks, or registered trademarks of their respective owners. IDG Books Worldwide is not associated with any product or vendor mentioned in this book.

is a trademark under exclusive license to IDG Books Worldwide, Inc., from International Data Group, Inc.

About the Author

If you're glancing at this page, you're probably either really bored or standing in a bookstore, trying to decide whether you should buy this book or not.

So to satisfy your curiosity about who writes these types of books, here's my biography so you can get to know me a little better:

Name: Wallace Evan Wang

Philosophy of This Book: "Computers are stupid and poorly designed, but this book will help you learn how to use them anyway."

Favorite Novels: *Catch-22* by Joseph Heller, *Another Roadside Attraction* by Tom Robbins, *Slaughterhouse-Five* by Kurt Vonnegut, *The Sotweed Factor* by John Barth, and *Birdy* by William Wharton.

Favorite Movies: *Pulp Fiction*, *The Sting*, *The Shawshank Redemption*, *Blood Simple*, *Fargo*, and *Babe* (the Australian talking pig movie).

Favorite Songs: "The Carpet Crawl" (Genesis), "Birdman" (Ian McDonald), "Fool's Overture" (Supertramp), "Bohemian Rhapsody" (Queen), "Turn the Page" (Bob Seger), "Heaven Tonight" (Cheap Trick), and "Brain Damage" (Pink Floyd).

Favorite Joke of Mine That Never Works on Stage: "The government has declared war on drugs to help protect the economy. That's good news because if too many people get addicted to crack or cocaine, there won't be enough people left to get hooked on cigarettes and alcohol."

E-mail addresses: 70334.3672@compuserve.com, bothekat@aol.com, bo_the_cat@msn.com, or bothecat@prodigy.net

ABOUT IDG BOOKS WORLDWIDE

Welcome to the world of IDG Books Worldwide.

IDG Books Worldwide, Inc., is a subsidiary of International Data Group, the world's largest publisher of computer-related information and the leading global provider of information services on information technology. IDG was founded more than 25 years ago and now employs more than 8,500 people worldwide. IDG publishes more than 275 computer publications in over 75 countries (see listing below). More than 60 million people read one or more IDG publications each month.

Launched in 1990, IDG Books Worldwide is today the #1 publisher of best-selling computer books in the United States. We are proud to have received eight awards from the Computer Press Association in recognition of editorial excellence and three from *Computer Currents'* First Annual Readers' Choice Awards. Our best-selling *...For Dummies®* series has more than 30 million copies in print with translations in 30 languages. IDG Books Worldwide, through a joint venture with IDG's Hi-Tech Beijing, became the first U.S. publisher to publish a computer book in the People's Republic of China. In record time, IDG Books Worldwide has become the first choice for millions of readers around the world who want to learn how to better manage their businesses.

Our mission is simple: Every one of our books is designed to bring extra value and skill-building instructions to the reader. Our books are written by experts who understand and care about our readers. The knowledge base of our editorial staff comes from years of experience in publishing, education, and journalism — experience we use to produce books for the '90s. In short, we care about books, so we attract the best people. We devote special attention to details such as audience, interior design, use of icons, and illustrations. And because we use an efficient process of authoring, editing, and desktop publishing our books electronically, we can spend more time ensuring superior content and spend less time on the technicalities of making books.

You can count on our commitment to deliver high-quality books at competitive prices on topics you want to read about. At IDG Books Worldwide, we continue in the IDG tradition of delivering quality for more than 25 years. You'll find no better book on a subject than one from IDG Books Worldwide.

John Kilcullen
CEO
IDG Books Worldwide, Inc.

Steven Berkowitz
President and Publisher
IDG Books Worldwide, Inc.

Eighth Annual Computer Press Awards ≥1992

Ninth Annual Computer Press Awards ≥1993

Tenth Annual Computer Press Awards ≥1994

Eleventh Annual Computer Press Awards ≥1995

IDG Books Worldwide, Inc., is a subsidiary of International Data Group, the world's largest publisher of computer-related information and the leading global provider of information services on information technology. International Data Group publishes over 275 computer publications in over 75 countries. Sixty million people read one or more International Data Group publications each month. International Data Group's publications include: **ARGENTINA:** Buyer's Guide, Computerworld Argentina, PC World Argentina; **AUSTRALIA:** Australian Macworld, Australian PC World, Australian Reseller News, Computerworld, IT Casebook, Network World, Publish, Webmaster; **AUSTRIA:** Computerwelt Österreich, Networks Austria, PC Tip Austria; **BANGLADESH:** PC World Bangladesh; **BELARUS:** PC World Belarus; **BELGIUM:** Data News; **BRAZIL:** Annuário de Informática, Computerworld, Connections, Macworld, PC Player, PC World, Publish, Reseller News, Supergamepower; **BULGARIA:** Computerworld Bulgaria, Network World Bulgaria, PC & MacWorld Bulgaria; **CANADA:** CIO Canada, Client/Server World, ComputerWorld Canada, InfoWorld Canada, NetworkWorld Canada, WebWorld; **CHILE:** Computerworld Chile, PC World Chile; **COLOMBIA:** Computerworld Colombia, PC World Colombia; **COSTA RICA:** PC World Centro America; **THE CZECH AND SLOVAK REPUBLICS:** Computerworld Czechoslovakia, Macworld Czech Republic, PC World Czechoslovakia; **DENMARK:** Communications World Danmark, Computerworld Danmark, Macworld Danmark, PC World Danmark, Techworld Denmark; **DOMINICAN REPUBLIC:** PC World Republica Dominicana; **ECUADOR:** PC World Ecuador; **EGYPT:** Computerworld Middle East, PC World Middle East; **EL SALVADOR:** PC World Centro America; **FINLAND:** MikroPC, Tietoverkko, Tietoviikko; **FRANCE:** Distributique, Hebdo, Info PC, Le Monde Informatique, Macworld, Reseaux & Telecoms, WebMaster France; **GERMANY:** Computer Partner, Computerwoche, Computerwoche Extra, Computerwoche FOCUS, Global Online, Macwelt, PC Welt; **GREECE:** Amiga Computing, GamePro Greece, Multimedia World; **GUATEMALA:** PC World Centro America; **HONDURAS:** PC World Centro America; **HONG KONG:** Computerworld Hong Kong, PC World Hong Kong, Publish in Asia; **HUNGARY:** ABCD CD-ROM, Computerworld Szamitastechnika, Internetto online Magazine, PC World Hungary, PC-X Magazin Hungary; **ICELAND:** Tolvuheimur PC World Island; **INDIA:** Information Communications World, Information Systems Computerworld, PC World India, Publish in Asia; **INDONESIA:** InfoKomputer PC World, Komputek Computerworld, Publish in Asia; **IRELAND:** ComputerScope, PC Live!; **ISRAEL:** Macworld Israel, People & Computers/Computerworld; **ITALY:** Computerworld Italia, Macworld Italia, Networking Italia, PC World Italia; **JAPAN:** DTP World, Macworld Japan, Nikkei Personal Computing, OS/2 World Japan, SunWorld Japan, Windows NT World, Windows World Japan; **KENYA:** PC World East African; **KOREA:** Hi-Tech Information, Macworld Korea, PC World Korea; **MACEDONIA:** PC World Macedonia; **MALAYSIA:** Computerworld Malaysia, PC World Malaysia, Publish in Asia; **MALTA:** PC World Malta; **MEXICO:** Computerworld Mexico, PC World Mexico; **MYANMAR:** PC World Myanmar; **NETHERLANDS:** Computer! Totaal, LAN Internetworking Magazine, LAN World Buyers Guide, Macworld Netherlands, Net, WebWereld; **NEW ZEALAND:** Absolute Beginners Guide and Plain & Simple Series, Computer Buyer, Computer Industry Directory, Computerworld New Zealand, MTB, Network World, PC World New Zealand; **NICARAGUA:** PC World Centro America; **NORWAY:** Computerworld Norge, CW Rapport, Datamagasinet, Financial Rapport, Kursguide Norge, Macworld Norge, Multimediaworld Norge, PC World Ekspress Norge, PC World Nettverk, PC World Norge, PC World ProduktGuide Norge; **PAKISTAN:** Computerworld Pakistan; **PANAMA:** PC World Panama; **PEOPLE'S REPUBLIC OF CHINA:** China Computer Users, China Computerworld, China InfoWorld, China Telecom World Weekly, Computer & Communication, Electronic Design China, Electronics Today, Electronics Weekly, Game Software, PC World China, Popular Computer Week, Software Weekly, Software World, Telecom World; **PERU:** Computerworld Peru, PC World Profesional Peru, PC World SoHo Peru; **PHILIPPINES:** Click!, Computerworld Philippines, PC World Philippines, Publish in Asia; **POLAND:** Computerworld Poland, Computerworld Special Report Poland, Cyber, Macworld Poland, Networld Poland, PC World Komputer; **PORTUGAL:** Cerebro/PC World, Computerworld/Correio Informático, Dealer World Portugal, Mac*In/PC*In Portugal, Multimedia World; **PUERTO RICO:** PC World Puerto Rico; **ROMANIA:** Computerworld Romania, PC World Romania, Telecom Romania; **RUSSIA:** Computerworld Russia, Mir PK, Publish, Seti; **SINGAPORE:** Computerworld Singapore, PC World Singapore, Publish in Asia; **SLOVENIA:** Monitor; **SOUTH AFRICA:** Computing SA, Network World SA, Software World SA; **SPAIN:** Communicaciones World España, Computerworld España, Dealer World España, Macworld España, PC World España; **SRI LANKA:** Infolink PC World; **SWEDEN:** CAP&Design, Computer Sweden, Corporate Computing Sweden, Internetworld Sweden, it.branschen, Macworld Sweden, MaxiData Sweden, MikroDatorn, Nätverk & Kommunikation, PC World Sweden, PCAktiv, Windows World Sweden; **SWITZERLAND:** Computerworld Schweiz, Macworld Schweiz, PCtip; **TAIWAN:** Computerworld Taiwan, Macworld Taiwan, NEW ViSiON/Publish, PC World Taiwan, Windows World Taiwan; **THAILAND:** Publish in Asia, Thai Computerworld; **TURKEY:** Computerworld Turkiye, Macworld Turkiye, Network World Turkiye, PC World Turkiye; **UKRAINE:** Computerworld Kiev, Multimedia World Ukraine, PC World Ukraine; **UNITED KINGDOM:** Acorn User UK, Amiga Action UK, Amiga Computing UK, Apple Talk UK, Computing, Macworld, Parents and Computers UK, PC Advisor, PC Home, PSX Pro, The WEB; **UNITED STATES:** Cable in the Classroom, CIO Magazine, Computerworld, DOS World, Federal Computer Week, GamePro Magazine, InfoWorld, I-Way, Macworld, Network World, PC Games, PC World, Publish, Video Event, THE WEB Magazine, and WebMaster; online webzines: JavaWorld, NetscapeWorld, and SunWorld Online; **URUGUAY:** InfoWorld Uruguay; **VENEZUELA:** Computerworld Venezuela, PC World Venezuela; and **VIETNAM:** PC World Vietnam.   3/24/97

Dedication

This book is dedicated to all Visual Basic programmers out there who can write better, faster, and more reliable programs using Visual Basic than other programmers using C++.

Author's Acknowledgments

Matt Wagner and Bill Gladstone at Waterside Productions both deserve a big thanks for getting me involved with this project. But in lieu of accolades, I'll just give them 15 percent of my royalties.

Clark Scheffy, Colleen Rainsberger, and Garrett Pease deserve a big thanks for reviewing this book for technical accuracy, grammatical correctness, and maximum joke potential to help make this book the best it could possibly be.

Thanks also go to all the wonderful people at The Comedy Store in La Jolla, California, including Fred Burns, Ron Clark, Frank Manzano, Dante, Karen Rontowski, Lamont Ferguson, Eric Schwandt and all the clueless waitresses there who keep whining because I never mention any of them in my books.

Final thanks go to Tasha, Scraps, and Bo the Cat. Anytime you see a "Bo the Cat" reference in any ...*For Dummies* computer book, you'll know that I had a hand in writing part of the text.

Publisher's Acknowledgments

We're proud of this book; please send us your comments about it by using the IDG Books Worldwide Registration Card at the back of the book or by e-mailing us at feedback/dummies@idgbooks.com. Some of the people who helped bring this book to market include the following:

Acquisitions, Development, and Editorial

Project Editor: Clark Scheffy

Senior Acquisitions Editor: Jill Pisoni

Acquisitions Editor:
Michael Kelly, Quality Control Manager

Product Development Director:
Mary Bednarek

Media Development Manager: Joyce Pepple

Technical Editor: Garrett Pease

Editorial Manager: Mary C. Corder

Editorial Assistant: Chris Collins

Production

Associate Project Coordinator:
E. Shawn Aylsworth

Layout and Graphics: Brett Black,
Angela F. Hunckler, Drew R. Moore,
Mark C. Owens, Brent Savage

Proofreaders: Ethel M. Winslow,
Laura L. Bowman, Joel K. Draper,
Dwight Ramsey, Robert Springer

Indexer: Richard Shrout

Special Help

Nancy DelFavero, Project Editor;

Colleen Rainsberger, Senior Project Editor;

Steve Hayes, Editorial Assistant

General and Administrative

IDG Books Worldwide, Inc.: John Kilcullen, CEO; Steven Berkowitz, President and Publisher

IDG Books Technology Publishing: Brenda McLaughlin, Senior Vice President and Group Publisher

Dummies Technology Press and Dummies Editorial: Diane Graves Steele, Vice President and Associate Publisher; Judith A. Taylor, Brand Manager; Kristin A. Cocks, Editorial Director

Dummies Trade Press: Kathleen A. Welton, Vice President and Publisher; Stacy S. Collins, Brand Manager

IDG Books Production for Dummies Press: Beth Jenkins, Production Director; Cindy L. Phipps, Supervisor of Project Coordination, Production Proofreading, and Indexing; Kathie S. Schutte, Supervisor of Page Layout; Shelley Lea, Supervisor of Graphics and Design; Debbie J. Gates, Production Systems Specialist; Tony Augsburger, Supervisor of Reprints and Bluelines; Leslie Popplewell, Media Archive Coordinator

Dummies Packaging and Book Design: Patti Sandez, Packaging Specialist; Lance Kayser, Packaging Assistant; Kavish + Kavish, Cover Design

✦

The publisher would like to give special thanks to Patrick J. McGovern,
without whom this book would not have been possible.

✦

Contents at a Glance

Cartoons at a Glance

By Rich Tennant • Fax: 508-546-7747 • E-mail: the5wave@tiac.net

page 209

page 7

page 313

page 361

page 103

page 263

page 167

Table of Contents

Introduction

●●

Since its introduction, Visual Basic has become one of the most popular ways to create Windows programs quickly and easily without losing your mind. Visual Basic is not only simple to use, it's also powerful enough to create programs that can rival almost anything the hard-core C++ programmers can put together.

Knowing that Visual Basic can create powerful programs is one thing, but being able to write these types of programs yourself is another. Just because you know how to use a hammer doesn't mean you know how to build a house.

The purpose of this book is to show you how to turn your Visual Basic knowledge and skill into practical applications. To give you a hand, each chapter covers a specific Visual Basic topic, and also contains plenty of source code to show you how Visual Basic programming works. By practicing with the sample programs provided in each chapter, you can gain experience using specific Visual Basic features in your own programs.

About This Book

This book is meant to be used as a quick reference to show you how to use certain features in Visual Basic. Some of the topics covered in this book are

- ✔ Using database files
- ✔ Creating animation
- ✔ Playing sound
- ✔ Compiling and distributing your Visual Basic programs for fun and profit

Although such topics might seem advanced and a little intimidating, relax. This book won't scare you away with lots of technical discussion and gibberish that only programmers care about and understand. Nor will it bombard you with page after page of program listings that only numb the senses and leave you with a feeling of despair and futility.

Instead, this book shows you how to do something in Visual Basic so you can use it in your own programs. Even though this book covers advanced topics, the explanations are short, simple, and easy to read. After all, programming can be a lot of fun once you know what you're doing, and this book will help you reach that level of competence as quickly as possible.

How to Use This Book

To help you use this book, all BASIC code appears in monospace type like this:

```
Printer.DrawWidth = Value
```

Type letter-for-letter anything that appears in **bold**. Any code that is not in bold is a placeholder where you can type your own information. In the preceding example, you would type `Printer.DrawWidth =` and then you would enter a number corresponding to the width of the line you wanted.

Because book margins are a fixed length, long lines of code may wrap to the next line. On your computer, those wrapped lines should appear as a single line of code, so don't insert a hard return when you see a wrapped line. You can identify wrapped lines because the second line appears indented like this:

```
Private Sub Form_KeyDown(KeyCode As Integer, Shift As Inte-
        ger)
```

Visual Basic doesn't care if you type everything in uppercase, lowercase, or both. However, it's a good idea to be consistent. All of the examples in this book use uppercase and lowercase in a style that Microsoft uses for their own Visual Basic examples. By following this style, you can ensure that other programmers can quickly understand your Visual Basic programs as well.

To make sure you understand the key ideas, each chapter provides a simple quiz, "Test your newfound knowledge." Unlike school quizzes that challenge you to fail, this book's quizzes emphasize real learning and enjoyment.

Each quiz presents four possible choices for each question. Although three of those choices will be so outrageously wrong that it will be easy for you to identify the correct answer, the questions will nevertheless help you remember specific Visual Basic topics, and the wrong answers can give you a good laugh as well.

Foolish Assumptions

If you're reading this book, it's obvious that you should know how to use Visual Basic well enough to load it, exit it, and create simple programs. If you're learning Visual Basic for the first time, pick up a copy of *Visual Basic 5 For Windows For Dummies* first. After you're familiar with the way Visual Basic works and want to create programs that can accomplish something worthwhile, you'll be ready for this book.

Besides knowing how to use Visual Basic and having a copy of Visual Basic loaded on your computer, a healthy dose of curiosity, fascination, and playfulness will come in handy too. After you start using Visual Basic, you'll find that programming can be as fun as creating structures out of Lego building blocks — except you won't have to pick up the pieces off the floor afterwards.

How This Book Is Organized

This book contains seven main parts. Each part focuses on a specific topic and contains several chapters. Each chapter explains the specific topic in more detail. Anytime you need help using Visual Basic, just browse through the table of contents to help you find the part and chapter containing the information you need.

To help you understand this book better, here are the seven parts of the book along with a brief description of what each part contains.

Part I: More on the User Interface

After a while, Visual Basic user interfaces can look depressingly similar. To provide a change of pace, Part I describes how to use several additional objects that can spice up your user interface and make your program even easier to use.

Part II: Holding, Storing, and Saving Information

Every program needs to store information at some point. In case your program needs to store lists of related information, you can create something useful called an array. Think of an array as an office filing cabinet, except you can actually find what you're looking for in an array.

Part III: Making Noise and Drawing Pictures

Multimedia has the become the latest fad by combining sound, graphics, and video so your computer can now mimic the educational content of MTV. If you've always wondered how to add sound, music, graphics, or video clips to your Visual Basic programs, look in Part III.

Part IV: Saving Stuff in and Retrieving Stuff from Files

After your Visual Basic program has accepted some data, it needs to find a place to store it. Part IV explains how to save and retrieve data as a text file, as a random access file, or an Access database file. In addition, this part also explains how to print pretty reports from your database files.

Part V: Using ActiveX Controls, OLE, DLL, API, and Other Confusing Acronyms

As powerful as Visual Basic may be, it still isolates you from the main features of Windows that allow C++ programmers to create dazzling programs. Fortunately, Part V explains how to combine Visual Basic with other programming languages, create your own ActiveX controls, and even tap into the hidden power of Windows itself.

Part VI: Polishing Your Program

When you complete your Visual Basic masterpiece and want to distribute it (for fun or profit) to others, you need to know how to test it for bugs and how to create an installation program so that complete novices can install your program on their own computer.

Part VII: Shortcuts and Tips Galore

Part VII contains tips for customizing Visual Basic along with sample programs that show you how to create certain effects such as splash screens, a Tip of the Day dialog box, or Easter Eggs (hidden features buried in a program). With the information in this part of the book, you can continue learning about Visual Basic until your head explodes with more knowledge than even Microsoft thought would be possible.

Icons Used in This Book

This icon highlights information that can get detailed (and sometimes amusing), but isn't necessary. Skip these if you want.

This icon flags some useful or helpful information that can make Visual Basic even easier to use.

Don't ignore these gentle reminders. These icons highlight important information that can be handy to know.

Watch out! Anytime you see this icon, it warns you of possible hazards that you can safely avoid as long as you follow the instructions carefully.

This icon points out step-by-step instructions that explain what is going on, such as explaining how each line of code in a program works.

Where to Go from Here

Now that you're ready to learn more about Visual Basic, turn on your computer, load Visual Basic, and get ready to start typing and practicing your newly acquired Visual Basic skills. The best way to learn anything is by doing (which explains why most people never forget about dissecting frogs in biology class).

So get ready to learn how to create even more powerful Visual Basic programs than ever before. Once you master some of Visual Basic's more advanced features, you'll be able to write better programs, ask for a raise, or even get a new job altogether.

Part I
More on the
User Interface

The 5th Wave   By Rich Tennant

"I TELL YA I'M STILL GETTING INTERFERENCE—
— COOKIE, RAGS? RAGS WANNA COOKIE? —
THERE IT GOES AGAIN."

In this part . . .

The best part about Visual Basic is that you can whip together a pretty and completely functional user interface in mere seconds. But what if you're tired of using the same objects to create your user interface? Well, Microsoft has loaded Visual Basic 5.0 with several new features and user interface objects to make your programs even fancier than before.

So let your imagination run wild and create the program of your dreams. Of course, after you create your user interface, you still have to use BASIC code to make it all work together, but that's covered in another part of this book.

Chapter 1

Manipulating Your
User Interface Objects

- -

- -

Sometimes the hardest part about writing a program is making it look halfway decent so people don't cringe every time they use it. Although no version of Visual Basic can design your user interface for you, Visual Basic 5 does provide several new features to help you create user interfaces with a minimal amount of trouble.

By taking advantage of user interface design shortcuts, you can spend less time doing tedious work and more time doing the fun stuff like writing BASIC code and seeing what happens when you try to run your program.

Selecting Multiple Objects

Before you can modify an object on your user interface, you must first select it. Visual Basic provides three ways to select a single object:

- ✔ Move the mouse pointer over the object and click the left mouse button (This is the easiest and simplest method, preferred by Visual Basic programmers the world over.)

- ✔ Click anywhere on the form containing the objects you want to select and press Tab (or Shift+Tab)

- ✔ Click on the downward-pointing arrow of the list box that appears in the top of the Properties window, and click on the object you want to select

To show which objects you've selected, Visual Basic displays little rect-angles, called handles, around the edges of the object.

While the previous three methods work for selecting a single object, what can you do if you want to select two or more objects? To select two or more objects, you have to use these methods:

✔ Hold down either the Shift or Ctrl key and click on each object that you want to select

✔ Move the mouse next to the objects you want to select, hold down the left mouse button, and drag the mouse. As you drag the mouse, Visual Basic displays a rectangle with a dotted line border and selects every object that this dotted line rectangle touches as soon as you release the left mouse button. Look at Figure 1-1 to see how you can select multiple objects with the mouse.

When you select two or more objects, only one object appears with dark handles around its edges while the remaining objects appear with "hollow" handles around the edges, as shown in Figure 1-2.

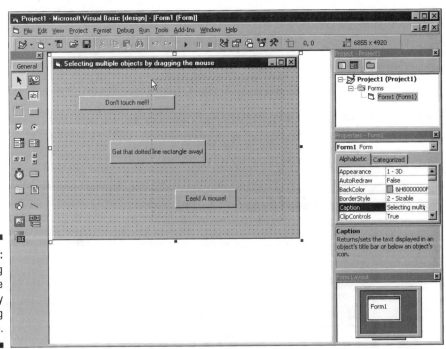

Figure 1-1:
Selecting
multiple
objects by
dragging
the mouse.

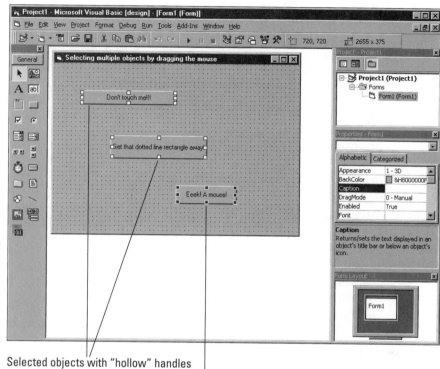

Figure 1-2:
Multiple
objects
selected on
a form.

Selected objects with "hollow" handles

Selected object with dark handles

Sizing Up Your Objects

Once you know how to select one or more objects, you can make all selected objects the same size, align all selected objects, or lock all selected objects so you (or another, obviously less-talented programmer) don't accidentally modify an object that shouldn't be changed.

If one object, such as a command button, is much bigger than another command button, the whole appearance of your user interface can look off-balance, distorted, or just plain amateur. Rather than spend your time measuring each object to make sure they're all the exact same size, let Visual Basic spend its time doing this tedious work for you.

If you select multiple objects by holding down the Shift or Ctrl key and clicking on each object, Visual Basic displays the last object with dark handles. This is the object that Visual Basic uses to determine the size of the other selected objects.

To make two or more objects the same size, follow these steps:

1. Select two or more objects using the methods described in the "Selecting Multiple Objects" section of this chapter. The selected object with the dark handles is the object that remains the same size; all other selected objects change to match this object's size.

2. Choose Format⇨Make Same Size and choose:

   • Width
   • Height
   • Both

Aligning Objects on Your User Interface

Despite everyone's best intentions, looks still make a difference, which explains why talentless actors and actresses can earn millions of dollars on TV shows by taking off their clothes while the rest of us have to work for a living. Since the appearance of your program can make a difference in the way people react to it, you should make your user interface look as pretty as possible.

To help you make your user interfaces aesthetically pleasing, Visual Basic lets you align your user interface objects in a variety of different ways. Aligning your objects alone doesn't necessarily make your user interface prettier, but it can be a first step to insuring that your user interface doesn't look ugly, awkward, or out of balance.

Aligning objects with one another

Besides making two or more objects the same size, you may also want to align two or more objects by the:

✔ Top of each object
✔ Bottom of each object
✔ Left edge of each object
✔ Right edge of each object
✔ Center of each object (measured vertically)
✔ Middle of each object (measured horizontally)

Figure 1-3 shows the six different ways to align objects on a form.

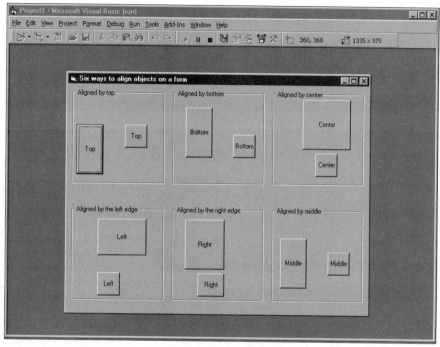

Figure 1-3:
The six different ways to align objects on a form.

If you select multiple objects by holding down the Shift or Ctrl key and clicking on each object, Visual Basic displays the last object with dark handles. This is the object that remains in place while the other selected objects move.

To align two or more objects, follow these steps:

1. Select two or more objects using the methods described in the "Selecting Multiple Objects" section in this chapter. The selected object with the dark handles is the object that stays put and that all other selected objects align themselves with.

2. Choose Format⇨Align and choose:

   • Lefts

   • Centers

   • Rights

   • Tops

   • Middles

   • Bottoms

Aligning objects to a form's grid

By default, Visual Basic already aligns objects to a default grid. However, if you really want to, you can tell Visual Basic never to align objects to the grid unless you specifically choose the Format⇨Align⇨to Grid command.

To set Visual Basic to never align objects to the grid unless you specifically tell it to, follow these steps:

1. Choose Tools⇨Options. An Options dialog box appears.

2. Click the General tab.

3. Make sure a check mark does not appear in the Align Controls to Grid check box and click OK.

Centering objects within a form

Visual Basic also gives you the choice of centering objects on a form, either horizontally or vertically. To center one or more objects on a form, follow these steps:

1. Select two or more objects using the methods described in the "Selecting Multiple Objects" section.

2. Choose Format⇨Center in Form and choose:

   • Horizontally

   • Vertically

Changing the spacing between two or more objects

Even if you align your objects perfectly on a form, you may still need to worry about the distance between your objects. Too large of a gap might look weird. Too small of a space between objects might make your user interface look crowded.

To avoid this problem, Visual Basic lets you adjust the spacing between multiple objects. To change the spacing between two or more objects on a form, follow these steps:

1. Select two or more objects using the methods described in the "Selecting Multiple Objects" section.

2. Choose Format⇨Horizontal Spacing or Vertical Spacing.

3. Choose one of the following:

- Make <u>E</u>qual — makes the spacing between all selected objects exactly the same

- <u>I</u>ncrease — slightly widens the space between all selected objects

- <u>D</u>ecrease — slightly narrows the space between all selected objects

- <u>R</u>emove — removes all spacing between all selected objects

You may have to choose the <u>I</u>ncrease or <u>D</u>ecrease command several times until the spacing between your selected objects looks exactly the way you want it to.

Locking Objects in Place

Occasionally you may draw an object on a form and decide that the object is perfectly positioned and sized just the way it is. To avoid moving or resizing an object by mistake, you can lock it in place. Once you lock an object in place, you can never move or resize that object again until you unlock the object.

To lock (or unlock) all objects on a single form, follow these steps:

1. Press Ctrl+R, choose <u>V</u>iew⇨<u>P</u>roject, or click the Project Explorer icon to display the Project Explorer window.

2. Highlight the .FRM Form file that contains the objects you want to lock (or unlock).

3. Choose F<u>o</u>rmat⇨<u>L</u>ock Controls. This command locks all objects that appear on the current form.

When you click on a locked object, Visual Basic displays the locked object with "hollow" handles around its edges. As long as you haven't selected two or more objects, "hollow" handles around an object tells you that the chosen object is locked.

Chapter 2

Drive, Directory, and File List Boxes

In This Chapter

▶ Creating drive, directory, and file list boxes

▶ Selecting files to display

▶ All about file attributes

*V*isual Basic gives you command buttons, check boxes, option buttons, list boxes, combo boxes, scroll bars, labels, pictures, and lines to adorn your user interface. Unfortunately, a pretty user interface is worthless if your program can't save and retrieve files from your disk. To do this, you need to write some Visual Basic code (see Chapters 16, 17, or 18) and use one or more of the following objects, as shown in Figure 2-1:

✔ Drive list box

✔ Directory list box

✔ File list box

Creating Drive, Directory, and File List Boxes

The drive list box displays a list of valid drives in a drop-down list box. The directory list box displays the directory tree of the current drive. The file list box displays a list of files stored in the current directory. By combining all three of these objects on a form, you can give users a way of selecting files stored on floppy, hard, or CD-ROM drives.

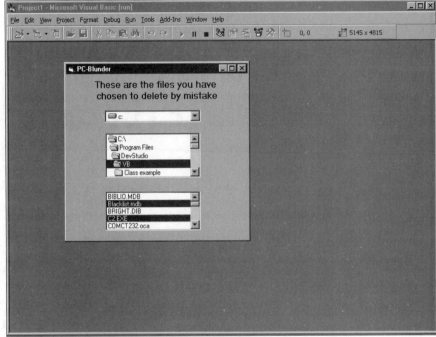

Figure 2-1:
The drive
list box, the
directory
list box, and
the file list
box working
in harmony
on a form.

To create a drive, directory, or file list box, follow these steps:

1. Click the Drive, Directory, or File list icon in the Visual Basic Toolbox as shown in Figure 2-2.

2. Move the mouse where you want to place the Drive, Directory, or File list box on the form.

3. Hold down the mouse button and move the mouse until the object is the size you want.

4. Let go of the mouse button.

The height for drive list boxes is always at 315 twips. In case you never learned about twips in elementary school, a twip is a screen-independent unit of measurement that Microsoft made up. There are approximately 1440 twips per inch or 567 twips per centimeter. If you draw a drive list box that's too big, Visual Basic automatically shrinks it back to a height of 315 twips whether you like it or not.

The Common Dialog control: a simpler alternative

Rather than wading through the problems of creating drive, directory, and file list boxes on your own, you can just use the Common Dialog control, which lets you create a standard Open or Save As dialog. If you want more flexibility, go ahead and learn to create drive, directory, and file list boxes. But if you just want to create an Open or Save As dialog box like you're used to seeing in Windows 95 programs, you're better off using the Common Dialog control.

The original *Visual Basic 5 For Windows For Dummies* book provides more detail on creating an Open or Save As dialog box. But to give you a quick idea of how to use the Common Dialog control without looking at another book, here are the steps you must follow to create an Open dialog box:

1. Draw the Common Dialog control on your form.

2. Write BASIC code to define the Filter property. For example:

```
CommonDialog1.Filter ="All
Files (*.*)|*.*| Text Files
(*.TXT)|*.TXT
```

3. Write BASIC code to define the FilterIndex, which determines what types of files the Open Dialog box displays first. For example:

```
CommonDialog1.FilterIndex = 2
'Displays Text Files
```

4. Write BASIC code to define the Action property of the Common Dialog control. For example:

```
CommonDialog1.ShowOpen  'Cre-
ates an Open dialog box
```

5. Create a variable to hold the file name the user chose, such as:

```
ChosenFile = Common
Dialog1.filename
```

Naming drive, directory, and file list boxes

As you might have just noticed, Visual Basic automatically names every object you create on a form. Because the names that Visual Basic chooses for objects are dull and unimaginative (such as Dir1 or Drive4), you should come up with your own names with the following restrictions:

- Names can be up to 40 characters long, including numbers or the underscore character (_).

- Names cannot include spaces, punctuation, or any naughty words that might upset censors.

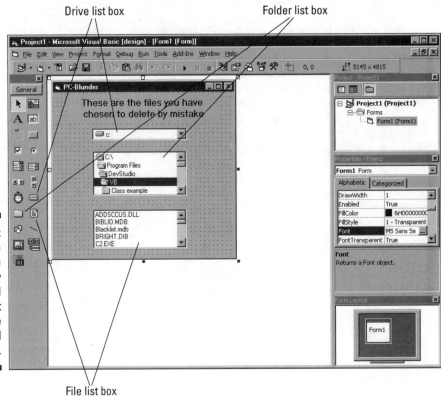

Figure 2-2:
The drive
list box, the
directory
list box, and
the file list
box on the
Toolbox and
form.

For drive list boxes, Visual Basic recommends that you begin the name with *drv*, such as

```
drvMeHome
drvOr_Take_The_42nd_Street_Bus
drvOr_Get_Off_The_Sidewalk
```

For directory list boxes, Visual Basic recommends that you begin the name with *dir*, such as

```
dirT
dire_Straits
dirtyWork66
```

For file list boxes, Visual Basic recommends that you begin the name with *fil*, such as

```
filPickAFile
filadelphia
fillip_ScrewDriver_Number_5
```

To change the name of a drive, directory, or file list box, follow these steps:

1. Click on the drive, directory, or file list box whose name you want to change.

2. Open the Properties window (by pressing F4, choosing View⇨Properties Window, or clicking on the Properties window icon on the toolbar).

3. Click on the Name property and type a new name.

Disabling drive, directory, and file list boxes

Every now and then, you still want to display a drive, directory, or file list box, but you may not want the user to be able to access a feature. This is known as *disabling,* or *graying out,* an item. From a user's point of view, this can also be known as confusion.

The appearance between a disabled and an enabled drive, directory, or file list box can be subtle and difficult to notice. To avoid confusion, it's probably a good idea not to disable these list boxes. So thank Microsoft for providing another virtually useless feature that most people will never need.

To disable a drive, directory, or file list box, follow these steps:

1. Click on the drive, directory, or file list box that you want to disable.

2. Open the Properties window (by pressing F4, choosing View⇨Properties Window, or clicking on the Properties window icon on the toolbar).

3. Click on the Enabled property and choose False.

When you disable a drive, directory, or file list box through the Property window, the chosen list box appears grayed whenever your program runs (though it may be hard to notice the difference). If a user clicks on a grayed drive, directory, or file list box, nothing happens.

Eventually, you have to enable (undim) a drive, directory, or file list box using BASIC code. To enable a list box, set the Enabled property to True. The following example enables a drive list box named drvMyComputer:

```
drvMyComputer.Enabled = True
```

To disable (dim) a list box through BASIC code, set the Enabled property to False. The following example disables a file list box named filListBox:

```
filListBox.Enabled = False
```

Once your program is running, you can disable and enable list boxes only through BASIC code. That way, you can disable and enable list boxes in response to whatever the user is doing (such as typing, moving the mouse, or pounding helplessly on the keyboard).

Making drive, directory, and file list boxes disappear

Rather than disabling a list box, you can make it disappear completely through the magic of invisibility.

To make a list box disappear, follow these steps:

1. Click on the list box you want to disappear.
2. Open the Properties window (by pressing F4, choosing <u>V</u>iew⇨Properties <u>W</u>indow, or clicking on the Properties window icon on the toolbar).
3. Click on the Visible property and set it to False.

Like disabled list boxes, invisible list boxes are absolutely useless unless you can make them visible once in a while. To make a list box visible again, you have to use BASIC code.

To make a list box disappear through BASIC code, set the list box's Visible property to False. The following example makes a directory list box named dirStructure disappear:

```
dirStructure.Visible = False
```

To make a list box appear again through BASIC code, set the Visible property to True. The following example makes a file list box named filFiles appear:

```
filFiles.Visible = True
```

Making text look pretty

For the sheer joy of it, Visual Basic lets you change the font, typestyle, and size of the text that appears in your drive, directory, or file list boxes. If you make it too weird, however, nobody will like using your program.

Fonts are different ways to display text, sometimes called typefaces. Normally, Visual Basic uses the MS Sans Serif font, but you can use any font in your computer. (MS Sans Serif is equivalent to the Helvetica font, and the MS Serif font is equivalent to the Times Roman font.)

To change the font of a drive, directory, or file list box, follow these steps:

1. Click on the drive, directory, or file list box whose text you want to modify.

2. Open the Properties window (by pressing F4, choosing View⇨Properties Window, or clicking on the Properties window icon on the toolbar).

3. Double-click on the Font property and click the ellipsis (. . .) that appears in the settings box. Visual Basic displays a Font dialog box like the one shown in Figure 2-3.

4. Click on the font, font style, size, or effects that you want. Visual Basic immediately shows you the appearance of your text in the Sample box.

5. Click OK.

Although fonts give you the chance to be creative, you can disorient users with bizarre fonts that don't look like anything normally found in nature. Unless you have a real good reason to use a different font, let Visual Basic use its default font of MS Sans Serif.

Coloring drive, directory, and file list boxes

Visual Basic believes in conserving colors by displaying text in boring black and white. For more color, spice, or kookiness, change the background or foreground colors of your list boxes.

The background color is defined by the BackColor property. The foreground color is defined by the ForeColor property. (Will wonders never cease?)

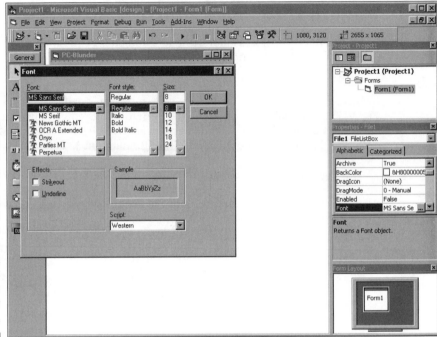

Figure 2-3:
The
Font dialog
box for
changing
the
appearance
of text in a
drive list
box, the
directory
list box, or
file list box.

To change the background or foreground color of a list box, follow these steps:

1. Click on the list box whose background or foreground color you want to change.

2. Open the Properties window (by pressing F4, choosing View⇨Properties Window, or clicking on the Properties window icon on the toolbar).

3. Double-click on the BackColor or ForeColor property in the Property Window.

4. Click the Palette tab. Visual Basic displays a color palette, as shown in Figure 2-4.

5. Click on the color you want. Visual Basic instantly obeys.

Selecting Files to Display in a File List Box

The drive list box always displays all the available drives on a computer without any help from you. Similarly, the directory list box always displays the directory structure of the current drive automatically.

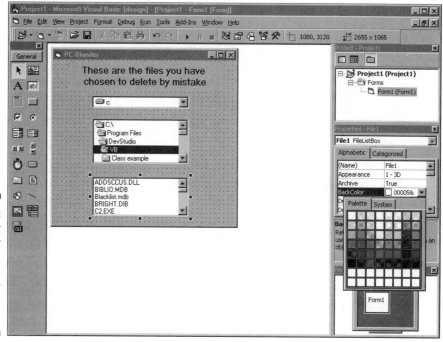

Figure 2-4:
The color palette for changing the foreground or background colors.

The file list box is different. A file list box displays only files that match its Pattern property. By default, the Pattern property is *.*, which means that the file list box will display every file it finds in a directory.

For those sharp DOS users out there, you may notice that the Pattern property works exactly like DOS wildcards. The asterisk (*) acts like a wildcard that represents one or more characters, and the question mark (?) acts like a wildcard that represents only one character.

For example, typing *.EXE in the Pattern property tells Visual Basic, "Find me all the files with the EXE file extension, and I don't care what the file names might be."

If the Pattern property were set to *.EXE, the file list box might display the following files:

```
VB.EXE
EXCEL.EXE
PROJECT.EXE
```

Typing H??.EXE in the Pattern property tells Visual Basic, "Find me all the files with a three-letter file name that begins with *H* and ends with the .EXE file extension."

If the Pattern property were set to H??.EXE, the file list box might display the following files:

```
HER.EXE
HLP.EXE
HOP.EXE
```

To change a file list box's Pattern property to display files selectively, follow these steps:

1. Click on the list box that you want to display files selectively.

2. Open the Properties window (by pressing F4, choosing <u>V</u>iew⇨Proper-ties <u>W</u>indow, or clicking on the Properties window icon on the toolbar).

3. Click on the Pattern property in the Property window.

4. Type a new pattern for choosing which files to display, such as *.EXE or H*.*.

Displaying files based on file attributes

Besides choosing files based on file names and file extensions, a file list box can also choose files based on five possible file attributes:

- ✔ Archive
- ✔ Hidden
- ✔ Normal
- ✔ Read-only
- ✔ System

To selectively display files based on their file attributes, follow these steps:

1. Click on the file list box that you want to selectively display files.

2. Open the Properties window (by pressing F4, choosing <u>V</u>iew⇨Proper-ties <u>W</u>indow, or clicking on the Properties window icon on the toolbar).

3. Click on the Archive, Hidden, Normal, ReadOnly, or System property in the Property window.

All about file attributes

The *archive attribute* marks files that have been previously copied with a backup program. Any new files you create or any old files that you modify will have their archive attribute set to False. Any old files that have already been copied by a backup program will have their archive attribute set to True.

The next time you back up your disk, the backup program can ignore all files with an archive attribute set to True and copy only files with an archive attribute set to False. By looking at the archive attribute, a backup program can avoid copying files that haven't changed since the last time you backed up your disk.

The *hidden attribute* hides a file from ordinary directory listing commands such as DIR or COPY. Hidden files are useful to keep users from accidentally erasing them.

The *read-only attribute* prevents a file from being modified, but lets it be viewed. This can be useful for preventing users from accidentally modifying a file.

The *system attribute* marks special files that do something useful with the operating system. Such files normally have both the hidden and system attributes set to True.

4. Change the property setting to True if you want to display files with a given attribute, or False if you don't want to display files with a given attributes.

5. Repeat Steps 3 and 4 to change multiple properties, such as changing both the Hidden and Archive attributes.

Letting the user select multiple files from the file list box

Normally, a file list box lets a user click and choose only a single file. Although this might be suitable in most cases (such as allowing a user to choose which file to open), you may want to let users select multiple files at once.

If you want to let users choose multiple files in a file list box, you have to change the file list box's MultiSelect property. The MultiSelect property offers three possible settings:

✔ 0 – None

✔ 1 – Simple

✔ 2 – Extended

0 – None is the default value and means that the file list box will let the user choose only one file at a time from the file list box.

1 – Simple means that the user can choose one or more files by clicking on them in the file list box.

2 – Extended means that the user can choose one or more files by holding down the Ctrl key and then clicking on a file. As an alternative, the user can also click on a file, hold down the Shift key, and then click another file. This selects a block of files, starting with the first file chosen and ending with the second file chosen, as shown in Figure 2-5.

To define how a user can select files displayed in a file list box, follow these steps:

1. Click on the file list box that you want to modify.

2. Open the Properties window (by pressing F4, choosing <u>V</u>iew⇨Proper-ties <u>W</u>indow, or clicking on the Properties window icon on the toolbar).

3. Click the MultiSelect property in the Property window.

4. Change its setting to 0 – None, 1 – Simple, or 2 – Extended.

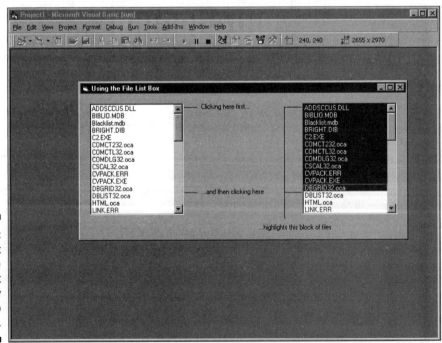

Figure 2-5:
A file list box with the MultiSelect property set to Extended.

Putting It to Practical Use

Drive, directory, and file list boxes must work together so that users can switch drives and directories to display files. But once you create a drive, directory, and file list box on a form, none of these three list boxes cooperate with one another. If you switch drives in the drive list box, the directory and file list boxes blindly displays the current directory and files.

To coordinate the drive, directory, and list boxes so that the currently displayed drive shows the correct directories and the files contained in those directories, you must connect all three list boxes using BASIC code.

To write BASIC code that synchronizes all three list boxes, follow these steps:

1. Draw a drive, directory, and file list box on a form.

2. Double click on the drive list box. Or click on the drive list box and press F7. Visual Basic displays an empty event procedure such as the following, where `Drive1` is the name of the drive list box:

```
Private Sub Drive1_Change ()
End Sub
```

3. Add a line in this event procedure so that it looks like this:

```
Private Sub Drive1_Change ()
   Dir1.Path = Drive1. Drive ' Set directory path
End Sub
```

In this example, `Drive1` is the name of the drive list box and `Dir1` is the name of the directory list box. If you've given your drive and directory list boxes different names, use those names instead of `Drive1` and `Dir1`.

4. Double click on the directory list box. Or click on the directory list box and press F7. Visual Basic displays an empty event procedure such as the following, where `Dir1` is the name of the directory list box:

```
Private Sub Dir1_Change ()
End Sub
```

5. Add a line in this event procedure so that it looks like this:

```
Private Sub Dir1_Change ()
   File1.Path = Dir1.Path ' Set file path
End Sub
```

In this example, `Dir1` is the name of the directory list box and `File1` is the name of the file list box. If you've given your directory and file list boxes different names, use those names instead of `Dir1` and `File1`.

Now if you run your program and change the drive in the drive list box, the program automatically displays the appropriate directory tree and files in the directory and file list boxes.

Which File Did the User Choose?

Once you have the drive, directory, and file list boxes synchronized to work together, you have one last task. When the user clicks on a file in the file list box, which one did he or she choose?

When the MultiSelect property is 0 – None

If the MultiSelect property of the file list box is set to 0 – None (which means users can select only one file), the answer is easy. When a user clicks on a file in the file list box, the file name gets stored in a property called FileName. So if the file list box name is `File1`, the name of the file that the user clicked on is stored in the following property:

```
File1.FileName
```

If you wanted to display the file name on the screen in a label named `Label1`, you could use the following event procedure:

```
Private Sub File1_Click ()
    Label1.Caption = File1.FileName
End Sub
```

This event procedure says, "Whenever the user clicks on a file in a file list box named File1, store this file name in the Caption property of a label named Label1," as shown in Figure 2-6.

When the MultiSelect property is 1 – Simple or 2 – Extended

If the MultiSelect property of the file list box is set to 1 – Simple or 2 – Extended, users can select one or more files displayed in the file list box. In these two cases, you can store the selected file names in a separate list box, as shown in Figure 2-7.

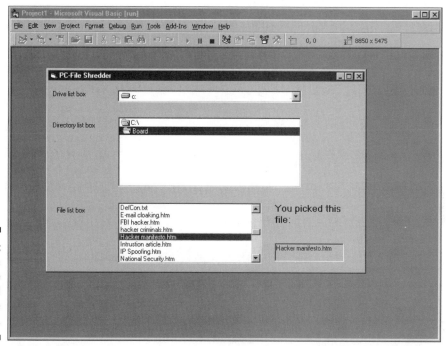

Figure 2-6:
Displaying a
file name
selected
from the file
list box.

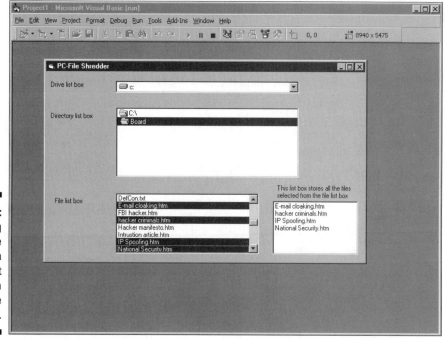

Figure 2-7:
Storing
multiple file
names from
a file list
box in a
separate
list box.

After creating a file list box and setting its MultiSelect property to 1 – Simple or 2 – Extended, you can store selected file names into the separate list box (named List1) by using the following event procedure:

```
Private Sub File1_Click ()
Dim Flag As Boolean
  Dim I As Integer
  InList = False
  For I = 0 To List1.ListCount - 1
    If File1.filename = List1.List(I) Then
      List1.RemoveItem I
      InList = True
    End If
  Next I

  If InList = False Then
    List1.AddItem File1.filename
  End If
End Sub
```

This event procedure works as follows:

1. The first line tells Visual Basic to use the following instructions any time the user clicks on a file list box named `File1`.

2. The second line declares a variable called `InList` as a Boolean, which means that `InList` can have a value of only True or False.

3. The third line declares a variable called `I` as an integer.

4. The fourth line sets the value of `InList` to False.

5. The fifth line tells Visual Basic to count from 0 to the number of items (minus 1 because Visual Basic is starting from 0) currently stored in a list box named `List1`.

6. The sixth line checks whether the file name that the user chose in the `File1` list box is already stored in the `List1` list box. If so, follow the instructions in lines 7, 8, and 9.

7. The seventh line removes the file name from the `List1` list box.

8. The eighth line sets the value of `InList` to True.

9. The ninth line marks the end of the If-Then statement that began on the sixth line.

10. The tenth line marks the end of the For-Next loop that began on the fourth line.

11. The eleventh line checks whether the value of InList is False. If so, follow the instructions in lines 12 and 13.

12. The twelfth line takes the file name selected in the File1 file list box and adds it to the List1 list box.

13. The thirteenth line marks the end of the If-Then statement that began on the eleventh line.

14. The fourteenth (last) line marks the end of the entire event procedure.

Try It Yourself

To give you a real-life, hands-on, hyphenated example that uses drive, directory, and file list boxes, create the following program, which lets you select multiple files from a file list box. By goofing around with this program and examining the BASIC code, you can better understand how drive, directory, and file list boxes can work together to make a better user interface for your own programs.

Test your newfound knowledge

1. What's one main advantage of the drive, directory, and file list boxes over ordinary list boxes?

   a. Ordinary list boxes require BASIC programming to get them to display anything useful. Drive, directory, and file list boxes automatically know how to display something useful right away.

   b. An ordinary list box will start displaying all your embarrassing memories unless you use BASIC code to program it differently.

   c. Drive, directory, and file list boxes don't work at all, but ordinary list boxes work on their own whether you like it or not.

   d. If you change the background color of an ordinary list box to black, you can see a list of all the people who your company has put on the blackball list.

2. How can you determine which types of files the file list box displays?

   a. Change the Pattern property of the file list box.

   b. Change your computer's hard disk.

   c. Erase all your files so you won't have to worry about different types of files any more.

   d. File list boxes never display anything. This is a trick question, isn't it?

Object	Property	Setting
Form	Caption	A drive, directory, and file list box example
	Height	4395
	Left	0
	Top	0
	Width	5145
Drive1	Left	240
	Top	120
	Width	2175
Dir1	Height	2350
	Left	240
	Top	720
	Width	2175
File1	Height	1650
	Left	2760
	MultiSelect	1 – Simple
	Top	120
	Width	1935
List1	Height	870
	Left	2760
	Top	2160
	Width	1935
Command1	Caption	E&xit
	Height	495
	Left	720
	Top	3360
	Width	1335
Label1	Caption	These are the files you selected
	Height	375
	Left	3000
	Top	3360
	Width	1575

Type the following in the *(General) (Declarations)* portion of the Code window:

```
Dim ShiftPressed As Boolean, ShiftFlag As Boolean,
         ControlPressed As Boolean
Dim FirstShift As String
```

Type the following in the Code window:

```
Private Sub Drive1_Change()
  Dir1.Path = Drive1.Drive
  List1.Clear
End Sub

Private Sub Dir1_Change()
  File1.Path = Dir1.Path
  List1.Clear
End Sub

Private Sub File1_Click()
  Dim Flag As Boolean
  Dim I As Integer, Start As Integer, Finish As Integer
  Flag = False
  Select Case File1.MultiSelect
    Case 0  ' MultiSelect is 0-None
      List1.Clear
      List1.AddItem File1.filename

    Case 1  ' MultiSelect is 1-Simple
      For I = 0 To List1.ListCount
        If File1.filename = List1.List(I) Then
          List1.RemoveItem I
          Flag = True
        End If
      Next I
      If Flag = False Then
        List1.AddItem File1.filename
      End If

    Case 2  ' MultiSelect is 2-Extended
      If (ControlPressed = False) And (ShiftPressed = False)
          Then
        List1.Clear
        List1.AddItem File1.filename
```

(continued)

(continued)

```
        FirstShift = File1.ListIndex
        ShiftFlag = True
    End If

    If (ControlPressed = True) And (ShiftPressed = False)
        Then
      For I = 0 To List1.ListCount - 1
        If File1.filename = List1.List(I) Then
          List1.RemoveItem I
          Flag = True
        End If
      Next I
      If Flag = False Then
        List1.AddItem File1.filename
      End If
    End If

    If (ControlPressed = False) And (ShiftPressed = True)
        Then
      If ShiftFlag = False Then
        List1.AddItem File1.filename
        FirstShift = File1.ListIndex
        ShiftFlag = True
      ElseIf ShiftFlag = True Then
        List1.Clear
        If FirstShift < File1.ListIndex Then
          Start = FirstShift
          Finish = File1.ListIndex
        Else
          Start = File1.ListIndex
          Finish = FirstShift
        End If
        For I = Start To Finish
          List1.AddItem File1.List(I)
        Next I
        ShiftFlag = False
      End If
    End If
  End Select
End Sub
```

```
Private Sub File1_KeyDown(KeyCode As Integer, Shift As
          Integer)
  If KeyCode = vbKeyShift Then ShiftPressed = True
  If KeyCode = vbKeyControl Then ControlPressed = True
End Sub

Private Sub File1_KeyUp(KeyCode As Integer, Shift As Inte-
          ger)
  If KeyCode = vbKeyShift Then ShiftPressed = False
  If KeyCode = vbKeyControl Then ControlPressed = False
End Sub

Private Sub Form_Load()
  ShiftFlag = False
  ShiftPressed = False
  ControlPressed = False
End Sub

Private Sub Command1_Click()
  Unload Me
End Sub
```

Chapter 3
Using the Bars:
Progress, Tool, and Status

· ·

In This Chapter

▶ Making your own Toolbar
▶ Creating a StatusBar
▶ Using the ProgressBar

· ·

*T*o help make programs easy to use, many programs utilize ProgressBars, Toolbars, and StatusBars. A ProgressBar appears whenever the program is busy doing something such as printing, saving a file, or erasing a hard disk. The ProgressBar shows the approximate amount of time remaining until a task is completed, as shown in Figure 3-1.

The Toolbar displays icons that represent program commands. Rather than forcing a user to wade through pull-down menus or memorize obscure keystroke commands, the Toolbar lets users click on a button containing an icon, or text as shown in Figure 3-1.

The StatusBar displays panels of information that the programmer thinks the user might want to see, such as the time, the date, or whether the Caps Lock key is pressed, as shown in Figure 3-1. A StatusBar isn't necessary, but it can make a program look more professional (or more cluttered, depending on your point of view).

The ProgressBar, Toolbar, and StatusBar are all ActiveX controls (which are separate files that end with the .OCX file extension) that must be added to your Visual Basic project before you can use them. ActiveX controls are a new Microsoft standard for defining miniature programs that you can plug into a program to save you the trouble of writing more code than absolutely necessary. To add one or more of these ActiveX controls to your program, follow these steps:

1. Choose Project⇨Components, or press Ctrl+T. A Components dialog box appears.

Toolbar

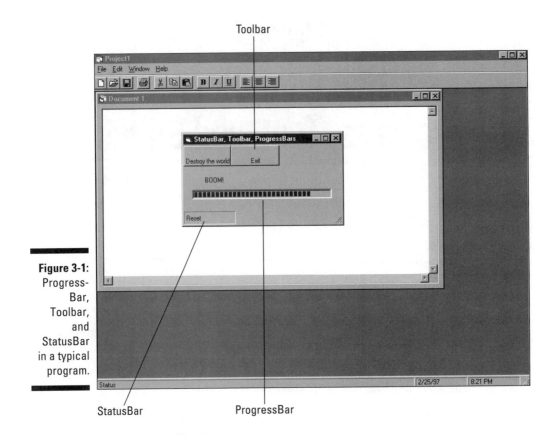

Figure 3-1:
Progress-
Bar,
Toolbar,
and
StatusBar
in a typical
program.

StatusBar   ProgressBar

2. Click in the Microsoft Windows Common Controls 5.0 check box and
click OK. Visual Basic displays the StatusBar, Toolbar, and ProgressBar
icons in the Toolbox, as shown in Figure 3-2.

Making Your Own Toolbar

A Toolbar consists of the following parts:

- ✔ One or more buttons
- ✔ Text description or graphics (or both) on each button
- ✔ ToolTips

The buttons of the Toolbar represent a specific command. When you first
create a Toolbar, it will not have any buttons.

The graphic on each button simply represents that button's function, such
as the Cut, Delete, or Copy command.

Toolbar icon

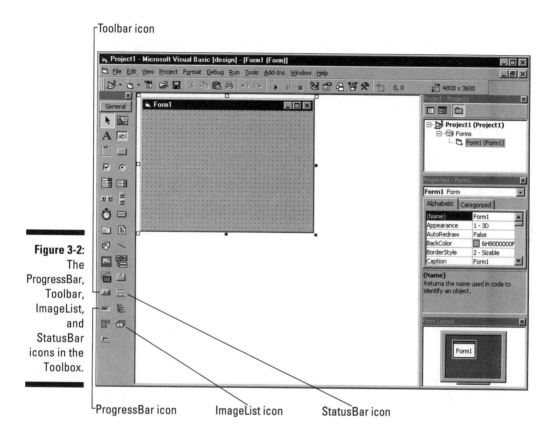

Figure 3-2:
The
ProgressBar,
Toolbar,
ImageList,
and
StatusBar
icons in the
Toolbox.

ProgressBar icon   ImageList icon   StatusBar icon

The text description provides a convenient label of the button's function so that the user doesn't have to figure out what the button's cryptic graphics might represent. In order to save space, though, many Toolbar buttons omit the text description, which is where a ToolTip comes in handy.

A ToolTip provides a short description of the button's function when the user points to the button with the mouse, as I describe later in this chapter.

If you use the VB Application Wizard to create your program, Visual Basic is normally set to create a Toolbar for you automatically. You can deselect the Toolbar option in the Wizard if you prefer not to create one for your application.

Adding buttons to the Toolbar

A Toolbar is useful only if you add buttons to it. Many programs such as Netscape Navigator, Microsoft Word, and Lotus 1-2-3 use Toolbars to provide a simple way to choose a command quickly and easily.

So if you want this same feature available in your own programs, you need to create a Toolbar and fill it in with buttons by following these steps:

1. Click the Toolbar icon in the Visual Basic Toolbox and draw the Toolbar anywhere on the form. Visual Basic automatically moves the Toolbar to the top of the form.

2. Open the Properties window (by pressing F4, choosing View➪ Properties Window, or clicking on the Properties window icon on the toolbar).

3. Double-click the *(Custom)* property to display the Property Pages dialog box as shown in Figure 3-3. Or, click on the Toolbar, press the right mouse button, and choose Properties.

4. Click the Buttons tab.

5. Click Insert Button. Visual Basic displays an empty button in your Toolbar as shown in Figure 3-4. Repeat this step for each button you want to create.

6. Click OK when you've finished creating all the buttons you want.

Toolbar drawn at the top of the form

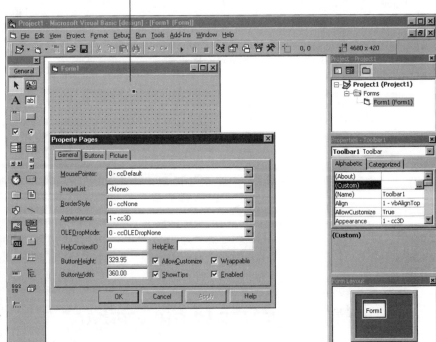

Figure 3-3:
The
Property
Pages
dialog box
as an
alternative
to using the
Property
Window.

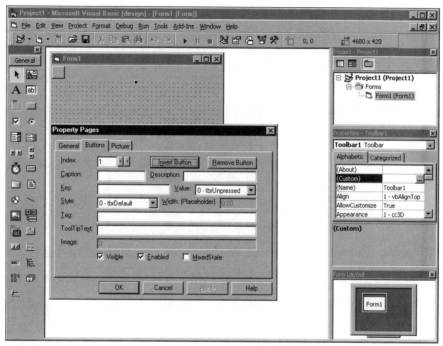

Figure 3-4:
Drawing
buttons on
a Toolbar.

If you want to separate groups of buttons, first create a new button to serve as a separator. Select the new button, then from the Toolbar Control Properties dialog box, change the Style property of this button to 3 – tbrSeparator and click Apply. Figure 3-5 shows six buttons where the fourth button appears as a separator.

Adding pictures to your Toolbar buttons

Once you create a Toolbar and add buttons to it, you may want to add pictures to the buttons so that they don't all look the same. You can use either bitmap (.BMP) or icon (.ICO) graphic files for your Toolbar.

To add pictures to your Toolbar, follow these steps:

1. Click the ImageList icon in the Visual Basic Toolbox, shown in Figure 3-2, and draw the ImageList anywhere on the form. Its location isn't important because it will be invisible when your program runs anyway.

2. Open the Properties window (by pressing F4, choosing View⇨ Properties Window, or clicking on the Properties window icon on the toolbar).

The fourth button appears as a separator

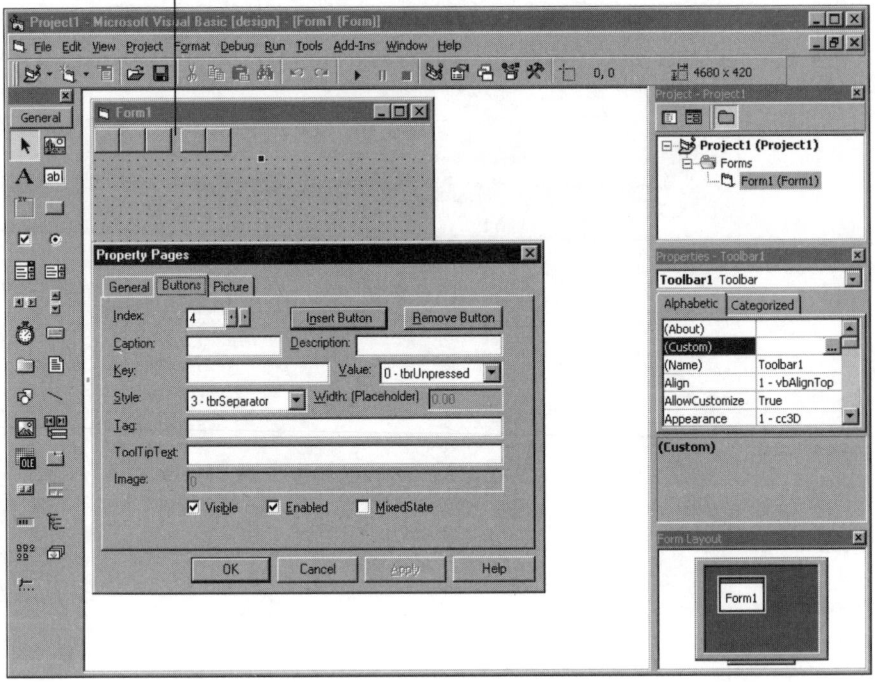

Figure 3-5:
Dividing
groups of
buttons on
a Toolbar.

3. Double-click on the *(Custom)* property to display the Property pages dialog box. Or click on the ImageList control, press the right mouse button, and choose Properties. A Property Pages dialog box appears.

4. Click the Images tab.

5. Click Insert Picture. A Select Picture dialog box appears. (If you don't want to use your own picture files, you can use the ones that come with Visual Basic, stored in the Graphics folder.)

6. Click on the bitmap or icon file that you want to use, and then click Open. Repeat this step for each picture you want to add to your Toolbar.

7. Click OK.

8. Click the Toolbar and open the Properties window (by pressing F4, choosing View⇨Properties Window, or clicking on the Properties window icon on the toolbar).

9. Double-click in the *(Custom)* property to display the Property Pages dialog box. Or click on the Toolbar, press the right mouse button, and choose Properties.

10. Click the General tab and click in the ImageList box to select the ImageList control you created in Step 1.

11. Click the Buttons tab.

12. Click the left or right arrow next to the Index box to choose a button number. The button that appears to the far left of the Toolbar has an index number of 1, the second button from the left has an index number of 2, and so on.

13. Type a number in the Image box. Typing 1 in the Image box displays the first graphic file you added in the ImageList control in Step 6, typing 2 in the Image box displays the second graphic file in the ImageList control, and so on.

14. Repeat Steps 12 and 13 for each button you want to bless with a graphic.

15. Click OK. Visual Basic displays pretty graphics on all your Toolbar buttons for all to see and admire as shown in Figure 3-6.

Adding text to your Toolbar buttons

Many programs don't display text on their Toolbar buttons to save space and force the user to guess what program command each cryptic button represents. However, if you want to provide a brief text description that explains what each button represents, Visual Basic has a way.

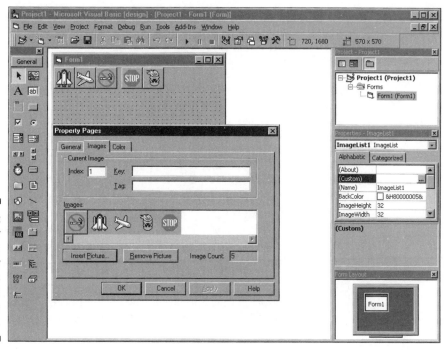

Figure 3-6:
A Toolbar
displaying
pretty
graphics
stored
in the
ImageList.

To add text to your Toolbar buttons, follow these steps:

1. Click the Toolbar and open the Properties window (by pressing F4, choosing View⇨Properties Window, or clicking on the Properties window icon on the toolbar)

2. Double-click on the *(Custom)* property to display the Property Pages dialog box. Or click on the Toolbar, press the right mouse button, and choose Properties.

3. Click the Buttons tab.

4. Click the left or right arrow next to the Index box to choose a button number. The button that appears to the far left of the Toolbar has an index number of 1, the second button from the left has an index number of 2, and so on.

5. In the Caption box, type the text that you want to appear on the button.

6. Repeat Steps 4 and 5 for each text description you want to add to a button.

7. Click OK.

Adding text descriptions to your Toolbar buttons makes the buttons taller, thus hogging up even more room on the screen. Many programs omit the text descriptions on buttons to avoid unsightly button swelling.

Adding ToolTips

ToolTips are little labels that pop up whenever you point to a Toolbar button. ToolTips are handy because they provide the user with a clue as to what each particular Toolbar button does.

To add ToolTips to your Toolbar buttons, follow these steps:

1. Click the Toolbar and open the Properties window (by pressing F4, choosing View⇨Properties Window, or clicking on the Properties window icon on the toolbar).

2. Double-click in the *(Custom)* property to display the Property Pages dialog box. Or click on the Toolbar, press the right mouse button, and choose Properties.

3. Click the Buttons tab.

4. Click the left or right arrow next to the Index box to choose a button number. The button that appears to the far left of the Toolbar has an index number of 1, the second button from the left has an index number of 2, and so on.

5. In the ToolTip Text box, type the text you want to appear as a ToolTip.

6. Repeat Steps 4 and 5 for each ToolTip you want to add to a button.

7. Click OK.

Responding to the user

After you create your Toolbar buttons, you need to write BASIC code to make them do something if a user clicks on them. The event procedure that identifies which button a user clicked on the Toolbar looks like this:

```
Private Sub Toolbar1_ButtonClick(ByVal Button As
          ComctlLib.Button)
End Sub
```

Then use a Select Case statement and the Button.Index property to identify which Toolbar button the user clicked. If the user clicks the first button, the Button.Index property is 1, if the user clicks the second button, the Button.Index property is 2, and so on. For example:

```
Private Sub Toolbar1_ButtonClick(ByVal Button As
          ComctlLib.Button)
  Select Case Button.Index
    Case 1
      ' Code to follow if user clicks the first button
    Case 2
      ' Code to follow if user clicks the second button
    Case 3
      ' Code to follow if user clicks the third button
  End Select
End Sub
```

Creating a StatusBar

A StatusBar usually serves no other purpose than to provide marginally useful information that the user can safely ignore. Word processors often use the StatusBar to display page, line, and column numbers. Other programs use the StatusBar to display the time, date, or keyboard status of the Caps Lock and Num Lock keys. A StatusBar consists of one or more panels, where each panel displays information, as shown in Figure 3-1.

Choosing a panel type

To make the StatusBar interesting, Visual Basic provides two panel types:

- ✔ 0 – sbrNormal
- ✔ 1 – sbrSimple

The 0 – sbrNormal style displays two or more panels in the StatusBar. That way, one panel can display the date, another panel can display the time, and still another panel can display page numbers.

The 1 – sbrSimple style displays a single panel in the StatusBar. When you choose a single panel, you can display text along the entire width of the StatusBar.

To choose a panel type, follow these steps:

1. Click the StatusBar icon in the Visual Basic Toolbox and draw the StatusBar anywhere on the form. Visual Basic automatically moves the StatusBar to the bottom of the form.

2. Click the StatusBar and open the Properties window (by pressing F4, choosing View⇨Properties Window, or clicking on the Properties window icon on the toolbar).

3. Click in the *(Custom)* property and then click the ellipsis button (. . .) to display the StatusBar Control Properties dialog box. Or click on the StatusBar, press the right mouse button, and choose Properties.

4. Click the General tab.

5. Click in the Style list box and choose one of the following:
   - 0 – sbrNormal
   - 1 – sbrSimple

6. Click OK.

Adding and removing StatusBar panels

If you choose to make a multiple panel StatusBar (0 – sbrNormal), you can create two or more panels for your StatusBar. To add panels to the StatusBar (or remove panels), follow these steps:

1. Click the StatusBar and open the Properties window (by pressing F4, choosing View⇨Properties Window, or clicking on the Properties window icon on the toolbar).

2. Double-click in the *(Custom)* property to display the Property Pages dialog box. Or click on the StatusBar, press the right mouse button, and choose P̲roperties.

3. Click the Panels tab.

4. Click I̲nsert Panel to add a panel. (Click R̲emove Panel to remove a panel.) Repeat this step for each panel you want to add (or remove).

5. Click OK.

Displaying text or graphics in a panel

After you create a panel in a StatusBar, it only makes sense to display information in that panel. There are two ways to display information in a panel:

- ✔ Using the Properties window at design time
- ✔ Using BASIC code at run-time

Displaying text in a single panel

If you create a single panel StatusBar (1 – sbrSimple), you can display text in the panel by following these steps:

1. Click the StatusBar and open the Properties window (by pressing F4, choosing V̲iew➪Properties W̲indow, or clicking on the Properties window icon on the toolbar).

2. Double-click in the *(Custom)* property to display the Property Pages dialog box. Or click on the StatusBar, press the right mouse button, and choose P̲roperties.

3. Click the General tab.

4. Make sure the S̲tyle list box contains 1 – sbrSimple.

5. In the SimpleT̲ext box, type the text that you want to appear in the StatusBar panel.

6. Click OK.

To display text in a single panel StatusBar using BASIC code, use the following command:

```
StatusBar1.SimpleText = "New string to appear"
```

This command displays the string New string to appear in a single panel StatusBar.

Displaying text or graphics in multiple panels

If you create a multiple panel StatusBar (0 – sbrNormal), you can display text in each panel by following these steps:

1. Click the StatusBar and open the Properties window (by pressing F4, choosing View⇨Properties Window, or clicking on the Properties window icon on the toolbar).

2. Double-click in the *(Custom)* property to display the Property Pages dialog box. Or click on the StatusBar, press the right mouse button, and choose Properties.

3. Click the General tab.

4. Make sure the Style list box contains 0 – sbrNormal.

5. Click the Panels tab.

6. Click the left or right arrow next to the Index box to choose a panel number. The panel that appears to the far left of the StatusBar has an index number of 1, the second panel from the left has an index number of 2, and so on.

7. In the Text box, type the text you want to appear in the panel.

8. If you want to add a picture to your panel, click the Browse button in the Picture group. A Select picture dialog box appears.

   Click on the bitmap (*.BMP) or icon (*.ICO) file that you want to display in your panel and click Open. Your chosen graphic appears in the Picture group.

9. Repeat Steps 6 through 8 for each text description and picture that you want to add to a panel.

10. Click OK.

To display text in a multiple panel StatusBar using BASIC code, use the following command:

```
StatusBar1.Panels(X).Text = "New string to appear"
```

where X represents the panel number. For example, if you wanted to change the text in the panel that appears to the far left of the StatusBar, X would be number 1. If you wanted to change the text in the panel that appears second from the left, X would be number 2, and so on.

You can only display text in panels by changing the Style property of a StatusBar to 0 – sbrText — this makes the StatusBar appear as one long panel for displaying text.

Visual Basic can automatically display in a panel the status of the following, without any additional help from you:

- ✔ Caps Lock
- ✔ Num Lock
- ✔ Insert
- ✔ Scroll Lock
- ✔ Time
- ✔ Date

To display any of this information in a panel, follow these steps:

1. Click the StatusBar and open the Properties window (by pressing F4, choosing View⇨Properties Window, or clicking on the Properties window icon on the toolbar).

2. Double-click in the *(Custom)* property and to display the Property Pages dialog box. Or click on the StatusBar, press the right mouse button, and choose Properties.

3. Click the Panels tab.

4. Click the left or right arrow next to the Index box to choose a panel number. The panel that appears to the far left of the StatusBar has an index number of 1, the second panel from the left has an index number of 2, and so on.

5. Click in the Style list box and choose one of the following:

   - 0 – sbrText
   - 1 – sbrCaps
   - 2 – sbrNum
   - 3 – sbrIns
   - 4 – sbrScrl
   - 5 – sbrTime
   - 6 – sbrDate
   - 7 – sbrKana (displays the letters *KANA*)

6. Repeat Steps 4 and 5 for each panel that you want to modify. Then click OK.

Responding to the user

Although the StatusBar usually only displays information, you can also let the user click on a panel to actually do something in your program. To do this, though, you need to write some BASIC code.

Clicking on a single panel StatusBar

If you have a StatusBar that displays a single panel (1 – sbrSimple), you just need to use the following event procedure to respond when a user clicks the StatusBar:

```
Private Sub Statusbar1_Click()
End Sub
```

Then insert code inside this event procedure to make your StatusBar do something when the user clicks on it.

Clicking on a multiple panel StatusBar

If you have a StatusBar that displays multiple panels (0 – sbrNormal), you need to identify which panel the user clicked on. The event procedure that identifies which StatusBar panel a user clicked looks like this:

```
Private Sub StatusBar1_PanelClick(ByVal Panel As
          ComctlLib.Panel)
End Sub
```

Then use a Select-Case statement and the Panel.Index property to identify which panel the user clicked on. If the user clicks on the first panel, the Panel.Index property is 1, if the user clicks on the second panel, the Panel.Index property is 2, and so on. For example:

```
Private Sub StatusBar1_PanelClick(ByVal Panel As
          ComctlLib.Panel)
  Select Case Panel.Index
    Case 1
      ' Code to follow if user clicks the first panel
    Case 2
      ' Code to follow if user clicks the second panel
    Case 3
      ' Code to follow if user clicks the third panel
  End Select
End Sub
```

Creating a ProgressBar

A ProgressBar shows the approximate amount of time remaining until a specific task is completed. When the task begins, the ProgressBar appears empty to show that the computer hasn't made any progress at all. As the program works at a task, the ProgressBar gradually fills up. When the task is finished, the ProgressBar appears full.

Three properties determine the appearance of the ProgressBar:

- ✔ Min
- ✔ Max
- ✔ Value

The Min property represents a number that determines when the ProgressBar is completely empty. The default value of Min is 0.

The Max property represents a number that determines when the ProgressBar is completely full. The default value of Max is 100.

The Value property represents a number greater than the Min property but less than the Max property. Changing the Value property changes the appearance of the ProgressBar.

To draw a ProgressBar, click the ProgressBar icon in the Visual Basic Toolbox and draw your ProgressBar on the form.

To fill up a ProgressBar, you have to use BASIC code such as the following:

```
If ProgressBar1.Value < ProgressBar1.Max Then
   ProgressBar1.Value = ProgressBar1.Value + 5
Else
   ProgressBar1.Visible = False
End If
```

1. The first line compares the number in the Value property to the number in the Max property. If the Value property is less than the Max property, Visual Basic follows the instructions in the second line.

2. The second line increases the Value property by increments of 5.

3. The third line marks the beginning of instructions to follow if the Value property is equal to or greater than the Max property (which means the ProgressBar is full).

4. The fourth line makes the ProgressBar disappear when the Value property is equal to or greater than the Max property (which means the ProgressBar is full).

5. The fifth line marks the end of the If-Then-Else statement started on the first line.

Try It Yourself

If you want to experiment with Toolbars, StatusBars, and ProgressBars on your own, create the following program, which is shown in Figure 3-7. Just create the following objects, modify their properties using the settings listed, and run the program so you can see how these fascinating new Visual Basic controls work.

Object	Property	Setting
Form	Caption	StatusBar, Toolbar, and ProgressBars
	Height	2535
	Left	2355
	Top	1365
	Width	4485
Label1	Caption	Seconds remaining until the end of the world
	Height	255

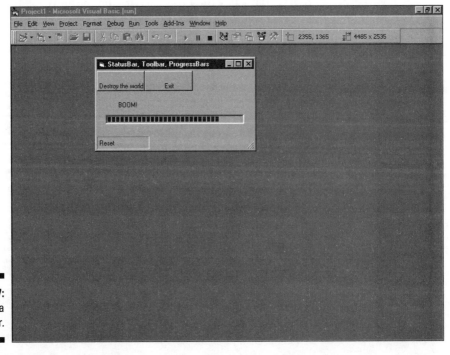

Figure 3-7:
Displaying a
ProgressBar.

Object	Property	Setting
	Left	600
	Top	840
	Width	3135
ProgressBar1	Height	255
	Left	240
	Max	1000
	Top	1200
	Width	3855
Toolbar1	Height	600
	Left	0
	Top	0
	Width	4365

Changes these properties from the Toolbar Property Pages dialog box:

	Index	1
	Caption	Destroy the world
	ToolTipText	Apocalypse
	Index	2
	Caption	Exit
	ToolTipText	Exit program
StatusBar1	Height	375
	Left	0
	Top	1755
	Width	4365

Changes these properties from the StatusBar Property Pages dialog box:

	Index	1
	Text	Reset

Type the following in the Code window:

```
Private Sub Toolbar1_ButtonClick(ByVal Button As
          ComctlLib.Button)
  Dim I As Integer
Select Case Button.Index
    Case 1
```

(continued)

(continued)

```
      For I = 1 To 1000
        If ProgressBar1.Value < ProgressBar1.Max Then
          ProgressBar1.Value = ProgressBar1.Value + 1
        End If
      Next I
      Label1.Caption = "BOOM!"
    Case 2
      End
  End Select
End Sub

Private Sub StatusBar1_PanelClick(ByVal Panel As
        ComctlLib.Panel)
  ProgressBar1.Value = 0
Label1.Caption = "Seconds remaining until the end of the
        world"
End Sub
```

Test your newfound knowledge

1. Why should you consider using Toolbars in your program?

   a. Because they exist and it's always important to load your program down with as many Visual Basic features as possible, just to keep the user guessing how your program really works.

   b. Toolbars provide a simple one-click access to your program's most commonly used commands.

   c. You shouldn't because a Toolbar is a corkboard that has hooks and silhouettes of each tool to show where they should be hanging.

   d. Toolbars make your program more confusing and harder to use, and that means your programs will look more professional and meet a typical user's expectations.

2. How can the StatusBar and ProgressBar help your program's users?

   a. The StatusBar can display useful information, and the ProgressBar can show how much of a task has been completed.

   b. Both the StatusBar and ProgressBar are great places for status-seeking business executives to visit and be seen so they can make more business deals to the detriment of the environment.

   c. The StatusBar and the ProgressBar both serve nonalcoholic beverages to conform with the health-conscious thinking of the future.

   d. The StatusBar erases any useful information that the ProgressBar tries to display on the screen.

Chapter 4

Making Sliders and Tabs

● ●

In This Chapter

▶ Using the Slider

▶ Toying with the Tabbed control

▶ Creating a TabStrip

● ●

*A*s an alternative to scroll bars and endless dialog boxes, Visual Basic now offers sliders and two types of tabbed controls called the Tabbed Dialog Control and the TabStrip. A slider works like a scroll bar except that it displays tick marks to let users choose discrete values, as shown in Figure 4-1.

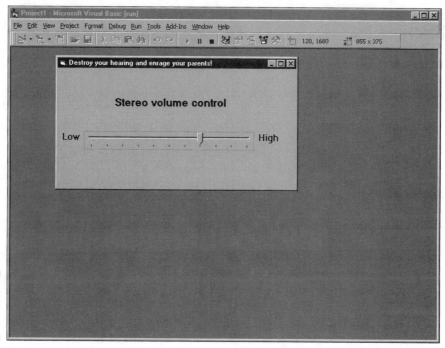

Figure 4-1:
A typical
slider.

A Tabbed Dialog Control or TabStrip lets you display related information in separate screens — without having to use multiple windows. Clicking on a tab displays a different screen, as shown in Figure 4-2.

The Slider, Tabbed Dialog Control, and the TabStrip are ActiveX controls, shown in Figure 4-3, that must be added to your Visual Basic project before you can use them. To add these ActiveX controls to your program, follow these steps:

1. Choose Project⇨Components (or press Ctrl+T). A Components dialog box appears.

2. Click in the Microsoft Windows Common Controls 5.0 check box. (This tells Visual Basic to display the Slider and TabStrip in the Toolbox.)

3. Click in the Microsoft Tabbed Dialog Control check box and click OK. (Choosing this check box tells Visual Basic to display the Tabbed Dialog Control in the Toolbox.)

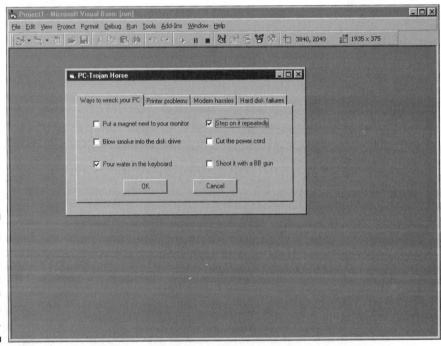

Figure 4-2:
The TabStrip organizes in separate screens in a dialog box.

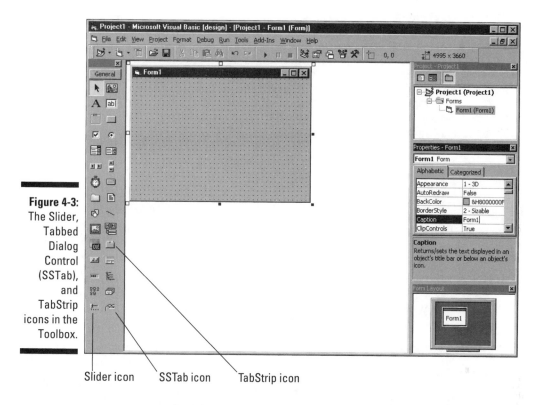

Figure 4-3:
The Slider,
Tabbed
Dialog
Control
(SSTab),
and
TabStrip
icons in the
Toolbox.

Slider icon   SSTab icon   TabStrip icon

Using the Slider

Although scroll bars and the Slider control let the user choose a specific
value by sliding a marker, the Slider limits the user to specific whole
number values such as 0, 5, 10, and 15. The Slider control consists of
seven main parts:

- ✔ Orientation
- ✔ Tick style
- ✔ Tick frequency
- ✔ Min
- ✔ Max
- ✔ Large change
- ✔ Small change

Choosing a slider's appearance

When you create a slider, you need to determine its orientation and the placement of the slider's tick marks, as shown in Figure 4-4. A slider can appear either horizontally or vertically. Here are the four ways to display tick marks on the slider:

- ✔ Bottom/Right
- ✔ Top/Left
- ✔ Both Bottom/Right and Top/Left
- ✔ No tick marks

To create a slider and with the appearance you want, follow these steps:

1. Click the Slider icon in the Visual Basic Toolbox and draw the slider anywhere on the form.

2. Open the Properties window (by pressing F4, choosing View⇨Properties Window, or clicking on the Properties window icon on the toolbar).

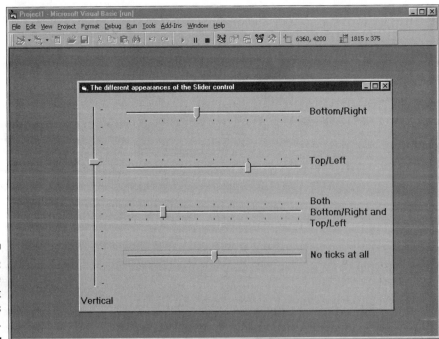

Figure 4-4: The different appearances of a Slider.

3. Click in the Orientation property and choose one of the following:

   - 0 – sldHorizontal

   - 1 – sldVertical

4. Click in the TickStyle property and choose one of the following:

   - 0 – sldBottomRight

   - 1 – sldTopLeft

   - 2 – sldBoth

   - 3 – sldNoTicks

The TickFrequency property determines the spacing of tick marks along the slider. By default, the TickFrequency is 1, which means a tick mark appears for every possible value on the slider. If you set the TickFrequency to 2, a tick mark appears for every other possible value on the slider, if the TickFrequency is 3, a tick mark appears for every third possible value on the slider, and so on, as shown in Figure 4-5.

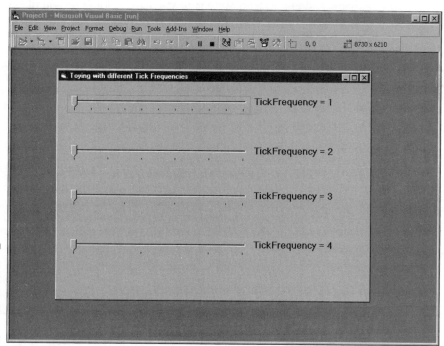

Figure 4-5:
Different tick frequencies on a slider.

Defining the slider tick mark values

The Min and Max properties of a slider determine the minimum and maximum values of the slider. By default, the minimum value is 0 and the maximum value is 10. So when the slider marker appears to the far left (or top) of the slider, the slider Value property is 0, and when the slider marker appears to the far right (or bottom), the slider Value property is 10.

The LargeChange property determines how far the slider marker moves when the user clicks the slider with the mouse. The SmallChange property determines how far the slider marker moves when the user presses the right or left arrow key.

Toying with the Tabbed Dialog Control

If you had a bunch of folders, you could scatter them across your floor in such a way that you could find them again, except they would take up a lot of space. A simpler alternative is to stack the folders on top of each other with separate tabs identifying each folder. Not only does this save space, but it lets you quickly choose a particular folder by searching for its tab.

The Tabbed Dialog Control works pretty much the same way. You can create multiple tabs and display different information on each one. Many programs use tabbed dialog controls, like the one shown in Figure 4-2, to provide the user with lots of choices without littering the entire screen with windows and dialog boxes.

Choosing a tabbed dialog appearance

The two properties that affect the appearance of a Tabbed dialog control are the TabOrientation and the Style properties. The TabOrientation property defines the four positions in which the tabs can appear, as shown in Figure 4-6:

- ✔ 0 – ssTabOrientationTop
- ✔ 1 – ssTabOrientationBottom
- ✔ 2 – ssTabOrientationLeft
- ✔ 3 – ssTabOrientationRight

If you choose either 2 – ssTabOrientationLeft or 3 – ssTabOrientationRight, you must choose a TrueType font that can rotate text correctly on the tab.

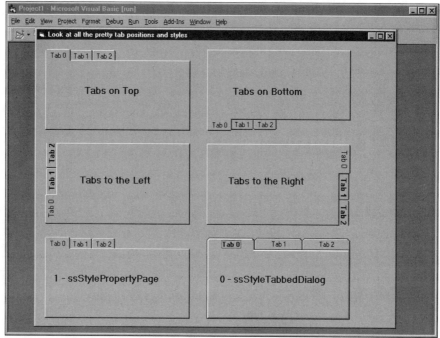

Figure 4-6:
The four
different tab
positions
and the two
different tab
styles.

The Style property defines the way tabs appear, as shown in Figure 4-6:

- ✔ 0 – ssStyleTabbedDialog
- ✔ 1 – ssStylePropertyPage

To create a tabbed dialog control and change its TabOrientation or Style property, follow these steps:

1. Click the SSTab icon in the Visual Basic Toolbox and draw your tabbed dialog control on a form. Figure 4-3 shows you where the icon is.

2. Click the Tabbed Dialog Control and open the Properties window (by pressing F4, choosing View➪Properties Window, or clicking on the Properties window icon on the toolbar).

3. Double-click in the *(Custom)* property to display the Property Pages dialog box. Or, click on the Tabbed dialog control, press the right mouse button, and choose Properties.

4. Click the General tab.

5. Click in the Orientation list box and choose one of the following:

- 0 – ssTabOrientationTop
- 1 – ssTabOrientationBottom
- 2 – ssTabOrientationLeft
- 3 – ssTabOrientationRight

6. Click in the Style list box and choose one of the following:

- 0 – ssStyleTabbedDialog
- 1 – ssStylePropertyPage

7. Click the Font tab.

8. Click the Font list box and choose a font.

9. Click in the Size list box and choose a type size.

10. Click OK.

Defining the number of tabs and each tab caption

You can display any number of tabs in your Tabbed dialog control. However, the more tabs you have, the more confusing the whole thing will look. When you create a Tabbed dialog control, Visual Basic blindly labels each tab with a caption like Tab 0 or Tab 5. Obviously, if you want to make your tabs more descriptive, you need to create your own tab captions.

To help organize your tabs, you may want to display tabs in two or more rows. The TabsPerRow property defines the maximum number of tabs that can appear in a row. The Tabs property defines the actual number of tabs that appear in each row.

To define the total number of tabs and each tab caption, follow these steps:

1. Click the Tabbed Dialog Control and open the Properties window (by pressing F4, choosing View⇨Properties Window, or clicking on the Properties window icon on the toolbar).

2. Double-click in the *(Custom)* property to display the Property Pages dialog box. Or, click on the Tabbed dialog control, press the right mouse button, and choose Properties.

3. Type the total number of tabs you want in the Tab Count box.

4. Type the number of tabs you want to appear per row in the TabsPerRow box.

5. Type a tab caption in the TabCaption box.

6. Click the right or left arrow button next to the Current Tab box to choose another tab.

7. Repeat Steps 5 and 6 for each tab caption you want to add.

8. Click OK.

Placing objects on your tabbed dialog control

The Tabbed dialog control is generally useless unless you put other objects on each tab, such as command buttons, check boxes, labels, text boxes, or picture boxes. To place an object on a tab, follow these steps:

1. Click the Tabbed dialog control and open the Properties window (by pressing F4, choosing View⇨Properties Window, or clicking on the Properties window icon on the toolbar).

2. Click in the Tab property, type the number of the tab on which you want to place objects, and press Enter.

3. Draw any objects you want (such as command buttons or check boxes) on the Tabbed dialog control.

4. Repeat Steps 2 and 3 for each tab.

If you delete a Tabbed dialog control, you also delete any objects stored on it, such as command buttons, check boxes, labels, or text boxes.

Creating a TabStrip

The TabStrip works much like the Tabbed Dialog Control except it gives you the option of displaying a tabbed dialog box or a row of buttons, as shown in Figure 4-8. A TabStrip is a much easier way to create, move, and write code for a row of buttons than cramming a bunch of separate command buttons together.

To create a TabStrip and define its Style property, follow these steps:

1. Click the TabStrip icon in the Visual Basic Toolbox and draw your TabStrip on a form, as shown in Figure 4-3.

2. Click on the TabStrip and open the Properties window (by pressing F4, choosing View⇨Properties Window, or clicking on the Properties window icon on the toolbar).

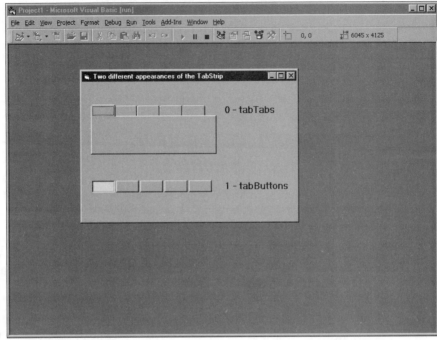

Figure 4-7:
The two
appearances
of a
TabStrip.

3. Double-click in the *(Custom)* property to display the Property Pages dialog box. Or click on the TabStrip control, press the right mouse button, and choose P̲roperties.

4. Click the General tab.

5. Click in the S̲tyle list box and choose one of the following:

   • 0 – tabTabs

   • 1 – tabButtons

6. Click OK.

Defining tab captions, ToolTips, and the number of tabs

You can display any number of tabs in a TabStrip. Unless you enjoy confusing your user, however, you probably want to limit the number of tabs. For example, displaying five tabs might be useful but trying to cram twenty tabs on the TabStrip might be overkill. When you create a TabStrip, each tab is blank. You can make your tabs more useful and descriptive by giving them captions.

To provide additional help to your program's hapless users, you may also want to create ToolTips for each tab as well. That way, when a user points to a tab, the ToolTip pops up, explaining what the tab will do.

To define the number of tabs, each tab caption, and any ToolTips, follow these steps:

1. Click on the TabStrip and open the Properties window (by pressing F4, choosing View⇨Properties Window, or clicking on the Properties window icon on the toolbar).

2. Double-click in the *(Custom)* property to display the Property Pages dialog box. Or click on the TabStrip control, press the right mouse button, and choose Properties.

3. Click the Tabs tab. (No, that's not a typo, but it does look funny, doesn't it?)

4. Click Insert Tab (or Remove Tab).

5. Type a tab caption in the Caption box.

6. Type a ToolTip for the tab in the ToolTipText box.

7. Repeat Steps 4 through 6 for each tab.

8. Click OK.

Displaying graphics on your TabStrip

To spice up the appearance of your tabs, you can also display graphics on them as shown in Figure 4-8. You have to complete two steps to display graphics on a TabStrip. First, you have to create and store the graphics in an ImageList control. Second, you have to define which graphic to use on each tab in your TabStrip.

Storing pictures in the ImageList

Before you can display graphics in a TabStrip, you have to add an ImageList control to your form and then add graphics to that ImageList control. To store graphics in an ImageList control, follow these steps:

1. Draw an ImageList control on the same form that contains your TabStrip control. (The location of the ImageList controls is not important because they aren't visible when your program is running.)

2. Click the ImageList control and open the Properties window (by pressing F4, choosing View⇨Properties Window, or clicking on the Properties window icon on the toolbar).

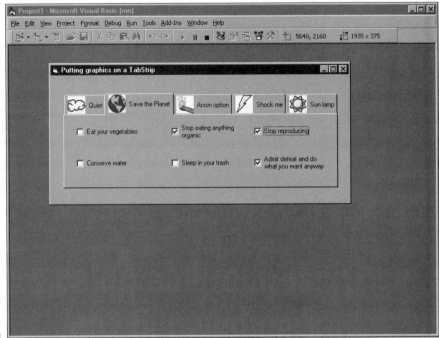

Figure 4-8:
Displaying
graphics on
a TabStrip.

3. Double-click the *(Custom)* property to display the Property Pages dialog box. Or click on the ImageList control, press the right mouse button, and choose P̲roperties.

4. Click the Images tab.

5. Click Insert P̲icture. A Select Picture dialog box appears, letting you choose a bitmap (*.BMP) or icon (*.ICO) file. Choose a file and click O̲pen.

6. Repeat Step 5 until you've stored all the pictures you want in the ImageList control.

7. Click OK.

Putting graphics on the TabStrip

After you've stored graphics in an ImageList control, you can choose which graphics will appear on which particular tab. To place graphics on a TabStrip, follow these steps:

1. Click the TabStrip control and open the Properties window (by pressing F4, choosing V̲iew⇨Properties W̲indow, or clicking on the Properties window icon on the toolbar).

2. Double-click the *(Custom)* property to display the Property Pages dialog box. Or click on the TabStrip control, press the right mouse button, and choose Properties.

3. Click the General tab.

4. In the ImageList list box, choose ImageList1.

5. Click the Tabs tab.

6. Click the left or right arrow button next to the Index box to choose a particular tab.

7. Type a number in the Image box that represents the graphic you want to appear on the tab. If you type 1, the first graphic stored in the ImageList control appears on the tab; if you type 2, the second graphic stored in the ImageList control appears, and so on.

8. Click OK.

Responding to the user

If the user clicks on a specific tab in the TabStrip, you need to write BASIC code to tell your program what to do next. Just use the `TabStrip1_Click` event procedure:

```
Private Sub TabStrip1_Click()
End Sub
```

Then use a Select-Case statement and the TabStrip1.SelectedItem.Index property to identify which item the user clicked on. If the user clicks the first item, the TabStrip1.SelectedItem.Index property is 1; if the user clicks the second item, the TabStrip1.SelectedItem.Index property is 2, and so on. For example:

```
Private Sub TabStrip1_Click()
  Select Case TabStrip1.SelectedItem.Index
    Case 1
      ' Code to follow if user clicks the first tab
    Case 2
      ' Code to follow if user clicks the second tab
    Case 3
      ' Code to follow if user clicks the third tab
  End Select
End Sub
```

Placing objects on the TabStrip

Like the Tabbed dialog control, the TabStrip lets you display multiple objects that the user can view just by clicking a particular tab. But unlike the Tabbed dialog control, the TabStrip forces you to write BASIC code to display and hide objects. For example, Figure 4-9 shows a TabStrip with both a check box and a command button displayed.

When the user clicks on the first tab, you want only the check box to appear. When the user clicks on the second tab, you want only the command button to appear. In this case, you need to write the following BASIC code:

```
Private Sub Form_Load()
  Command1.Visible = False
  Check1.Visible = True
End Sub

Private Sub TabStrip1_Click()
  Select Case TabStrip1.SelectedItem.Index
    Case 1
      Command1.Visible = False
      Check1.Visible = True
    Case 2
      Command1.Visible = True
      Check1.Visible = False
  End Select
End Sub
```

The `Form_Load` event procedure works like this:

1. The first line defines the start of an event procedure that runs when the form first loads.

2. The second line makes the `Command1` command button invisible.

3. The third line makes the `Check1` check box visible.

4. The fourth line marks the end of the `Form_Load` event procedure.

The `TabStrip1_Click` event procedure works like this:

1. The first line defines the start of an event procedure that runs whenever the user clicks on any tab displayed in a TabStrip named `TabStrip1`.

2. The second line checks which tab the user clicked. If the user clicked the first tab, the value of `TabStrip1.SelectedItem.Index` is 1. If the user clicked on the second tab, the value of `TabStrip1.SelectedItem.Index` is 2, and so on.

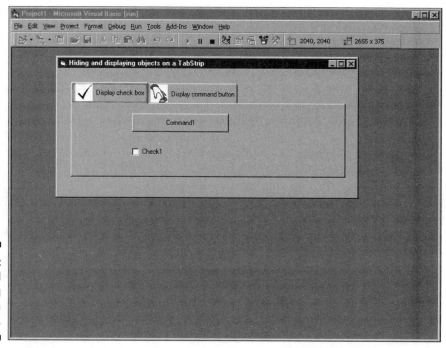

Figure 4-9:
Hiding and
displaying
objects on a
TabStrip.

3. The third line marks the beginning of instructions to follow if the user clicked the first tab.

4. The fourth line hides the Command1 command button.

5. The fifth line makes the Check1 check box visible.

6. The sixth line marks the beginning of instructions to follow if the user clicked the second tab.

7. The seventh line makes the Command1 command button visible.

8. The eighth line hides the Check1 check box.

9. The ninth line marks the end of the Select-Case statement.

10. The tenth line marks the end of the entire event procedure.

Try It Yourself

If you want to toy with sliders, Tabbed Dialog Controls, and TabStrips, create the following program, shown in Figure 4-10.

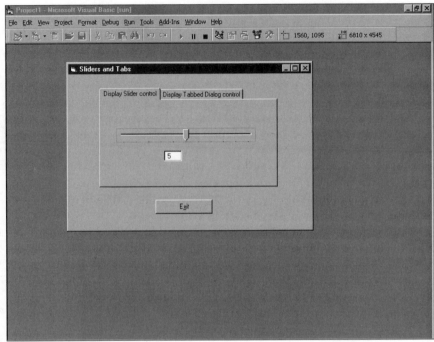

Figure 4-10:
What the
sample
program is
supposed to
look like.

Draw the TabStrip1 control first, and then draw the Text1, Slider1, and SSTab1 controls over the TabStrip1 control.

Object	*Property*	*Setting*
Form	Caption	Sliders and Tabs
	Height	4545
	Left	1560
	Top	1095
	Width	6810
TabStrip1	Caption (for Index 1)	Display Slider control
	Caption (for Index 2)	Display Tabbed Dialog control
	Height	2655
	Left	840
	Top	360
	Width	4935

Note: *To modify the Captions for the TabStrip1 control, you must use the Property Pages dialog box of the TabStrip1 control.*

Test your newfound knowledge

1. What is the main difference between the Slider control and a scroll bar?

   a. The scroll bar lets the user scroll up and down, but the Slider only lets the user slide a desk chair back and forth.

   b. A scroll bar works with the now-obsolete practice of printing manuscripts on long scrolls. The Slider control is what small children use to slide down hot metal playground slides in the middle of the summer.

   c. The Slider control forces the user to choose only specific whole number values such as 10, 20, and 30. Scroll bars let users choose a range of values such as any number between 10 and 30

   d. The Slider control is completely useless and is included with Visual Basic 5 only to give you the illusion that you actually got your money's worth.

2. What is the main difference between the Tabbed dialog control and the TabStrip?

   a. The TabStrip requires that you write BASIC code to display and hide objects in the TabStrip. The Tabbed dialog control does not require BASIC code to display or hide information.

   b. The TabStrip was written by Microsoft so it's superior to the Tabbed dialog control, which was written by another company that Microsoft probably will buy soon.

   c. Both the TabStrip and the Tabbed dialog control let you create programs that nobody can understand.

   d. The TabStrip contains the word *Strip*, so it's been banned in many parts of the world that deal harshly with pornography.

Object	*Property*	*Setting*
Text1	Height	285
	Left	2640
	Text	(Empty)
	Top	2040
	Width	495
Slider1	Height	375
	Left	1320
	Max	10
	Min	0
	Top	1440
	Width	3855

Object	Property	Setting
SSTab1	Height	1695
	Left	2040
	Top	1080
	Width	2775
Command1	Caption	E&xit
	Height	375
	Left	2400
	Top	3360
	Width	1575

Type the following in the Code window:

```
Private Sub TabStrip1_Click()
  Select Case TabStrip1.SelectedItem.Index
    Case 1
      Text1.Visible = True
      Slider1.Visible = True
      SSTab1.Visible = False
    Case 2
      Text1.Visible = False
      Slider1.Visible = False
      SSTab1.Visible = True
  End Select
End Sub



Private Sub Slider1_Change()
  Text1.Text = Str(Slider1.Value)
End Sub



Private Sub Command1_Click()
  Unload Me
End Sub
```

Chapter 5

Displaying Lists in Pretty Ways

. . . .

In This Chapter
▶ Using the ListView
▶ Using the TreeView
▶ Adding pretty pictures with the ImageList

. . . .

*I*f your program needs to display a list of items and you want to be creative, you can display your lists using the ListView or TreeView controls. The ListView control displays items similar to the Windows 95 desktop. Each item appears in rows and columns with (or without) an accompanying icon, as shown in Figure 5-1.

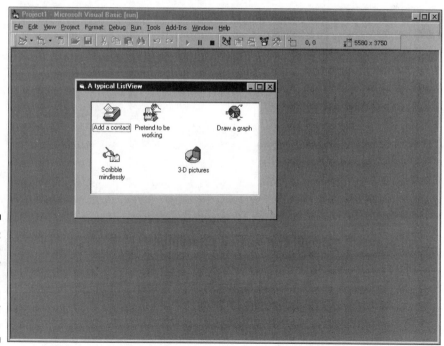

Figure 5-1:
The
ListView
on a form
displaying
ordinary
size icons.

Because lists of items may be related, you may want to display your list using a more structured approach. Rather than the helter-skelter appearance of the ListView, use the TreeView, which displays your lists in an outline complete with indentation and connecting lines, as shown in Figure 5-2.

The ListView and TreeView are ActiveX controls that must be added to your Visual Basic project before you can use them. To add these ActiveX controls to your program, follow these steps:

1. Choose Project⇨Components (or press Ctrl+T). A Components dialog box appears.

2. Click in the Microsoft Windows Common Controls 5.0 check box and click OK. Visual Basic displays the ListView and TreeView icons in the Toolbox as shown in Figure 5-3.

With the Visual Basic 5 Application Wizard, you can quickly create a program that uses the ListView and TreeView if you choose to create a Windows Explorer style user interface.

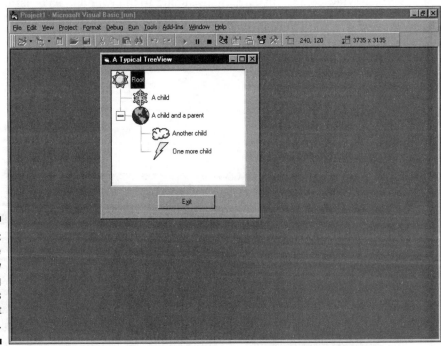

Figure 5-2:
The
TreeView
showing
child nodes
and parent
nodes.

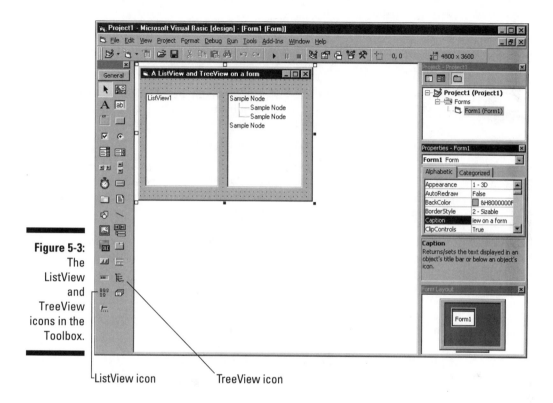

Figure 5-3:
The
ListView
and
TreeView
icons in the
Toolbox.

ListView icon   TreeView icon

Using the ListView

Normally, the ListView displays items as plain, boring text as shown in
Figure 5-3. However, it's usually more interesting to display items as a
combination of text and icons instead, as shown in Figure 5-2.

Adding items to the ListView

Of course, to make the ListView display anything at all, you first have to tell
the ListView control what you want to display. Each ListView control stores
its list of displayed items in an array of objects called `ListItems`. Until you
stuff objects in the `ListItems` array, the `ListItems` array is empty.
(Chapter 7 explains arrays in more detail if you feel like skipping ahead.)

To display stuff into the `ListItems` array, you must draw a ListView
control on your form and then use these commands to stuff items in the
`ListItems` array:

```
Dim MyStuff As ListItem
Set MyStuff = ListView1.ListItems.Add()
MyStuff.Text = "First Item"
```

1. The first line declares the MyStuff variable as a ListItem data type. Although Visual Basic doesn't require that you include this line, it's a good idea just to clarify the code in case other programmers look at it.

2. The second line creates a blank array element in the ListItems array.

3. The third line assigns the string First Item into the text property of the MyStuff variable. Because MyStuff represents a blank array element in the ListItems array, First Item gets stuffed into this array element in the ListItems array.

If you leave the parentheses empty in the second line, Visual Basic simply adds the First Item string to the end of the ListItems array. If you specify a number, Visual Basic will display the First Item string in the location you specify.

For example, the following code adds the Next Item string as the first element displayed in the ListView control:

```
Set MyStuff = ListView1.ListItems.Add(1)
MyStuff.Text = "Next Item"
```

Any text located in the first element gets pushed back to the second element in the ListItems array.

What do you think happens if you have only five items stored in the ListItems array and you decide to use the following code?

```
Set MyStuff = ListView1.ListItems.Add(7)
MyStuff.Text = "Next Item"
```

The above code causes Visual Basic to choke because if you only have five items stored in the ListItems array, you can't specify a location greater than 5. Because array element 7 doesn't exist, Visual Basic doesn't know what to do and just displays an error message.

To make it even easier to add items to the ListView, you can use just one line as follows:

```
ListView1.ListItems.Add(index, key, text, icon, smallicon)
```

index specifies the position where you want to add the item.

key specifies a string that can be used to access this item.

text is the string that is added to the ListView control.

icon is an integer that determines which icon to use in the ImageList control when the ListView control is set to Icon view.

smallicon is an integer that determines which icon to use in the ImageList control when the ListView control is set to SmallIcon view.

For example, instead of using the following multiple lines of code:

```
Set MyStuff = ListView1.ListItems.Add(7)
MyStuff.Text = "Next Item"
```

You could use this single line of code instead:

```
Set MyStuff = ListView1.ListItems.Add(7, ,"Next Item")
```

Removing items from the ListView

You may one day find that you want to remove one or more items from the ListView. To remove an item from the ListView, you just have to use these magical commands:

```
Set MyStuff = ListView1.ListItems
MyStuff.Remove 1
```

1. The first line defines `MyStuff` as a variable that represents the `ListItems` array.

2. The second line removes the array element specified. In this case, the number 1 tells Visual Basic to remove the first array element.

Although it sounds as logical as a peace-keeping missile, you can't remove an array element that doesn't exist. For example, suppose you have only seven items stored in the `ListItems` array and you try removing the tenth item:

```
Set MyStuff = ListView1.ListItems
MyStuff.Remove 10
```

This code will cause Visual Basic to scream and display an error message because ten or more elements do not exist in the `ListItems` array.

Adding icons to the ListView

Without icons, the ListView looks pretty dull, plain, and downright boring. Because people respond faster to pictures than words (which explains the popularity of television over books), you may want to represent each item with a descriptive icon as well as text.

Storing pictures in the ImageList

Before you can display icons in your ListView, you have to add an ImageList control to your form and then add icons to that ImageList control. Typically, you need two ImageList controls, one to represent Icons and the second to represent SmallIcons.

To store icons in an ImageList control, follow these steps:

1. Draw an ImageList control on the same form that contains your ListView control. (The location of the ImageList controls is not important because they won't be visible when your program is running.)

2. Click the ImageList control and open the Properties window (by pressing F4, choosing View⇨Properties Window, or clicking on the Properties window icon on the toolbar).

3. Double-click in the *(Custom)* property to display the Property Pages dialog box. Or click on the ImageList control, press the right mouse button, and choose Properties.

4. Click the General tab; then click in the 32 x 32 radio button for regular icons, or the 16 x 16 radio button for small icons.

5. Click the Images tab.

6. Click Insert Picture. A Select Picture dialog box appears, letting you choose a bitmap (*.BMP) or icon (*.ICO) file. Choose a file and click Open.

7. Repeat Step 6 until you've stored all the pictures you want in both ImageList controls.

   Note: When you're storing pictures in an ImageList, the pictures must be of the same format, that is, all bitmap files (*.BMP) or all icon files (*.ICO).

8. Click OK.

9. Repeat Steps 1 through 8 to create a second ImageList control. (Remember, the images and order of the images in the first ImageList control should be similar to the images and order in the second

ImageList control. This way, when the user switches between large and small icons, the programs they represent will be equally cryptic.)

10. Add the following code in the `Form_Load` event procedure:

```
Private Sub Form_Load()
   ListView1.Icons = ImageList1
   ListView1.SmallIcons = ImageList2
End Sub
```

11. Use the following code when adding an item to the ListView:

```
Set MyStuff = ListView1.ListItems.Add()
MyStuff.Text = "Bo the Cat"
MyStuff.Icon = 1
MyStuff.SmallIcon = 1
```

Or if you want to use just one line of code, use the following:

```
Set MyStuff = ListView1.ListItems.Add(, , "Bo the Cat",
   1, 1)
```

Choosing Icons or SmallIcons for the ListView

The ListView can display two types of icons, unimaginatively called:

 Icons

Smalllcons

 When you choose to display SmallIcons, guess what? Visual Basic simply displays the icons in a different position. If you actually want to display smaller icons, you have to store a second set of icons with smaller pictures in the ImageList control to define the SmallIcons group, as shown in Figure 5-4.

To choose which types of icons to display in the ListView, you can change the View property of the ListView control by using the Properties window or Visual Basic code.

To change the View property using the Properties window, follow these steps:

1. Click the ListView control and open the Properties window (by pressing F4, choosing View⇨Properties Window, or clicking on the Properties window icon on the toolbar).

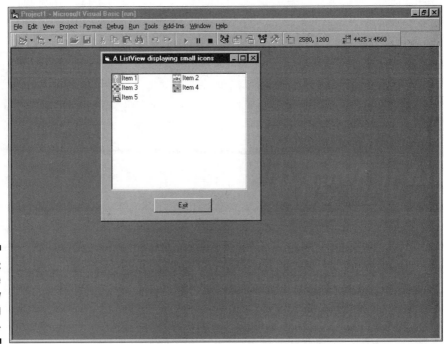

Figure 5-4:
The same
ListView
displaying
small icons.

2. Click in the <u>V</u>iew property and choose one of the following:

>   0 – lvwIcon

>   1 – lvwSmallIcon

To change the View property using BASIC code, use the following:

```
ListView1.View = lvwIcon
```

This command displays Icons in the ListView control. If you want to display SmallIcons, use the following instead:

```
ListView1.View = lvwSmallIcon
```

Responding to the user

If the user clicks on a specific item displayed in the ListView, you need to write BASIC code to tell your program what to do next. So how does your program know which item the user clicked on?

The answer is easier than you might think. First, you need to use the
ItemClick event procedure for your ListView control. Initially, the
ItemClick event procedure looks like this:

```
Private Sub ListView1_ItemClick(ByVal Item As
          ComctlLib.ListItem)
End Sub
```

Then use a Select-Case statement and the Item.Index property to identify
which item the user clicked. If the user clicks the first item, the Item.Index
property is 1, if the user clicks the second item, the Item.Index property is 2,
and so on. For example:

```
Private Sub ListView1_ItemClick(ByVal Item As
          ComctlLib.ListItem)
  Select Case Item.Index
    Case 1
      ' Code to follow if the user clicks the first item
    Case 2
      ' Code to follow if user clicks the second item
    Case 3
      ' Code to follow if user clicks the third item
  End Select
End Sub
```

Using the TreeView

The TreeView displays items in a hierarchical list combining text and
optional graphics, like what you see in Figure 5-2. Using computer science
lingo, a *hierarchical list* consists of nodes connected by lines. The three
types of nodes are:

- Root
- Parent
- Child

There can be only one root node in every TreeView, and that root appears at
the very top of the tree.

You can have zero or more parent nodes. A parent node is any node that has
child nodes attached to it. Sometimes a node can be both a parent and a child
as shown in Figure 5-2.

Adding nodes to the TreeView

To make the TreeView display anything, you have to store items in the TreeView control. Because the TreeView stores items in a hierarchical list, when you add a new node you must specify:

- ✔ The existing node under which you want to place your new node
- ✔ Whether to make the new node a child indented under the existing node or a sibling node at the same level as the existing node

Creating a root node

You need to create only one root node because the TreeView can have only one root node anyway. To create a root node, use the following code:

```
Dim MyNodes As Node
Set MyNodes = TreeView1.Nodes.Add( , , "R", "Root")
```

1. The first line declares the MyNodes variable as a Node.

2. The second line adds the string Root to the root node of the MyNodes variable. The R string simply labels the root node so that in the future you can tell Visual Basic to retrieve the root node contents by looking for the R node.

Creating a child node

After you create a root node, you need to create one or more child nodes. To create a child node, use the following code:

```
Set MyNodes = TreeView1.Nodes.Add("R", tvwChild, "C1",
          "Child 1")
MyNodes.EnsureVisible
```

1. The first line provides Visual Basic with four important clues on where to add this node:

   - The R string tells Visual Basic to place this new node next to the existing node identified by the R string.

   - The tvwChild constant tells Visual Basic to make this node a child of another node.

   - The C1 string simply identifies this new node as C1. This string can be any name that you care to give your node.

   - The Child 1 string appears in the TreeView to identify your new node.

2. The second line tells Visual Basic to make sure the newly created node appears in the TreeView control.

There is no special method for creating parent nodes. A parent node is nothing more than a child node that contains its own child node.

Creating a sibling node

A sibling node appears at the same level as an existing node. When you create a sibling node, you can place it in one of three locations in relation to an existing node:

- Directly before an existing node (tvwPrevious)
- Directly after an existing node (tvwNext)
- Last on the same level as an existing node (tvwLast)

To create a sibling node, use the following code:

```
Set MyNodes = TreeView1.Nodes.Add("C1", tvwPrevious, "C2",
        "Child 2")
MyNodes.EnsureVisible
```

1. The first line provides Visual Basic with four important clues on where to add this node:

   - The C1 string tells Visual Basic to place this new node next to the existing node identified by the C1 string.

   - The tvwPrevious constant tells Visual Basic to place this node on the same level but before the node identified by C1. (To place this node directly after the C1 node, replace tvwPrevious with tvwNext. If you want this node to appear last on the same level as the C1 node, replace tvwPrevious with tvwLast.)

   - The C2 string simply identifies this new node as C2. This string can be any name that you care to give your node.

   - The Child 2 string appears in the TreeView to identify your new node.

2. The second line tells Visual Basic to make sure the newly created node appears in the TreeView control.

Removing nodes from the TreeView

After you add nodes to the TreeView, you may want to remove one or more nodes later. To remove a node from the TreeView, you just have to use this magical command:

```
TreeView1.Nodes.Remove "C2"
```

This line simply tells Visual Basic to remove the node identified by the string C2.

If you delete a node that's a parent to one or more child nodes, you also wipe out those child nodes, so be careful when deleting nodes.

Adding icons to the TreeView

Without icons, the TreeView displays items as dull, plain, boring text. To spice up the appearance of your TreeView items, you can have each item display an icon as well. To display pictures in a TreeView control, you must first store the pictures you want to use in an ImageList control.

Storing pictures in the ImageList

After drawing your TreeView control, draw an ImageList control on your form and then add icons to that ImageList control.

To store icons in an ImageList control, follow these steps:

1. Draw an ImageList control on the same form that contains your TreeView control. (The location of the ImageList controls is not important because they won't be visible when your program is running.)

2. Click the ImageList control and open the Properties window (by pressing F4, choosing <u>V</u>iew⇨Properties <u>W</u>indow, or clicking on the Properties window icon on the toolbar).

3. Click in the *(Custom)* property and then click the ellipsis button (. . .) to display the ImageList Control Properties dialog box. Or click the ImageList, press the right mouse button, and choose P<u>r</u>operties.

4. Click the Images tab.

5. Click Insert <u>P</u>icture. A Select Picture dialog box appears, letting you choose a bitmap (*.BMP) or icon (*.ICO) file. Choose a file and click <u>O</u>pen.

6. Repeat Step 5 until you've stored all the pictures you want in the ImageList control.

   Note: When you're storing pictures in an ImageList, the pictures must be of the same format, that is, all bitmap files (*.BMP) or all icon files (*.ICO).

7. Click OK.

8. Add the following code before the code that adds any nodes:

```
Set TreeView1.ImageList = ImageList1
```

You can also set the ImageList property through the Property window if you'd rather not mess around with any more BASIC code than absolutely necessary.

9. When you add a node to the TreeView control, include the index number as follows:

```
Set MyNodes = TreeView1.Nodes.Add("C1", tvwPrevious,
     "C2", "Child 2", 1)
```

This code includes the number 1 at the end of the line. This number 1 tells Visual Basic to display the first picture stored in the ImageList control. If you change this number to 2, Visual Basic displays the second picture stored in the ImageList control, and so on.

Displaying icons in the TreeView

After you store pictures in an ImageList control and write BASIC code to include a picture with each node that you add, the final step is to tell the TreeView control to display icons as well.

The TreeView can display eight types of trees as shown in Figure 5-5:

- 0 – tvwTextOnly
- 1 – tvwPictureText
- 2 – tvwPlusMinusText
- 3 – tvwPlusMinusPictureText
- 4 – tvwTreelinesText
- 5 – tvwTreelinesPictureText
- 6 – tvwTreelinesPlusMinusText
- 7 – tvwTreelinesPlusMinusPictureText

To choose the tree style property of the TreeView control at design time, follow these steps:

1. Click the TreeView control and open the Properties window (by pressing F4, choosing View➪Properties Window, or clicking on the Properties window icon on the toolbar).

2. Click in the Style property and choose one of the following:

   1 – tvwPictureText

   3 – tvwPlusMinusPictureText

   5 – tvwTreelinesPictureText

   7 – tvwTreelinesPlusMinusPictureText

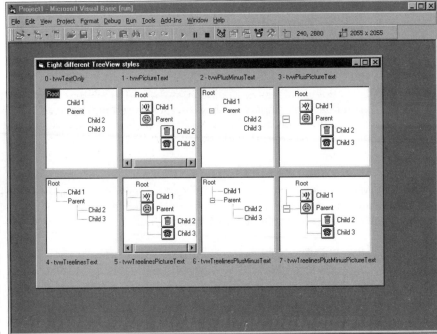

Figure 5-5:
Different
ways to
display a
TreeView
with
treelines
and
pictures.

To change the View property at run-time using BASIC code, use the following:

```
TreeView1.Style = x
```

where x can equal a constant such as tvwPictureText or tvwTreelines-PictureText.

Responding to the user

When the user clicks on a specific item displayed in the TreeView, nothing happens unless you've written BASIC code to tell your program what to do next. The event procedure that can tell which node a user clicked is the NodeClick event procedure. Initially, the NodeClick event procedure looks like this:

```
Private Sub TreeView1_NodeClick(ByVal Node As
          ComctlLib.Node)
End Sub
```

Then toss in a Select-Case statement and use the Node.Index property to identify which item the user clicked on. If the user clicks the root node, the Node.Index property is 1, if the user clicks the second node you created, the Node.Index property is 2, and so on. For example:

```
Private Sub TreeView1_NodeClick(ByVal Node As
        ComctlLib.Node)
Select Case Node.Index
    Case 1
       ' Code to follow if the user clicks the root node
    Case 2
       ' Code to follow if user clicks the first node Case 3
       ' Code to follow if user clicks the second node End
            Select
End Sub
```

The Node.Index value is based on the order that you created the nodes, not their appearance in the TreeView control. The root node always has a Node.Index value of 1. Each time you create a new node, that node gets a Node.Index value one greater than the last node no matter where its location may be in the TreeView control.

If you want to reference nodes by name, you can use the Key property instead. For example, you could rewrite the preceding code as follows:

```
Private Sub TreeView1_NodeClick(ByVal Node As
        ComctlLib.Node)
Select Case Node.Key
    Case "R"
       ' Code to follow if the user clicks the node desig-
            nated as " R"
    Case "C1"
       ' Code to follow if user clicks the node designated
            as "C1"
    Case "C2"
       ' Code to follow if user clicks the node designated
            as "C2"
  End Select
End Sub
```

Try It Yourself

To see how the ListView, TreeView, and ImageList controls work, here's a real-life program that you can create.

Test your newfound knowledge

1. How does the ListView control store items?

   a. The ListView control is so sloppy that it stores items in the garage, the attic, the basement, and other places where nobody will ever find them again.

   b. The ListView control stores items in an array of objects.

   c. The ListView control doesn't work at all because it has bugs in it, so there.

   d. I didn't know the ListView control could store any items at all. Wait, let me buy another Visual Basic book to tell me more about this.

2. What are the two ways to identify nodes in the TreeView control?

   a. You can identify them by name or by their Node.Index value.

   b. TreeView control nodes are unidentified and the subject of an intense government investigation that some people believe is a conspiracy to keep the public ignorant of the real facts.

   c. There is no way to identify nodes in a TreeView control because the TreeView control can never store anything worthwhile.

   d. Nodes must carry two forms of identification with them at all times, such as a driver's license, passport, or birth certificate.

Object	Property	Setting
Form	Caption	A ListView, TreeView, and ImageList
	Height	5370
	Left	2580
	Top	1200
	Width	4425
TreeView1	Height	2055
	Left	240
	Top	120
	Width	3735
ListView1	Height	2055
	Left	240
	Top	2280
	Width	3735

Object	Property	Setting
Command1	Caption	E&xit
	Height	375
	Left	1440
	Top	4440
	Width	1575
ImageList1	Left	120
	Top	4320

In the ImageList1 Control Properties dialog box, insert the smiley face icon. (If you let Visual Basic install itself in its own directories, the smiley face icon can be found in `icons\misc\Face03.ico`.)

Type the following in the Code window:

```
Private Sub Form_Load()
  Dim MyNode As Node
  Set TreeView1.ImageList = ImageList1
  Set MyNode = TreeView1.Nodes.Add(, , "R", "Root", 1)
  Set MyNode = TreeView1.Nodes.Add("R", tvwChild, "C1",
          "Child 1", 1)
  Set MyNode = TreeView1.Nodes.Add("R", tvwChild, "C2",
          "Child 2", 1)
  Set MyNode = TreeView1.Nodes.Add("C2", tvwChild, "C3",
          "Child 3", 1
  Set MyNode = TreeView1.Nodes.Add("C3", tvwLast, "C4",
          "Child 4", 1)
  MyNode. EnsureVisible
  TreeView1.Style = 7

  Dim MyItem As ListItem
  Dim I As Integer
  ListView1.Icons = ImageList1
  ListView1.View = 0
  For I = 1 To 5
    Set MyItem = ListView1.ListItems.Add()
    MyItem.Text = "Item " & I
    MyItem.Icon = 1
  Next I
End Sub
```

(continued)

(continued)

```
Private Sub ListView1_ItemClick(ByVal Item As
          ComctlLib.ListItem)
  MsgBox "You clicked item " & Item.Index, 64,
          "Generic Message"
End Sub

Private Sub TreeView1_NodeClick(ByVal Node As
          ComctlLib.Node)
  MsgBox "You clicked node " & Node.Index, 64,
          "Generic Message"
End Sub

Private Sub Command1_Click()
  Unload Me
End Sub
```

Chapter 6

Using the Rich TextBox

· ·

· ·

*T*o give you more options for displaying text, Visual Basic provides a special text box called a Rich TextBox. The main difference between an ordinary text box and a Rich TextBox is that a Rich TextBox can load and display text trapped in a Rich Text Format (RTF) file.

Unlike the old ASCII file format that stores only text and no fonts, underlining, or point sizes, a Rich Text Format file can store text, fonts, underlining, bold face, and point sizes. As a result, nearly all word processors (such as Microsoft Word 97 and WordPerfect) can share files if they are saved as RTF files.

Two reasons to use a Rich TextBox instead of an ordinary text box are:

✔ When you need to display more than 64K of text

✔ When you need to display text along with any special formatting (such as italics or fonts)

Creating a Rich TextBox

Before you can add a Rich TextBox to a form, you have to add the Rich TextBox ActiveX control to your Visual Basic project:

1. Choose Project➪Components (or press Ctrl+T). A Components dialog box appears.

2. Click in the Microsoft Rich TextBox Control 5.0 check box and click OK. Visual Basic displays the Rich TextBox icon in the Toolbox as shown in Figure 6-1.

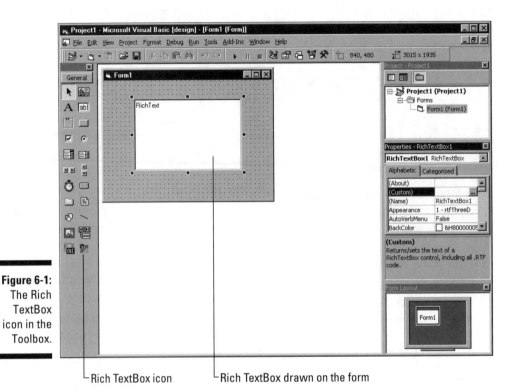

Figure 6-1:
The Rich
TextBox
icon in the
Toolbox.

Rich TextBox icon   Rich TextBox drawn on the form

Once you add the Rich TextBox to the Toolbox, you can draw it on a form
just like any other Toolbox object. Just click on the Rich TextBox icon in the
Toolbox, move the mouse pointer anywhere on a form, hold down the left
mouse, drag the mouse to draw the Rich TextBox, and release the mouse.

Stuffing Text in a Rich TextBox

After you draw a Rich TextBox, the next obvious step is to put text in it. Just
like with an ordinary text box, you can add text to a Rich TextBox by modifying the Text property of the Rich TextBox like this:

```
RichTextBox1.Text = "Cats rule the world"
```

This BASIC command simply puts the string "Cats rule the world" in a Rich
TextBox named RichTextBox1.

Of course, modifying the Text property of a Rich TextBox doesn't make it
any more useful than an ordinary text box unless you use the Rich TextBox
to display text trapped in a Rich Text Format (RTF) file, or if you want the
user to type formatted text.

Most word processors can save documents in a Rich Text Format. Just choose File➪Save As. When a Save As dialog box appears, click in the Save as type list box and choose Rich Text Format.

Loading an RTF file into a Rich TextBox

To load an RTF file, you have to use the magic LoadFile BASIC command:

```
RichTextBox1.LoadFile Pathname, Filetype
```

Pathname is a string that defines the path and filename. If you want to load a file called FBI.RTF, located in your C:\SECRETS directory, the pathname would be C:\SECRETS\FBI.RTF.

Filetype specifies the type of file to load. The two choices for Filetype are shown in Table 6-1.

Table 6-1 Constant values for loading a file into a Rich TextBox.

Constant	Value	Description
rtfRTF	0	Loads an RTF file.
rtfText	1	Loads a plain, ASCII text file.

To load the FBI.RTF file into a Rich TextBox, you could use the following:

```
RichTextBox1.LoadFile "C:\SECRETS\FBI.RTF", rtfRTF
```

You may want to use the Common Dialog control to display an Open dialog box. That way users can pick a file they want to load into the Rich TextBox, rather than forcing you to "hard code" a specific RTF file to load into the Rich TextBox.

Loading text from the Clipboard into a Rich TextBox

Besides loading text from a file, you can also load text from the Windows Clipboard. (Naturally, before you can load text from the Clipboard into a Rich TextBox, the user must have copied something to the Clipboard first.)

To copy text from the Clipboard and paste it into a Rich TextBox, use the following BASIC command:

```
RichTextBox1.Text = Clipboard.GetText (vbCFText)
```

Remember that when you copy text into the Clipboard, the Clipboard is stupid and doesn't keep all the formatting such as bold face, italics, fonts, or point sizes. So if you paste text from the Clipboard into a Rich TextBox, you just get plain ASCII text without any formatting.

Linking a Rich TextBox to a database

Ordinary text boxes can only hold a maximum of 64K of text. The Rich TextBox can store more than 64K, so you may want to use a Rich TextBox to display text stored in a database memo field.

To connect a Rich TextBox to a database, follow these steps:

1. Click on the Data control in the Toolbox and draw the Data control on the form.

2. Open the Properties window (by pressing F4, choosing View⇨Properties Window, or clicking on the Properties window icon on the toolbar).

3. Double-click the DatabaseName property. A DatabaseName dialog box appears.

4. Click on the database file you want to use and click Open. (You may have to dig through folders to find the database file you want to use.)

5. Click on the RecordSource property and choose a database table to use.

6. Draw a Rich TextBox on the form and open the Properties window (by pressing F4, choosing View⇨Properties Window, or clicking on the Properties window icon on the toolbar).

7. Click on the DataSource property and choose the name of the data control you created in step 1.

8. Click on the DataField property and choose a field that you want to display in the RichTextbox.

Changing Text Inside a Rich TextBox

Once you fill a Rich TextBox with text, you may want to modify the text appearance by choosing a different font or making text appear underlined. That way your text can look more eye-catching or aesthetically pleasing in case you need to display a message to the user, or if you just want to make your program look really neat.

Your computer most likely has tons of fonts buried on its hard disk. Before you can display text in a particular font, you have to know the exact font name you want to use.

If you don't know the exact name of a particular font on your computer, click the Start button on the Windows 95 taskbar and choose Settings⇨Control Panel. When the Control Panel window appears, double-click on the Fonts icon. This displays a Font window that lists all the fonts loaded on your computer.

To specify a font to use for all the text inside a Rich TextBox, use the following BASIC command:

```
RichTextBox1.SelFontName = Fontname
```

Where the Font is specified by the Fontname. So if you wanted to change the text in a Rich TextBox to the Times New Roman font, you would use the following command:

```
RichTextBox1.SelFontName = "Times New Roman"
```

When you change the font, any existing text in a Rich TextBox retains its font. Changing the font only changes any highlighted text or text typed into the Rich TextBox after specifying a new font.

Changing the point size

The point size determines the actual size of text and typically ranges from 8 (approximately very tiny) all the way up to 72 (approximately 1 inch tall). To change the point size of text in a Rich TextBox, use the following BASIC command:

```
RichTextBox1.SelFontSize = Number
```

Where Number is an actual number such as 12, 26 or 13.5.

When you change the point size, any existing text in a Rich TextBox retains its original point size. Changing the point size only changes any highlighted text or text typed into the Rich TextBox after specifying a new point size.

Making text bold, italic, strikethrough, or underline

If you want to display text in boldface, italic, strikethrough, or underline, you have to set the appropriate typestyle property to True or False to turn off that typestyle. Table 6-2 shows the properties that affect the appearance of text in a Rich TextBox.

Table 6-2	Rich TextBox properties that change the appearance of text.
Property	*Typestyle*
SelBold	**Bold**
SelItalic	*Italic*
SelStrikethru	~~Strikethrough~~
SelUnderline	<u>Underline</u>

For example, to change the text in a Rich TextBox to bold, use the following:

```
RichTextBox1.SelBold = True
```

To turn off bold face, use the following:

```
RichTextBox1.SelBold = False
```

When you change the text style (such as bold or underline), any existing text in a Rich TextBox retains its original text style. Changing the text style only changes any highlighted text or text typed into the Rich TextBox after specifying a new text style.

Saving the Contents of a Rich TextBox

Once you store text inside a Rich TextBox, you may want to print or save it. To save text, just use the handy SaveFile command such as:

```
RichTextBox1.SaveFile Pathname, Filetype
```

Pathname is a string that defines the path and filename. If you want to save a file called SAVEME.RTF, in your C:\WINDOWS directory, the pathname would be C:\WINDOWS\SAVEME.RTF.

Filetype specifies the type of file to load. The two choices for Filetype are shown in Table 6-3.

Table 6-3	Constant values for saving a file in a Rich TextBox.	
Constant	*Value*	*Description*
rtfRTF	0	Saves text as an RTF file.
rtfText	1	Saves text as a plain, ASCII text file.

So combining the above into a real-life BASIC command, you get:

```
RichTextBox1.SaveFile "C:\WINDOWS\SAVEME.RTF", rtfRTF
```

Try It Yourself

To see how you can play around with a Rich TextBox, create the following program, shown at run-time in Figure 6-2.

Object	Property	Setting
Form	Caption	Playing with a Rich TextBox
	Height	3915
	Left	105
	Top	105
	Width	6990
RichTextBox1	Height	2775
	Left	240

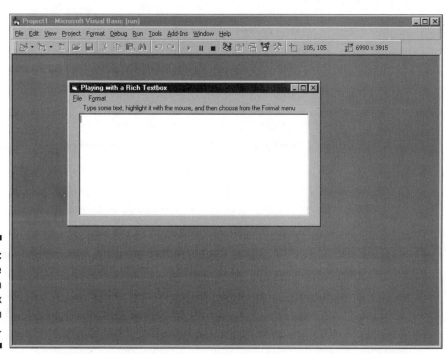

Figure 6-2:
What the sample Rich Textbox program looks like.

Object	Property	Setting
	Top	240
	Width	6375
Label1	Caption	Type some text, highlight it with the mouse, and then choose from the Format menu
	Height	255
	Left	360
	Top	0
	Width	6255

Draw a Common Dialog Control anywhere on the form (its exact location doesn't matter). Then create a pull-down menu with the following menu structure:

Menu Caption	Name
&File	mnuFile
...&Open	mnuFileOpen
...&Save	mnuFileSave
...-	mnuBar
...E&xit	mnuFileExit
F&ormat	mnuFormat
...&Font	mnuFormatFont
......Ariel	mnuFormatFontAriel
......Courier New	mnuFormatFontCourierNew
......Times New Roman	mnuFormatFontTimesNewRoman
...&Size	mnuFormatSize
......8	mnuFormatSize8
......10	mnuFormatSize10
......12	mnuFormatSize12
......14	mnuFormatSize14
......18	mnuFormatSize18
...S&tyle	mnuFormatStyle
......&Bold	mnuFormatStyleBold
......&Italic	mnuFormatStyleItalic
......&Strikethru	mnuFormatStyleStrikethru
......&Underline	mnuFormatStyleUnderline

Type the following in the Code window:

```
Private Sub mnuFileExit_Click()
  Unload Me
End Sub

Private Sub mnuFileOpen_Click()
  CommonDialog1.Filter = "RTF files (*.rtf)|*.RTF"
  CommonDialog1.FilterIndex = 1
  CommonDialog1.ShowOpen
  RichTextBox1.LoadFile CommonDialog1.filename, rtfRTF
End Sub

Private Sub mnuFileSave_Click()
  CommonDialog1.Filter = "RTF files (*.rtf)|*.RTF"
  CommonDialog1.FilterIndex = 1
  CommonDialog1.ShowSave
  RichTextBox1.SaveFile CommonDialog1.filename, rtfRTF
End Sub

Private Sub mnuFormatFontAriel_Click()
  RichTextBox1.SelFontName = "Ariel"
End Sub

Private Sub mnuFormatFontCourierNew_Click()
  RichTextBox1.SelFontName = "Courier New"
End Sub

Private Sub mnuFormatFontTimesNewRoman_Click()
  RichTextBox1.SelFontName = "Times New Roman"
End Sub

Private Sub mnuFormatSize10_Click()
  RichTextBox1.SelFontSize = 10
End Sub

Private Sub mnuFormatSize12_Click()
  RichTextBox1.SelFontSize = 12
End Sub

Private Sub mnuFormatSize14_Click()
  RichTextBox1.SelFontSize = 14
End Sub
```

(continued)

(continued)

```
Private Sub mnuFormatSize18_Click()
  RichTextBox1.SelFontSize = 18
End Sub

Private Sub mnuFormatSize8_Click()
  RichTextBox1.SelFontSize = 8
End Sub

Private Sub mnuFormatStyleBold_Click()
  If RichTextBox1.SelBold = True Then
    RichTextBox1.SelBold = False
  Else
    RichTextBox1.SelBold = True
  End If
End Sub

Private Sub mnuFormatStyleItalic_Click()
  If RichTextBox1.SelItalic = True Then
    RichTextBox1.SelItalic = False
  Else
    RichTextBox1.SelItalic = True
  End If
End Sub

Private Sub mnuFormatStyleStrikethru_Click()
  If RichTextBox1.SelStrikeThru = True Then
    RichTextBox1.SelStrikeThru = False
  Else
    RichTextBox1.SelStrikeThru = True
  End If
End Sub

Private Sub mnuFormatStyleUnderline_Click()
  If RichTextBox1.SelUnderline = True Then
    RichTextBox1.SelUnderline = False
  Else
    RichTextBox1.SelUnderline = True
  End If
End Sub
```

Part II
Holding, Storing, and Saving Information

In this part . . .

Every program needs to store information in one form or another. To give you the full power of storage and retrieval that other languages offer, Part II explains how to use arrays in Visual Basic.

Arrays simply let you organize lists of related information in one convenient location. If you can't resist even more rigid segmentation of data, Part II also shows you how to create and use structures.

Essentially, a structure lets you create your own way of organizing information such as name, address, age, height, and other data that upsets people if the government stores it on their computers.

Chapter 7

Storing Stuff in Arrays

- -

- -

*E*very program needs to work with data such as numbers, letters, or pictures. The trick with data is that your Visual Basic program needs a place where it can store the data temporarily and then find it again. Because Visual Basic can't store data in your desk drawer, it needs to create its own storage containers called *data structures*. A data structure is nothing more than a way for your program to organize information for quick retrieval.

The most common data structure is something called an *array*. Essentially, an array is like a row of buckets, each labeled with a number as shown in Figure 7-1.

Each row of buckets can hold only one type of data, such as Integer, Single, Double, or Strings. You can create one row of buckets to hold just Integers, another to hold just Strings, and so on. For convenience's sake, you can give a name to this row of buckets.

To store or retrieve data in an individual bucket, you must first identify the name of the row of buckets, and then use the number of the individual bucket. Once again, fancy programming terminology calls each bucket an *array element*.

To create an array, you must define the array's

> ✔ Name
>
> ✔ Size
>
> ✔ Data type (Integer, Long, Single, Double, Currency, or String)
>
> ✔ Scope (local, module, or global)

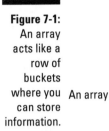

Figure 7-1:
An array acts like a row of buckets where you can store information.

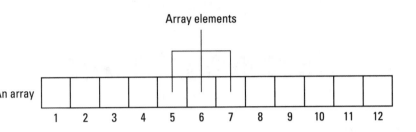

Naming an Array

The name of an array must meet the following criteria:

✔ Be 255 characters or less

✔ Consist of any combination of letters, numbers, and the underscore (_) character

✔ Begin with a letter

✔ Not be a Visual Basic reserved word

Some valid array names include:

```
Bucket_of_Strings

NumberArray

ThisHolds6Numbers
```

Here are some invalid array names:

```
99BottlesOfBeer (Doesn't begin with a letter)

What'sWrong? (Uses invalid characters)

Function (Uses a Visual Basic reserved word)
```

Defining the Size of an Array

After you name an array, you must define its size to specify the number of array elements in your array. The size of an array is determined by two numbers: Its lower bound and its upper bound. The values of the lower and upper bounds must be in the range of -2^{31} to 2^{31} minus 1, although if you use arrays this big, you ought to have your head examined.

To define an array's size, specify the lower and upper bound in parentheses like this:

```
Bucket_of_Strings (1 To 10)

NumberArray (15 To 26)

ThisHolds6Numbers (-34 To -29)
```

As shown in Figure 7-2, the `Bucket_of_Strings` array consists of ten array elements numbered 1 to 10. The `NumberArray` array consists of twelve array elements numbered 15 to 26. The `ThisHolds6Numbers` array consists of six array elements numbered –34 to –29.

Bucket_of_Strings (1 To 10)

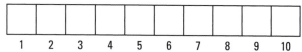

| 1 | 2 | 3 | 4 | 5 | 6 | 7 | 8 | 9 | 10 |

NumberArray (15 To 26)

| 15 | 16 | 17 | 18 | 19 | 20 | 21 | 22 | 23 | 24 | 25 | 26 |

Figure 7-2:
All the
arrays with This Holds6Numbers (-34 To -29)
their
elements
numbered.

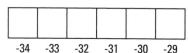

| -34 | -33 | -32 | -31 | -30 | -29 |

Unless the lower and upper bound numbers have some meaning to your program, you're best off simplifying your arrays:

```
NumberArray (1 To 12)

ThisHolds6Numbers (1 To 6)
```

If you feel lazy, you don't have to specify the lower bound at all. Instead, you can just specify the upper bound and Visual Basic automatically assumes that the lower bound will be zero. For example:

```
Bucket_of_Strings (9)

NumberArray (11)

ThisHolds6Numbers (5)
```

As you can see in Figure 7-3, the `Bucket_of_Strings` array still holds ten array elements, but now they're numbered 0 to 9. The `NumberArray` array holds twelve array elements, but they're numbered 0 to 11. The `ThisHolds6Numbers` array holds six array elements, but they're numbered 0 to 5.

Bucket_of_Strings (9)

NumberArray (11)

Figure 7-3:
All the
arrays with
their
elements
numbered
from zero
on up.

This Holds6Numbers (5)

Although the default method of defining an array size is simpler, it can be confusing if you don't remember that the first array element is numbered 0.

When using arrays, it's a good idea to define arrays consistently throughout your program. For example, you could define an array to hold ten elements in the following ways:

```
MyArray (1 To 10)
MyArray (9)
```

The method you choose doesn't matter just as long as you use the method you like best and you are consistent.

Defining a default lower bound

To change the lower bound from the default 0 to 1, follow these steps:

1. Press F7, choose View⇨Code from the menu bar to display the Code window, or click on the View Code icon in the Project Explorer window.

2. Choose *(General)* from the Object list box. Visual Basic automatically displays *(Declarations)* in the Proc list box.

3. Type **Option Base 1**.

With the Option Base 1 statement in the declarations part of your Visual Basic code, the lower bound of all arrays will be 1 unless otherwise specified. Suppose that the Option Base 1 statement was defined for the following arrays:

```
Bucket_of_Strings (9)

NumberArray (11)

ThisHolds6Numbers (5)
```

The `Bucket_of_Strings` array would have nine array elements numbered 1 to 9. The `NumberArray` array would have eleven array elements, numbered 1 to 11. The `ThisHolds6Numbers` array would have five array elements, numbered 1 to 5.

Rather than use Option 1, for clarity you're best off specifically identifying lower and upper array bounds, such as:

```
ArrayName (1 To 10)
```

If you like risking confusion, use the other methods, but don't say I didn't warn you.

Using constants in array bounds

Although you can specify the size of an array using numbers, you can also use constants. For example, the following code defines an array of size 10:

```
Const LOWER = 1
Const UPPER = 10
ArrayName (LOWER To UPPER)
```

This is equivalent to the following:

```
ArrayName (1 To 10)
```

By using constants to define the size of an array, you can quickly change the array size by changing the constant. For example, two arrays might have different lower bounds but have identical upper bounds:

```
FirstArray (1 To 20)
SecondArray (5 To 20)
```

Changing the upper bounds of both arrays requires editing two lines. But if you define the upper bound with a constant, you have to change only the constant value, such as:

```
Const UPPER = 20
FirstArray (1 To UPPER)
SecondArray (5 To UPPER)
```

Anytime two or more parts of your program needs to share the same number, you can save time and risk fewer errors by using a constant.

Defining the Data Type of an Array

Before an array can hold anything, you have to specify the data type it can hold. Arrays can hold all kinds of data, including:

- Integer
- Long
- Single
- Double
- Currency
- String
- Boolean
- Any user-defined data types

To specify the data type of an array, you have to specify the array name, its size, and finally its data type. For example:

```
Bucket_of_Strings (1 To 10) As String

NumberArray (1 To 12) As Integer

ThisHolds6Numbers (1 To 6) As Double
```

The `Bucket_of_Strings` array can hold ten strings. The `NumberArray` array can hold twelve integers. The `ThisHolds6Numbers` array can hold six double numbers.

If you try to store a different data type in an array that expects another data type, it doesn't work. However, you can define an array to be of a Variant data type, such as:

```
JunkArray (1 To 25) As Variant
```

Since a Variant data type can hold numbers, strings, or dates, an array declared as a Variant data type can hold a variety of different items. For example, `JunkArray (3)` might hold a currency value, `JunkArray(21)` might hold a string, and so on.

Defining the Scope of an Array

The scope of an array determines where it can be used. The three choices for an array's scope are

- ✔ Local
- ✔ Module
- ✔ Public

Local arrays can be used only in the procedure where they are declared. To create a local array, declare the array inside a procedure and use the Dim keyword, such as:

```
Private Sub StoreNames ()
  Dim Bucket_of_Strings (1 To 10) As String
End Sub
```

In this example, the array can be used only inside the `StoreNames` procedure.

Module arrays can be declared in the declarations part of an .FRM form or in a .BAS module or .CLS class module file using the Dim keyword. If an array is declared in an .FRM form file, only procedures stored in that same .FRM form file can use that array. If an array is declared in a .BAS module or .CLS class module file, only procedures stored in that same .BAS module file can use that array.

To create a module array, follow these steps:

1. Press Ctrl+R, choose View⇨Project, or click the Project Explorer icon to display the Project Explorer window.

2. Highlight the .FRM form or .BAS module file where you want to declare the module array.

3. Press F7, choose View⇨Code from the menu bar to display the Code window, or click on the View Code icon in the Project Explorer window.

4. Choose *(General)* from the Object list box. Visual Basic automatically displays *(Declarations)* in the Proc list box.

5. Type your array. For example:

```
Dim NumberArray (1 To 12) As Integer
```

Public arrays can be declared in the declarations part of any .BAS module file using the Public keyword. A public array can be used by any procedure stored in any .FRM form or .BAS module file in the same .VBP project file.

To create a public array, follow these steps:

1. Press Ctrl+R, choose View⇨Project, or click the Project Explorer icon to display the Project Explorer window.

2. Highlight the .BAS module file where you want to declare the public array.

3. Press F7, choose View⇨Code from the menu bar to display the Code window, or click on the View Code icon in the Project Explorer window.

4. Choose *(General)* from the Object list box. Visual Basic automatically displays *(Declarations)* in the Proc list box.

5. Type your array. For example:

```
Public ThisHolds6Numbers (1 To 6) As Double
```

Storing and Retrieving Array Data

Any array you create automatically contains zeros or empty strings (" ") until you store your own data in the array.

To put data in (or yank data out of) an array, you have to specify the array name and the array element number that you want to use, such as:

```
Dim NumberArray (1 To 12) As Integer
NumberArray(1) = 23
VariableName = NumberArray(1)
```

1. The first line defines an array called NumberArray, defines its size as 12, and specifies that it can hold only integers.

2. The second line stores the number 23 in the first element of the NumberArray.

3. The third line retrieves the value of the first element of NumberArray and stores it into a variable called VariableName.

To reference a specific array element, just identify it by its number (such as 1, 2, or 3). To reference all of the array's elements, the easiest thing to do is use a For-Next loop. For example:

```
Private Sub InitializeArray ()
Static Bucket_of_Strings (1 To 10) As String
Dim I As Integer
   For I = 1 To 10
       Bucket_of_Strings (I) = "Letters"
   Next I
End Sub
```

1. The first line defines a general procedure called `InitalizeArray`.

2. The second line defines a local array called `Bucket_of_Strings` that contains 10 array elements and can hold only Strings.

3. The third line declares a variable called `I` that can hold an integer value.

4. The fourth line is the start of a For-Next loop that counts from 1 to 10.

5. The fifth line stores the string `Letters` into the array element identified by the value of I (such as 1, 2, or 3) in the `Bucket_of_Strings` array.

6. The sixth line increases the value of `I` by 1 and loops back to line 4.

7. The seventh line defines the end of the general procedure.

Test your newfound knowledge

1. What are the three parts of an array that you must define?

   a. You never have to define any parts of an array because the dictionary has already defined the word *array* for you.

   b. The height, width, and length.

   c. The array's color, age, and capability to cause headaches in laboratory rats.

   d. The array's name, its size, and the type of data it can hold.

2. What is the size of the following two arrays?

```
Const SMALL = 2
Const LARGE = 23
```

```
FirstArray = (1 To LARGE) As
    String
SecondArray = (SMALL To LARGE)
    As Integer
```

   a. One size fits all, so both arrays are the same length.

   b. The size of `FirstArray` is 1 to 23. The size of `SecondArray` is 2 To 23.

   c. Both arrays are infinite in size and can be used to hold all the garbage currently being stored in landfills across the country.

   d. One array is larger than the other, but I don't know which array that is and I don't care either.

Try It Yourself

To give you experience in creating, storing, and retrieving data in arrays, the following program asks you to store numbers in an array and then displays those numbers on the screen for you to see, as shown in Figure 7-4. So load Visual Basic, create the following objects, set the properties as defined in the following list, and see for yourself how arrays really work.

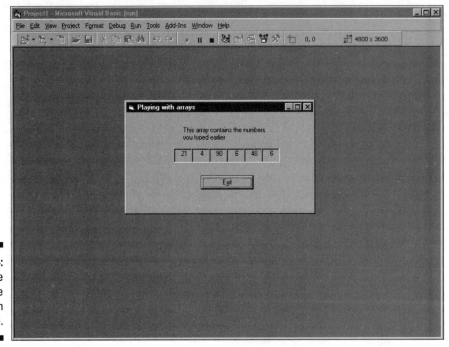

Figure 7-4:
What the sample program looks like.

Object	Property	Setting
Form	Caption	Playing with arrays
	Height	3060
	Left	1575
	Top	1215
	Width	5265
Label1	Alignment	2 – Center
	BorderStyle	1 – Fixed Single
	Caption	(Empty)
	Height	375

Object	*Property*	*Setting*
	Left	1320
	Top	960
	Width	495
Label2	Alignment	2 – Center
	BorderStyle	1 – Fixed Single
	Caption	(Empty)
	Height	375
	Left	1800
	Top	960
	Width	495
Label3	Alignment	2 – Center
	BorderStyle	1 – Fixed Single
	Caption	(Empty)
	Height	375
	Left	2280
	Top	960
	Width	495
Label4	Alignment	2 – Center
	BorderStyle	1 – Fixed Single
	Caption	(Empty)
	Height	375
	Left	2760
	Top	960
	Width	495
Label5	Alignment	2 – Center
	BorderStyle	1 – Fixed Single
	Caption	(Empty)
	Height	375
	Left	3240
	Top	960
	Width	495
Label6	Alignment	2 – Center

(continued)

Object	Property	Setting
	BorderStyle	1 – Fixed Single
	Caption	(Empty)
	Height	375
	Left	3720
	Top	960
	Width	495
Label7	Caption	This array contains the numbers you typed earlier
	Height	375
	Left	1560
	Top	360
	Width	2415
Command1	Caption	E&xit
	Height	375
	Left	2040
	Top	1680
	Width	1455

Type the following in the *(General) (Declarations)* part of the Code window:

```
Const UPPER = 6
Dim NumberArray(1 To UPPER) As Integer
```

Type the following in the Code window:

```
Private Sub Form_Load()
  Dim I As Integer
  For I = 1 To UPPER
  NumberArray(I) = InputBox("Type a number to stuff into
            the array:",
    "Stuff a number into array element number" & Str(I))
          Next I  Label1.Caption = CStr(NumberArray(1))
  Label2.Caption = CStr(NumberArray(2))
  Label3.Caption = CStr(NumberArray(3))
  Label4.Caption = CStr(NumberArray(4))
  Label5.Caption = CStr(NumberArray(5))
  Label6.Caption = CStr(NumberArray(6))
End Sub
```

```
Private Sub Command1_Click()
  Unload Me
End Sub
```

Chapter 8

Multidimensional Arrays

● ●

In This Chapter

▶ Creating multidimensional arrays

▶ Defining the scope of multidimensional arrays

▶ Storing data in multidimensional arrays

▶ Retrieving data from multidimensional arrays

● ●

A simple one-dimensional array can hold information like a row of buckets can hold water (or whatever else you might pour into them), as described in the previous chapter. Sometimes, however, you may find it more convenient to use a multidimensional array. For more bizarre storage capability, you can create a three-, four-, five-, or even sixty-dimensional array. But if you create anything as complicated as that, your brain will likely explode from the mental exertion.

For simplicity's sake, you're best off sticking to one-, two-, or three-dimensional arrays unless you really *need* to create a larger type. If you've ever seen a piece of graph paper, you've seen a two-dimensional array. If you've ever seen a Rubik's Cube, you've seen a three-dimensional array. And if you've ever seen a four-dimensional array, you may want to check what substances you've been ingesting.

Each element of a multidimensional array, like each element in a single (one-dimensional) array, can hold only one type of data, such as Integer, Single, Double, or String.

To create an array, you need to define the array's

✔ Name

✔ Size

✔ Dimension (two, three, four, and so on)

✔ Data type (Integer, Long, Single, Double, Currency, or String)

✔ Scope (local, module, or global)

Naming an Array

The name of an array must meet the following criteria:

- ✔ Be 255 characters or less
- ✔ Consist of any combination of letters, numbers, and the underscore (_) character
- ✔ Begin with a letter
- ✔ Not be a Visual Basic reserved word

Some valid array names include:

```
BattleshipGrid
Post_Office_Boxes
A_3_D_Array
```

Here are some invalid array names:

```
3DArray     (Doesn't begin with a letter)
Big-Array   (Uses an invalid character)
Sub         (Uses a Visual Basic reserved word)
```

Defining the Size of a Multidimensional Array

The size of an array is determined by two numbers: the array's lower bound and upper bound. The value of the lower and upper bounds must be in the range of -2^{31} to 2^{31} minus 1. Of course, any number big enough to approach the limit of this range is going to make your array more complicated to use and understand. If you enjoy complication and that's what you want, fine. Otherwise, stick to smaller numbers whenever possible for both clarity and efficiency.

To define a multidimensional array, you have to specify the size of the array for each dimension. The syntax for defining a multidimensional array is

```
ArrayName (Dimension1, Dimension2, Dimension3, etc.)
```

To define a two-dimensional array, you have to define the two dimensions, such as:

```
TwoDimensions (1 To 6, 1 To 5)
```

One side of the array ranges from 1 to 6. The other side of the array ranges from 1 to 5, as shown in Figure 8-1.

TwoDimensions [1 To 6, 1 To 5]

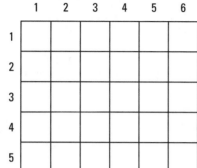

Figure 8-1:
How a two-dimensional array stores data.

To define a three-dimensional array, you have to define the size of all three dimensions, such as:

ThreeD (1 To 6, 1 To 5, 1 To 3)

One side of the array ranges from 1 to 6. The second side of the array ranges from 1 to 5. The third side of the array ranges from 1 to 3, as shown in Figure 8-2.

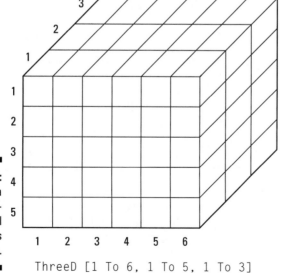

Figure 8-2:
How a three-dimensional array stores data.

ThreeD [1 To 6, 1 To 5, 1 To 3]

Rather than listing both the lower and upper bounds of a range, you can use the shortcut method:

```
ThreeD (9, 19, 2)
```

This defines a three-dimensional array ranging from 0 to 9, 0 to 19, and 0 to 2. Of course, leaving out the lower bounds can be confusing if you keep forgetting that the lower bound is 0.

Just as with single-dimension arrays, multidimensional arrays can use different values for their lower and upper bounds. For example:

```
BattleshipGrid (1 To 10, 1 To 5)
Post_Office_Boxes (3 To 6, 5 To 10)
A_2_D_Array (-9 To -4, 4 To 8)
```

The `BattleshipGrid` array consists of a 10 (1 To 10) by 5 (1 To 5) two-dimensional array. The `Post_Office_Boxes` array consists of a 4 (3 To 6) by 6 (5 To 10) two-dimensional array. The `A_2_D_Array` array consists of a 6 (-9 To -4) by 5 (4 To 8) two-dimensional array.

Unless the lower and upper bound numbers have some meaning to your program, you're best off simplifying arrays, like this:

```
Post_Office_Boxes (1 To 4, 1 To 6)
A_2_D_Array (1 To 6, 1 To 5)
```

If you don't feel like specifying the lower bound, you don't have to. Instead, you can just specify the upper bound and Visual Basic automatically assumes that the lower bound will be 0. For example:

```
BattleshipGrid (9, 4)
Post_Office_Boxes (7, 5)
A_2_D_Array (7, 6)
```

The `BattleshipGrid` array consists of a 10 (0 To 9) by 5 (0 To 4) two-dimensional array. The `Post_Office_Boxes` array consists of an 8 (0 To 7) by 6 (0 To 5) two-dimensional array, as shown in Figure 8-3. The `A_2_D_Array` array consists of an 8 (0 To 7) by 7 (0 To 6) two-dimensional array.

Although this method of defining an array size is simpler, it can be confusing if you don't remember that the first array element is numbered 0. You can change the lower bound to 1 if you think it would make it easier to deal with the code.

To change the default lower bound to 1, follow these steps:

1. Press F7, choose View⇨Code from the menu bar to display the Code window, or click on the View Code icon in the Project Explorer window.

2. Choose *(General)* from the Object list box. Visual Basic automatically displays *(Declarations)* in the Proc list box.

3. Type **Option Base 1**.

With the Option Base 1 statement in the declarations, the lower bound of all arrays will be 1 unless otherwise specified. Suppose that Option Base 1 was defined for the following arrays:

```
BattleshipGrid (9, 4)
Post_Office_Boxes (5, 7)
A_2_D_Array (7, 6)
```

The BattleshipGrid array would consist of a 9 (1 To 9) by 4 (1 To 4) two-dimensional array. The Post_Office_Boxes array would consist of a 5 (1 To 5) by 7 (1 To 7) two-dimensional array as shown in Figure 8-3. The A_2_D_Array array would consist of a 7 (1 To 7) by 6 (1 To 6) two-dimensional array.

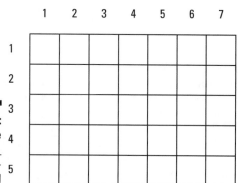

TwoDimensions [1 To 5, 1 To 7]

Figure 8-3:
The Post_Office_Boxes two-dimensional array.

Post_Office_Boxes [5,7]

Defining the Data Type of an Array

Before an array be filled, you have to specify the data type it can hold. Arrays can hold all kinds of data, including:

- ✔ Integer
- ✔ Long
- ✔ Single
- ✔ Double
- ✔ Currency
- ✔ String
- ✔ Boolean
- ✔ Any user-defined data types

The following examples show arrays designed to hold specific types of data:

```
BattleshipGrid (1 To 10, 1 To 10) As Integer
Post_Office_Boxes (1 To 12, 1 To 100) As String
A_3_D_Array (1 To 5, 1 To 10, 1 To 7) As Currency
```

The `BattleshipGrid` array is a two-dimensional, 10-by-10 array that can hold only Integers. The `Post_Office_Boxes` array is a two-dimensional, 12-by-100 array that can hold only Strings. The `A_3_D_Array` array is a three-dimensional, 5-by-10-by-7 array that can hold only Currency values.

If you try to store a String data type in an array that expects a Currency data type, Visual Basic will scold you with an error message. If you insist on storing all types of data in an array, however, define the array to be of a Variant data type, such as the following array:

```
JunkArray (1 To 25, 1 To 14) As Variant
```

Because a Variant data type can hold either numbers, strings, or dates, an array declared as a Variant data type can hold a variety of different items. For example, `JunkArray (1, 2)` might hold a String, `JunkArray (20, 12)` might hold an Integer, and so on.

Defining the Scope of an Array

The scope of an array determines where it can be used. You have three choices for an array's scope:

- ✔ Local
- ✔ Module
- ✔ Public

The maximum number of dimensions for local, module, and public arrays is 60.

Local arrays can be used only in the procedure where they are declared.

To create a local array, declare the array inside a procedure and use the Static keyword. For example:

```
Private Sub StoreNames ()
   Dim BattleshipGrid (1 To 10, 1 To 10) As String
End Sub
```

In this example, the `BattleshipGrid` array can be used only inside the `StoreNames` procedure.

Module arrays can be declared in the declarations part of an .FRM form or a .BAS module file using the Dim keyword.

If an array is declared in an .FRM form file, only procedures stored in that same .FRM form file can use the array. If an array is declared in a .BAS module or .CLS class module file, only procedures stored in that same .BAS module or .CLS class module file can use the array.

To create a module array, follow these steps:

1. Press Ctrl+R, choose View⇨Project, or click the Project Explorer icon to display the Project Explorer window.

2. Highlight the .FRM form, BAS module, or .CLS class module file where you want to declare the module array.

3. Press F7, choose View⇨Code from the menu bar to display the Code window, or click on the View Code icon in the Project Explorer window.

4. Choose *(General)* from the Object list box. Visual Basic automatically displays *(Declarations)* in the Proc list box.

5. Type your array. For example:

```
Dim TwoDArray (1 To 12, 1 To 9) As Integer
```

You can declare public arrays in the declarations part of any .BAS module file using the Public keyword. A public array can be used by any procedure stored in any .FRM form or .BAS module file in the same .VBP project file.

To create a public array, follow these steps:

1. Press Ctrl+R, choose View⇨Project, or click the Project Explorer icon to display the Project Explorer window.

2. Highlight the file (such as a .BAS module or .CLS class module file) where you want to declare the public array.

3. Press F7, choose View⇨Code from the menu bar to display the Code window, or click on the View Code icon in the Project Explorer window.

4. Choose *(General)* from the Object list box. Visual Basic automatically displays *(Declarations)* in the Proc list box.

5. Type your array. For example:

```
Public ThreeDArray (1 To 6, 1 To 4, 1 To 90) As Double
```

Storing and Retrieving Data in Multidimensional Arrays

When you create an array, your array automatically contains zeros or empty strings (" ") until you store your own data in the array.

To put data in or yank data out of an array, you have to specify the array name and the element number that you want to use, such as:

```
Dim BigArray (1 To 12, 1 To 9) As Integer
BigArray(3, 8) = 23
VariableName = BigArray(3, 8)
```

1. The first line defines a two-dimensional array called BigArray, defines its size as 12 by 9, and specifies that it can hold only Integers.

2. The second line stores the number 23 in the (3, 8) element of the BigArray.

3. The third line retrieves the value of the (3, 8) element of BigArray and stores it into a variable called VariableName.

To reference specific array elements, just identify the element by its number (such as 1, 2, or 3). If you want to reference all of the array's elements, the easiest thing to do is use a For-Next loop. For example:

```
Private Sub InitializeArray ()
  Dim BigArray (1 To 10, 1 To 8) As String
  Dim I, J As Integer
  For I = 1 To 10
    For J = 1 To 8
      BigArray(I, J) = "Kitty"
    Next J
  Next I
End Sub
```

1. The first line defines a general procedure called `InitalizeArray`.

2. The second line defines a local array called `BigArray` that contains 10-by-8 array elements and can hold only Strings.

3. The third line declares two variables called `I` and `J` that can hold Integer values.

4. The fourth line is the start of a For-Next loop that counts from 1 to 10.

5. The fifth line is the start of a second For-Next loop that counts from 1 to 8.

6. The sixth line stores the string `Kitty` into the array element identified by the value of I and J (such as 1, 2) into the `BigArray` array.

7. The seventh line increases the value of J by 1 and loops back to line 5.

8. The eighth line increases the value of `I` by 1 and loops back to line 4.

9. The ninth line defines the end of the general procedure.

Try It Yourself

Here's a program to give you some experience in creating, storing, and retrieving data in a 3-by-2, two-dimensional array. The program asks you to store numbers in an array and then displays those numbers on the screen for you to see, as shown in Figure 8-4.

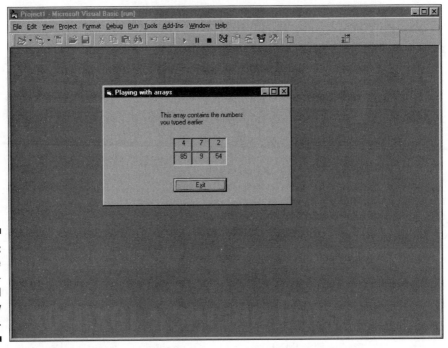

Figure 8-4:
The sample multi-dimensional array program.

Object	Property	Setting
Form	Caption	Playing with arrays
	Height	3240
	Left	1575
	Top	1215
	Width	5220
Label1	Alignment	2 – Center
	BorderStyle	1 – Fixed Single
	Caption	(Empty)
	Height	375
	Left	1920
	Top	1080
	Width	495

Object	Property	Setting
Label2	Alignment	2 – Center
	BorderStyle	1 – Fixed Single
	Caption	(Empty)
	Height	375
	Left	1920
	Top	1440
	Width	495
Label3	Alignment	2 – Center
	BorderStyle	1 – Fixed Single
	Caption	(Empty)
	Height	375
	Left	2400

Test your newfound knowledge

1. What is the maximum number of dimensions you can have for local, module, and public multidimensional arrays?

   a. Multidimensional arrays can be so vast that they defy the imagination, hence I refuse to answer this question on the grounds that it may reveal the fact that I didn't read this chapter very carefully.

   b. Local, module, and public multidimensional arrays can be up to 60 dimensions.

   c. There is no limit to the size of multidimensional arrays because the universe is expanding and there will always be room.

   d. If you create too many dimensions, you may wind up in another dimension.

2. What does the following code do?

```
Const SMALL = 2
Const MEDIUM = 5
Const LARGE = 7
Dim Big = (1 To SMALL, 1 To
MEDIUM, 1 To LARGE) As String
```

   a. This declares a 2-by-5-by-7 three-dimensional array named Big that can contain strings.

   b. This defines the only three sizes of men's shirts that you can buy in today's market.

   c. This code doesn't do anything except confuse me and everyone else who hates being questioned.

   d. This code contains the three most vital instructions for getting Windows to run properly on your computer.

Object	Property	Setting
	Top	1080
	Width	495
Label4	Alignment	2 – Center
	BorderStyle	1 – Fixed Single
	Caption	(Empty)
	Height	375
	Left	2400
	Top	1440
	Width	495
Label5	Alignment	2 – Center
	BorderStyle	1 – Fixed Single
	Caption	(Empty)
	Height	375
	Left	2880
	Top	1080
	Width	495
Label6	Alignment	2 – Center
	BorderStyle	1 – Fixed Single
	Caption	(Empty)
	Height	375
	Left	2880
	Top	1440
	Width	495
Label7	Caption	This array contains the numbers you typed earlier
	Height	375
	Left	1560
	Top	360
	Width	2415

Object	Property	Setting
Command1	Caption	E&xit
	Height	375
	Left	1920
	Top	2160
	Width	1455

Type the following in the *(General) (Declarations)* part of the Code window:

```
Const X = 3
Const Y = 2
Dim NumberArray(1 To X, 1 To Y) As Integer
```

Type the following in the Code window:

```
Private Sub Form_Load()
  Dim I As Integer, J As Integer
  For I = 1 To X
    For J = 1 To Y
  NumberArray(I,J) = InputBox("Type a number to stuff into
          the array:",
    "Stuff a number into array element number" & Str(I) &
          "," & Str(J))
    Next J
  Next I
  Label1.Caption = CStr(NumberArray(1,1))
  Label2.Caption = CStr(NumberArray(1,2))
  Label3.Caption = CStr(NumberArray(2,1))
  Label4.Caption = CStr(NumberArray(2,2))
  Label5.Caption = CStr(NumberArray(3,1))
  Label6.Caption = CStr(NumberArray(3,2))
End Sub

Private Sub Command1_Click()
  Unload Me
End Sub
```

Chapter 9

Dynamic Arrays

• •

In This Chapter

▶ Defining a dynamic array

▶ Defining the size of a dynamic array

▶ Preserving the contents of a dynamic array

• •

*N*ormally when you create an array, you must specify its size. Unfortunately, if you specify an array size that's too small, you may run out of room. If you specify an array size that's too large, you can waste memory and make your program run more slowly.

To avoid the possible problems related to array size, you can create dynamic arrays which adjust their sizes to whatever your program needs at the moment. Dynamic arrays can be simple or multi-dimensional just like standard arrays.

To create a dynamic array, you need to define the array's:

✔ Name

✔ Data type (Integer, Long, Single, Double, Currency, or String)

✔ Scope (local, module, or global)

Naming an Array

The name of an array must meet the following criteria:

✔ Be 255 characters or less

✔ Consist of any combination of letters, numbers, and the underscore character (_)

✔ Begin with a letter

✔ Not be a Visual Basic reserved word

Some valid array names include the following examples:

```
ChameleonArray
Doppleganger_Array
ShapeShifterArray2
```

Here are some invalid array names:

$MoneyArray (Doesn't begin with a letter)

Changing Array (Uses an invalid character)

End (Uses a Visual Basic reserved word)

Defining a Dynamic Array

Normally, you must define the size and dimension of an array. However, dynamic arrays are defined by empty parentheses. For example:

```
ChameleonArray ()
Doppleganger_Array ()
ShapeShifterArray2 ()
```

The empty parentheses tell Visual Basic that this is a dynamic array and that you want to define its size later.

Defining the Data Type of an Array

Before an array can hold anything, you must specify the type of data it can hold. Arrays can hold all kinds of data, including the following types:

- Integer
- Long
- Single
- Double
- Currency
- String
- Boolean
- Any user-defined data types

Here are the examples of dynamic arrays with their data types declared:

```
ChameleonArray () As Long
Doppleganger_Array () As String
ShapeShifterArray2 () As Double
```

The `ChameleonArray` array can hold only Long values. The `Doppleganger_Array` array can hold only Strings. The `ShapeShifterArray2` array can hold only Double values.

If you try to store a Double data type in an array that expects a String data type, or try to mix types any other way, Visual Basic complains with an error message.

However, if you absolutely must store multiple types of data in an array, define the array to be of the Variant data type, such as the following:

```
JunkArray () As Variant
```

A Variant data type can hold either numbers, strings, or dates.

Defining the Scope of an Array

The scope of an array determines where it can be used. Local arrays can be used only in the procedure where they are declared.

To create a local array, declare the array inside a procedure and use the Dim keyword. For example:

```
Private Sub StoreNames ()
   Dim ChameleonArray () As Long
End Sub
```

In this example, the `ChameleonArray` array can be used only inside the `StoreNames` procedure.

Module arrays can be declared in the declarations part of an .FRM form, a .BAS module, or a .CLS class module file by using the Dim keyword. If an array is declared in an .FRM form file, only procedures stored in that same .FRM form file can use the array. If an array is declared in a .BAS module or .CLS class module file, only procedures stored in that same .BAS module file can use the array.

To create a module array, follow these steps:

1. Press Ctrl+R, choose View⇨Project, or click the Project Explorer icon to display the Project Explorer window.

2. Highlight the .FRM form or .BAS module file where you want to declare the module array.

3. Press F7, choose View⇨Code from the menu bar to display the Code window, or click on the View Code icon in the Project Explorer window.

4. Choose *(General)* from the Object list box. Visual Basic automatically displays *(Declarations)* in the Proc list box.

5. Type your array. For example:

```
Dim Doppleganger_Array () As String
```

Public arrays can be declared in the declarations part of any .BAS module file by using the Public keyword. A public array can be used by any procedure stored in any .FRM form or .BAS module file in the same .VBP project file.

To create a public array, follow these steps:

1. Press Ctrl+R, choose View⇨Project, or click the Project Explorer icon to display the Project Explorer window.

2. Highlight the .BAS module file where you want to declare the public array.

3. Press F7, choose View⇨Code from the menu bar to display the Code window, or click on the View Code icon in the Project Explorer window.

4. Choose *(General)* from the Object list box. Visual Basic automatically displays *(Declarations)* in the Proc list box.

5. Type your array. For example:

```
Public ShapeShifterArray2 () As Double
```

Defining the Size of a Dynamic Array

After you define an array to be a dynamic array, it doesn't know how many items you want it to hold. Before you can start stuffing values into a dynamic array, you must define its size.

You use the ReDim keyword to define a dynamic array's size and dimensions. Suppose that you had previously defined three dynamic arrays, as follows:

```
Dim ChameleonArray () As Long
Dim Doppleganger_Array () As String
Public ShapeShifterArray2 () As Double
```

You need to define each array's size and dimensions before you can stuff data into it, for example, like this:

```
ReDim ChameleonArray (1 To 5)
ReDim Doppleganger_Array (9, 11)
ReDim ShapeShifterArray2 (1 To 8)
```

The ChameleonArray is now defined as a one-dimensional array consisting of 5 elements that can hold Long values. The Doppleganger_Array is now defined as a two-dimensional, 10 (0 To 9) by 12 (0 To 11) array consisting of String values. The ShapeShifterArray2 is now defined as a one-dimensional array consisting of 8 elements that can hold Double values.

Later, you could redefine the size of each of these arrays, for example:

```
ReDim ChameleonArray (1 To 50)
ReDim Doppleganger_Array (3, 5)
ReDim ShapeShifterArray2 (1 To 12)
```

The ChameleonArray is now defined as a one-dimensional array consisting of 50 elements that can hold Long values. The Doppleganger_Array is now defined as a two-dimensional, 4 (0 To 3) by 6 (0 To 5) array consisting of String values. The ShapeShifterArray2 is now defined as a one-dimensional array consisting of 12 elements that can hold Double values.

Each time you redefine a dynamic array, Visual Basic conveniently loses all the data stored in the dynamic array. So before redefining a dynamic array, make sure that you can afford to lose your data. (The next section, "Preserving the Contents of a Dynamic Array," explains how to keep your data from disappearing.)

After you define the number of dimensions for a dynamic array, you can't change it later. For example, after you define the ChameleonArray as a one-dimensional array, you can never change it to a two-dimensional array. Likewise, after you define the Doppleganger_Array as a two-dimensional array, you can never change it to a one-dimensional or a three-dimensional array. It must be a two-dimensional array from the time you defined it as such.

Preserving the Contents of a Dynamic Array

Each time you use the ReDim statement to redefine the size of an array, Visual Basic automatically sets the values of all array elements to zero or an empty string, depending on the array's data type. The first time you define a dynamic array, this is okay because you didn't have anything stored in the array anyway.

But if you store values in a dynamic array and then decide to redefine its size, guess what? Visual Basic dumps out all the values stored in the array, and sets all the array elements back to zero or empty strings.

If you want to save the contents of your dynamic array but still redefine its size, you need to follow these two simple rules:

- ✔ Redefine your dynamic array with the ReDim Preserve keywords.
- ✔ Only increase (don't decrease) the size of your dynamic array.

Visual Basic doesn't allow you to save the contents of a dynamic array if you shrink its size.

To increase the size of a dynamic array while preserving its contents, you do this:

```
Redim Preserve ChameleonArray (1 To 6)
```

This command says, "Resize the ChameleonArray so it contains 6 array elements, and preserve the contents already stored in the array."

When increasing the size of a multidimensional dynamic array, you can only increase the size of the last dimension if you want to preserve any data stored in the other dimensions of the multidimensional array. For example, if you define a dynamic array:

```
Dim ThreeDArray () As String
```

and then redefine it as a three-dimensional array:

```
ReDim ThreeDArray (1 To 10, 1 To 8, 1 To 7)
```

you can increase the size of only the third dimension, like this:

```
Redim Preserve ThreeDArray (1 To 10, 1 To 8, 1 To 10)
```

In this example, the last (third) dimension of the array is increased from its original size of 7 to 10.

If you try increasing the size of the first or second dimension, Visual Basic screams and causes a run-time error because you can increase the size of only the last dimension.

When you increase an array's size, the values stay in their old locations. For example, if you have a single-dimensional array of three elements that contain the numbers 1, 23, and 4 and you increase its size to five elements, the first three elements still contain the numbers 1, 23, and 4, but the last two elements are empty.

Try It Yourself

To give you experience in creating, saving data in, and expanding a dynamic array, the following program asks you to store six numbers in an array and then displays those numbers on the screen, as shown in Figure 9-1.

Test your newfound knowledge

1. What is the advantage of using dynamic arrays?

   a. Dynamic arrays are more exciting than lethargic arrays.

   b. Dynamic arrays are more likely to crash your computer.

   c. Dynamic arrays enable you to define the size of an array as you need it.

   d. There is no advantage to using dynamic arrays. Why don't you learn C++ instead?

2. What does the following code do?

   ```
   Dim MyArray () As String
   ReDim MyArray (1 To 3, 1 To 6)
   Redim Preserve MyArray (1 To
   3, 1 To 10)
   ```

   a. The first line defines a dynamic array called MyArray that can hold Strings. The second line defines MyArray as a 3-by-6, two-dimensional array. The third line preserves any values stored in MyArray and increases its second dimension by 4 so that it is now a 3-by-10, two-dimensional array.

   b. This code can be used to reverse your telephone bill charges, change your high school grades, and delete your name from the IRS computers.

   c. This code is making my head dizzy. Can I go home now?

   d. The first line directly contradicts the second and third lines, so your Visual Basic program dies a horrible death in front of your eyes.

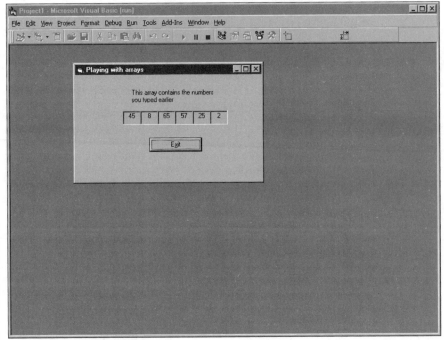

Figure 9-1:
What the
sample
program is
supposed to
look like.

Object	Property	Setting
Form	Caption	Playing with arrays
	Left	1575
	Top	1215
	Width	5265
Label1	Alignment	2 – Center
	BorderStyle	1 – Fixed Single
	Caption	(Empty)
	Height	375
	Left	1320
	Top	960
	Width	495
Label2	Alignment	2 – Center
	BorderStyle	1 – Fixed Single
	Caption	(Empty)
	Height	375
	Left	1800

Object	Property	Setting
	Top	960
	Width	495
Label3	Alignment	2 – Center
	BorderStyle	1 – Fixed Single
	Caption	(Empty)
	Height	375
	Left	2280
	Top	960
	Width	495
Label4	Alignment	2 – Center
	BorderStyle	1 – Fixed Single
	Caption	(Empty)
	Height	375
	Left	2760
	Top	960
	Width	495
Label5	Alignment	2 – Center
	BorderStyle	1 – Fixed Single
	Caption	(Empty)
	Height	375
	Left	3240
	Top	960
	Width	495
Label6	Alignment	2 – Center
	BorderStyle	1 – Fixed Single
	Caption	(Empty)
	Height	375
	Left	3720
	Top	960
	Width	495
Label7	Caption	This array contains the numbers you typed earlier

Object	Property	Setting
	Height	375
	Left	1560
	Top	360
	Width	2415
Command1	Caption	E&xit
	Height	375
	Left	2040
	Top	1680
	Width	1455

Type the following in the *(General) (Declarations)* part of the Code window:

```
Dim NumberArray() As Integer
```

Type the following in the Code window:

```
Private Sub Form_Load()
  Dim I As Integer
   ReDim NumberArray(1 To 3)
  For I = 1 To 3
    NumberArray(I) = InputBox("Type a number to stuff into
          the array:",
     "Stuff a number into array element number" & Str(I))
  Next I
  Label1.Caption = CStr(NumberArray(1))
  Label2.Caption = CStr(NumberArray(2))
  Label3.Caption = CStr(NumberArray(3))
  ReDim Preserve NumberArray(1 To 6)
  For I = 4 To 6
    NumberArray(I) = InputBox("Type a number to stuff into
          the array:",
      "Stuff a number into array element number" & Str(I))
  Next I
  Label4.Caption = CStr(NumberArray(4))
  Label5.Caption = CStr(NumberArray(5))
  Label6.Caption = CStr(NumberArray(6))
End Sub

Private Sub Command1_Click()
  Unload Me
End Sub
```

Chapter 10
Control Arrays

*W*hen you draw objects for your user interface, you may create two or more objects that perform virtually identical functions. However, in Visual Basic, you still need to write separate event procedures for each of them unless you use a *control array*.

For example, Figure 10-1 shows six radio buttons. If you click a radio button, it moves the scroll box in the horizontal scroll bar.

Though the event procedures are nearly identical, you must to write a separate event procedure for each radio button. If you group all radio buttons in a control array, however, you can write one generic event procedure that works for all six radio buttons.

There are two main advantages to using a control array:

✔ Two or more objects can share the same event procedures

✔ Your program can add or remove objects while it is running

Creating a Control Array

All objects in a control array must be of the same type, such as all command buttons, all check boxes, or all text boxes. Objects in a control array always share:

✔ The same object name

✔ The same event procedures

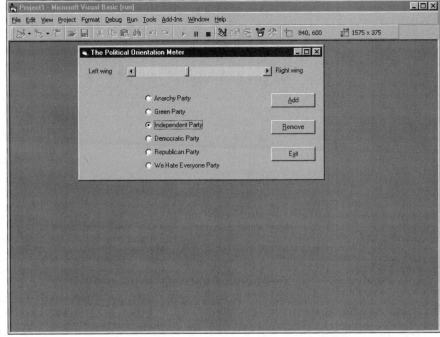

Figure 10-1:
Six radio
buttons
organized in
a control
array.

Visual Basic provides two ways to create a control array:

✔ Assign the same name to more than one object of the same type

✔ Copy an existing object and paste it on the form

To create a control array by assigning the same name to an object, follow these steps:

1. Draw all the objects that you want to group in a control array. Make sure that all objects are of the same type (such as all command buttons, check boxes, or radio buttons).

2. Select the object that you want to be the first element in your control array.

3. Open the Properties window (by pressing F4, choosing View⇨Properties Window, or clicking on the Properties window icon on the toolbar).

4. Click on the Name property and type the name that you want to call your control array.

5. Click on the next object that you want to be in the control array.

6. Repeat Steps 3 to 5 until you've selected all the items you want to be part of the control array. When Visual Basic displays a dialog box, asking whether you want to create a control array, click Yes.

To create a control array by copying an object and pasting a copy on a form, follow these steps:

1. Draw the first object that you want to group in a control array.

2. Open the Properties window (by pressing F4, choosing View⇨ Properties Window, or clicking the Properties window icon on the toolbar).

3. Click the Name property and type the name you want to use for your control array.

4. Select the object that you want to group in a control array. Make sure that the black "handles," or rectangles, surround the object.

5. Press Ctrl+C or choose Edit⇨Copy from the menu bar.

6. Press Ctrl+V or choose Edit⇨Paste from the menu bar. Visual Basic displays a dialog box asking if you want to make this new object part of a control array.

7. Type Y or click the Yes button.

8. Repeat Steps 4 to 7 until you create all the items you want to be part of a control array.

After you create a control array, don't change the name of its objects. If you have three objects in a control array but change the name of only one of them, the newly named object is no longer part of your control array, although its Index property remains the same, and you effectively destroy the purpose of using a control array in the first place.

Sharing Event Procedures

After you create a control array, Visual Basic automatically creates event procedures like the following:

```
Private Sub ControlArrayName_Event (Index As Integer)
End Sub
```

You can always identify shared event procedures in a control array by looking for (Index As Integer) at the end of the first line.

Because all objects in a control array share the same event procedures, the Index value determines which object the event procedure affects. If the Index value is 0, the event procedure affects the first object in the control array; if the Index value is 1, the event procedure affects the second object, and so on.

In Figure 10-1, six radio buttons are grouped in a control array called
Option1. After you click one of the six radio buttons, Visual Basic
immediately looks for the following shared event procedure:

```
Private Sub Option1_Click(Index As Integer)
  HScroll1.Value = Index * 10
End Sub
```

1. The first line defines the start of an event procedure that runs whenever the user clicks any of the radio buttons in the control array called
   Option1.

2. The second line tells Visual Basic to multiply the Index value by 10 and
   store the result in the Value property of a horizontal scroll bar called
   HScroll1. If the user clicks the first radio button of the control array,
   the Index is 0. The second radio button has an Index of 1, and so on.

3. The third line marks the end of the event procedure.

Although all six radio buttons use the same code, the program is still able to
keep track of which button the user clicked with the Index value.

Adding Objects While Your Program Is Running

Besides enabling you to share event procedures, control arrays also let you
add objects while your program is running. After you define a control array,
you can add objects by using:

- ✔ The Load keyword
- ✔ The control array's name
- ✔ The index number of the new object

For example, if you had a control array of three text boxes called txtLock,
you could create a new text box by using the following command:

```
Load txtLock(3)
```

This command creates a fourth text box. (Remember, the first object in a
control array has an index value of 0, the second has a value of 1, the third, 2,
and so on.) If you try creating a new object and give it an index number of an
existing object in the control array, Visual Basic shudders and displays an
error message.

After you create a new object using the Load command, you still have to define at least two more properties of your newly created object for it to appear on screen:

- ✔ Define the Top property (so that the newly created object appears in a specific location on the screen)
- ✔ Set the Visible property to True

The complete code may look like this:

```
Load txtLock(3)
txtLock(3).Top = txtLock(2).Top + 360
txtLock(3).Visible = True
```

If you don't define the Height, Width, and Left properties of your newly created object, Visual Basic just assigns your new object the same values as the first object in your control array.

Removing Objects While Your Program Is Running

You can remove objects from a control array only if they were created using the Load command. You can never remove an object that was drawn on the user interface.

To remove an object, you must use:

- ✔ The Unload keyword
- ✔ The control array's name
- ✔ The index number of the object you want to remove

For example, suppose you had a control array of three text boxes called txtLock, and you created a new text box by using the following command:

```
Load txtLock(3)
```

This command would create a fourth text box. (Remember, the first object in a control array has an index value of 0, the second, 1, the third, 2, and so on.)

If you want to remove this fourth text box, use the following command:

```
Unload txtLock(3)
```

If you try removing an object that the programmer drew on the user interface, Visual Basic doesn't let you. You can only remove objects that were added to the user interface with the Load command.

Try It Yourself

To show you how shared event procedures work with control arrays and how to add (and remove) objects while your program is running, create the following program. Figure 10-1 shows what the program looks like after you click on the Add button a few times.

Object	Property	Setting
Form	Caption	The Political Orientation Meter
	Height	3630
	Left	1995
	Top	1215
	Width	6810
Label1	Caption	Left wing
	Height	255
	Left	240
	Top	240
	Width	1095

Test your newfound knowledge

1. What are the two advantages of using control arrays?

   a. Control arrays can help your computer grow bigger and faster in twelve different ways.

   b. Control arrays are cheap to buy and they're recyclable, too.

   c. Control arrays enable multiple2 objects to share the same event procedures, and add or remove objects while your program is running.

   d. I know two advantages to using control arrays but I'm not going to tell you, so don't bother trying to ask again.

2. What is the main limitation of control arrays?

   a. Control arrays can only consist of two or more objects of the same type, such as two or more command buttons.

   b. Control arrays, work only as long as your program doesn't threaten the monopoly of Microsoft's software market.

   c. The phrase "control arrays" starts to look funny if you stare at it long enough.

   d. Control arrays have no limits and no fear.

Object	Property	Setting
Label2	Caption	Right wing
	Height	255
	Left	5400
	Top	240
	Width	1095
HScroll1	Height	255
	Left	1320
	Max	50
	Top	240
	Width	3975
Option1(0)	Caption	Anarchy Party
	Height	255
	Left	1800
	Top	960
	Width	2175
Option1(1)	Caption	Green Party
	Height	255
	Left	1800
	Top	1320
	Width	2175
Command1	Caption	&Add
	Height	375
	Left	5280
	Top	960
	Width	1215
Command2	Caption	&Remove
	Height	375
	Left	5280
	Top	1680
	Width	1215
Command3	Caption	E&xit
	Height	375
	Left	5280
	Top	2400
	Width	1215

Type the following in the *(General) (Declarations)* part of the Code window:

```
Dim MaxParties As Integer
```

Type the following in the Code window:

```
Private Sub Form_Load()
  MaxParties = 1
End Sub

Private Sub Option1_Click(Index As Integer)
  HScroll1.Value = Index * 10
End Sub

Private Sub Command1_Click()
  Dim Name As String
  If MaxParties > 4 Then
    MsgBox "Only six political parties allowed", 16, "Error
          message"
    Exit Sub
  End If
  MaxParties = MaxParties + 1
  Load Option1(MaxParties)
  Option1(MaxParties).Top = Option1(MaxParties - 1).Top +
          360
  Option1(MaxParties).Visible = True
  Select Case MaxParties
    Case 2
      Name = "Independent Party"
    Case 3
      Name = "Democratic Party"
    Case 4
      Name = "Republican Party"
    Case 5
      Name = "We Hate Everyone Party"
  End Select
  Option1(MaxParties).Caption = Name
End Sub

Private Sub Command2_Click()
  If MaxParties = 1 Then Exit Sub
  Unload Option1(MaxParties)
  MaxParties = MaxParties - 1
End Sub

Private Sub Command3_Click()
  Unload Me
End Sub
```

Chapter 11

Making Structures to Hold Stuff

*W*hen you write a Visual Basic program, you may need to create several variables to hold information. For example, you may need to keep track of such information as names, addresses, age, and salary. You could create separate variables for each, such as:

```
Dim Name, Address As String
Dim Age As Integer
Dim Salary As Currency
```

Unfortunately, creating a separate variable for each little piece of information is like writing each bit on separate slips of paper and scattering it across your desk. The information may be there, but it's not organized very well.

Rather than scatter separate bits of information, a better solution is to stuff all this information in one place, such as an envelope. Visual Basic doesn't come with envelopes, but it does enable you to organize separate variables in something called a *structure*. A structure can hold different information in one place and looks like the following example:

```
Type PersonRecord
  Name As String
  Address As String
  Age As Integer
  Salary As Currency
End Type
```

Basically, a structure organizes related bits of data together in one place by storing multiple variables (`Name`, `Address`, `Age`, and `Salary`) inside a single variable (`PersonRecord`).

Creating a Structure

Structures can be stored in the declarations portion of a .BAS module or a .CLS class module file, or in the declarations of a .FRM form file. If you store a structure in a .BAS module file, the structure is global in scope, which means that any procedure located anywhere in the program can access it. If you store a structure in a .FRM form file, the structure is local in scope, which means that only procedures stored in that same .FRM form file can access it.

To create a structure in an existing .BAS module, .CLS class module, or .FRM form file, follow these steps:

1. Press F7, choose View⇨Code from the menu bar to display the Code window, or click on the View Code icon in the Project Explorer window.

2. Highlight the .BAS module, .CLS class module or .FRM form file where you want to store your structure.

3. Press F7, choose View⇨Code from the menu bar to display the Code window, or click on the View Code icon in the Project Explorer window.

4. Choose *(General)* from the Object list box. Visual Basic automatically displays *(Declarations)* in the Proc list box.

5. Start typing your structure.

To create a structure and store it in a new .BAS module file, follow these steps:

1. Choose Project⇨Add Module. Visual Basic displays the Code window.

2. Choose *(General)* from the Object list box. Visual Basic automatically displays *(Declarations)* in the Proc list box.

3. Start typing your structure.

Declaring a Structure

Defining a structure in the declarations portion of a .BAS module file essentially means that you create your own data type. Of course, you can't use your structure until you declare a variable to represent your structure:

```
Dim VariableName As StructureName
```

If you created a structure named `PersonRecord`, you could declare a variable to be a `PersonRecord`, such as:

```
Dim Employees As PersonRecord
```

This command defines the variable `Employees` as a `PersonRecord` data type, as shown in Figure 11-1. In this case, the `PersonRecord` data type is defined as:

```
Type PersonRecord
    Name As String
    Address As String
    Age As Integer
    Salary As Currency
End Type
```

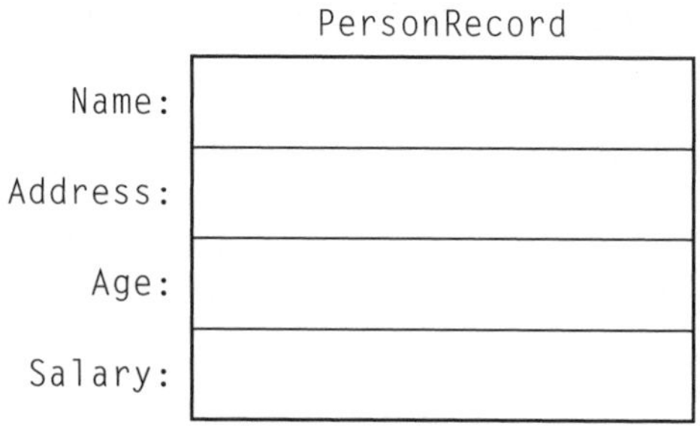

Figure 11-1: The PersonRecord structure.

Stuffing and Retrieving Data

To stuff data into a structure, you need to use the variable name along with the property name:

```
VariableName.StructureProperty
```

For example, the following example assigns the name Tasha to the Name property.

```
Dim Employees As PersonRecord
Employees.Name = "Tasha"
```

1. The first line tells Visual Basic to create a new variable called Employees and make it represent the structure defined by PersonRecord.

2. The second line stuffs the string Tasha into the Name property of the Employees variable.

After you stuff data into a structure, you probably want to get it back out again. To retrieve data from a structure, assign a variable of the right data type to the structure property that you want to retrieve. For example:

```
Dim Employees As PersonRecord
Dim Who As String
Who = Employees.Name
```

1. The first line tells Visual Basic to create a new variable called Employees and make it represent the structure defined by PersonRecord.

2. The second line creates a new variable called Who that can hold strings.

3. The third line takes the string stored in the Name property of the Employees structure and stuffs it into the Who variable. If the Name property stores the string Tasha, the Who variable would also store the string Tasha.

Structure properties can be defined also as a fixed-size array, such as:

```
Type Vengeance
   BlackList (1 To 5) As String
   Location As String
End Type
```

This structure defines a single property that consists of an array of five strings.

To stuff data in an array that is buried inside a structure, you must do the following:

```
Dim Mad As Vengeance
Mad.BlackList(2) = "My boss"
```

1. The first line tells Visual Basic to create a new variable called Mad and make it represent the structure defined by Vengeance.

2. The second line stuffs the string My boss into the second array element that's part of the Mad variable, as shown in Figure 11-2.

Figure 11-2: Stuffing a string in the second array element of the Mad structure.

Vengeance

BlackList:		"My Boss"			
Location:					

Using an Array of Structures

By itself, a structure is pretty limited — much like a filing cabinet that can hold only one folder in each drawer. To make structures useful, you need to create an array which, instead of holding individual bits of data, holds structures.

Rather than define an array as a certain data type, such as:

```
Dim DogFood (1 To 4) As String
```

you can define an array as a structure data type, as shown in Figure 11-3. The following code shows is an example of an array defined as a structure data type:

	DogFood[1]	DogFood[2]	DogFood[3]	DogFood[4]
Name:		"Mailman"		
Address:				
Age:				
Salary:				

Figure 11-3: The DogFood array of structures.

```
Type PersonRecord
   Name As String
   Address As String
   Age As Integer
   Salary As Currency
End Type

Dim DogFood (1 To 4) As PersonRecord
```

To store data in a property, such as the Name property, you would use:

```
DogFood(2).Name = "Mailman"
```

This command stores the Mailman string in the Name property of the second array element in the DogFood array.

Creating a Collection

As another way to organize multiple variables in one convenient location, Visual Basic offers something called a collection. A collection simply stores a related group of items as a single object. The big difference between creating an array of structures and using a collection is that you don't have to define the size of a collection beforehand like you have to do with an array.

To create a collection, just use this magic BASIC command:

```
Dim VariableName As New Collection
```

For example, if you want to create a collection to store random information, you might use this command:

```
Dim MyPets As New Collection
```

Adding information to a collection

Once you create a collection, you need to add information to it. To add information to a collection, you have to use the Add command like this:

```
MyPets.Add Item:="Female orange cat"
```

The previous command stores the string "Female orange cat" in a collection defined by the variable name `MyPets`.

Identifying information with a key string

The above command effectively dumps your information into the collection much like tossing your socks in a laundry basket. To better organize the information stored in your collection, you might want to identify your information with a unique key string, which acts like a name.

By using a key string, you can use BASIC code to tell the computer, "I don't know where the information may be stored in the collection, but you can identify it by a specific key string."

For example, the following BASIC command uses the key string "Bo" to identify the string "Female orange cat" in the MyPets collection:

```
MyPets.Add Item:="Female orange cat", Key:="Bo"
```

Every chunk of data stored in a collection requires a different key string. In other words, you can't give two chunks of data the same key string and save them in the same collection.

Specifying a location to add information in a collection

When you add information to a collection, Visual Basic organizes information much like a stack of cards. As you add more information to a collection, the information simply piles up in the order you add it. (Ever play fifty-two card pick-up?)

If you want, you can tell Visual Basic a specific location in which to add information to a collection. By being precise, you can tell Visual Basic, "See this information? I want to store it before (or after) another chunk of information already stored in my collection."

To add information before a specific chunk of data already stored in a collection, you have to use the following command:

```
MyPets.Add Item:="Male orange cat", Key:="Scraps",
          before:="Bo"
```

This command tells Visual Basic, "Look in a collection called MyPets and find a chunk of data identified by the key string 'Bo'. When you find the data identified by the key string 'Bo', insert the string 'Male orange cat' in front of the data identified by 'Bo' and call identify this new information by the key string 'Scraps'."

To add information after a specific chunk of data already stored in a collection, you have to use the following command:

```
MyPets.Add Item:="Male gray cat", Key:="Tasha", after:="Bo"
```

This command tells Visual Basic, "Look in a collection called MyPets and find a chunk of data identified by the key string 'Bo'. When you find the data identified by the key string 'Bo', insert the string 'Male gray cat' after the data identified by 'Bo' and identify this new information by the key string 'Tasha'." Figure 11-4 shows what the MyPets collection looks like after the following three commands:

```
MyPets.Add Item:="Female orange cat", Key:="Bo"
MyPets.Add Item:="Male orange cat", Key:="Scraps",
           before:="Bo"
MyPets.Add Item:="Male gray cat", Key:="Tasha", after:="Bo"
```

Figure 11-4:
Inserting data in a collection.

	Index = 1	Index = 2	Index = 3
Key string:	"Scraps"	"Bo"	"Tasha"
Item:	"Male orange cat"	"Female orange cat"	"Male gray cat"

Retrieving information from a collection

After storing data in a collection, you probably need to retrieve the information later. Visual Basic provides two ways to retrieve information from a collection:

✔ By the order they are stored

✔ By key string

Using index numbers

The first chunk of data stored in a collection is assigned an index number of 1, the second chunk of data is assigned an index number of 2, and so on, as shown in Figure 11-4.

If you insert a new chunk of data before the first item stored in a collection, that new chunk of data gets assigned an index number of 1.

To retrieve information from a collection using index numbers, just use the following command:

```
VariableName = CollectionName.Item(IndexNumber)
```

So if you want to retrieve the first chunk of data stored in the collection called MyPets, you use the following command:

```
WhichPet = MyPets.Item(1)
```

If the MyPets collection contained three chunks of data as shown in Figure 11-4, the value of WhichPet would be "Female orange cat."

Using key strings

Index numbers are fine as long as you know the order of the data stored in a collection. Since your program may be inserting and removing data from a collection, you may find it easier to retrieve data from a collection using key strings instead.

To retrieve information from a collection using key strings, just use the following command:

```
VariableName = CollectionName.Item(Key string)
```

So if you want to retrieve the chunk of data identified by the key string "Tasha" and stored in a collection named MyPets, you use the following command:

```
WhichPet = MyPets.Item("Tasha")
```

Deleting information from a collection

In case you've stored something in a collection and decide you want to get rid of it, you can delete it by using the magical Remove command like this:

```
CollectionName.Remove(IndexNumber)
```

or this:

```
CollectionName.Remove(Key string)
```

So if you want to remove the second item stored in a collection called MyPets, you use this command:

```
MyPets.Remove(2)
```

And if you want to remove an item identified by the key string "Bo", you use this command:

```
MyPets.Remove("Bo")
```

Try It Yourself

To see for yourself how structures work, create the following program consisting of two forms (Form1 and Form2) and one module (Module1) file. When you run it, this program looks like the one displayed in Figure 11-5.

Test your newfound knowledge

1. Why should you use structures in your Visual Basic programs?

   a. Because they are available and you should use every Visual Basic feature in your programs whenever possible.

   b. Structures let you create your own buildings so you can charge rent and quit your job.

   c. Structures let you organize related variables inside a single variable.

   d. Structures prop up your Visual Basic program and keep it from falling over on its side.

2. What is the main difference between using an array of structures and using a collection?

   a. An array of structures makes it easier for your programs to lose data, which can be especially useful if you're writing a Visual Basic program for the government.

   b. A collection is something that people use to store coins, stamps, and dead butterflies. An array of structures is a complicated computer science term that requires four years of college education to figure out what it means.

   c. Arrays of structures and collections never get along, so it's we must force them to integrate whether they like it or not.

   d. An array of structures requires that you specify the data type to store. A collection can store any type of information without specifying a data type.

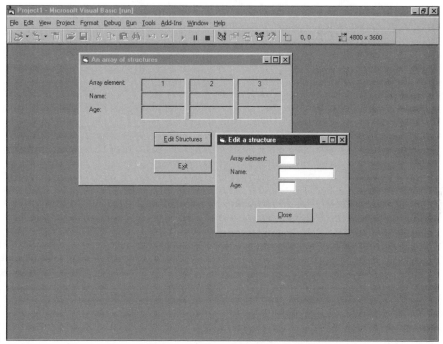

Figure 11-5:
What the
sample
program
looks like.

Object	Property	Setting
Form1	Caption	An array of structures
	Height	3585
	Left	1995
	Top	1260
	Width	5910
Label1	Alignment	2 – Center
	BorderStyle	1 – Fixed Single
	Caption	1
	Height	375
	Left	1680
	Top	360
	Width	1215
Label2	BorderStyle	1 – Fixed Single
	Caption	(Empty)
	Height	375
	Left	1680

Object	Property	Setting
	Top	720
	Width	1215
Label3	BorderStyle	1 – Fixed Single
	Caption	(Empty)
	Height	375
	Left	1680
	Top	1080
	Width	1215
Label4	Alignment	2 – Center
	BorderStyle	1 – Fixed Single
	Caption	2
	Height	375
	Left	3000
	Top	360
	Width	1215
Label5	BorderStyle	1 – Fixed Single
	Caption	(Empty)
	Height	375
	Left	3000
	Top	720
	Width	1215
Label6	BorderStyle	1 – Fixed Single
	Caption	(Empty)
	Height	375
	Left	3000
	Top	1080
	Width	1215
Label7	Alignment	2 – Center
	BorderStyle	1 – Fixed Single
	Caption	3

Object	Property	Setting
	Height	375
	Left	4320
	Top	360
	Width	1215
Label8	BorderStyle	1 – Fixed Single
	Caption	(Empty)
	Height	375
	Left	4320
	Top	720
	Width	1215
Label9	BorderStyle	1 – Fixed Single
	Caption	(Empty)
	Height	375
	Left	4320
	Top	1080
	Width	1215
Label10	Caption	Array element:
	Height	255
	Left	240
	Top	360
	Width	1215
Label11	Caption	Name:
	Height	255
	Left	240
	Top	720
	Width	1215
Label12	Caption	Age:
	Height	255
	Left	240
	Top	1080
	Width	1215

Object	Property	Setting
Command1	Caption	&Edit Structures
	Height	375
	Left	2040
	Top	1800
	Width	1575
Command2	Caption	E&xit
	Height	375
	Left	2040
	Top	2520
	Width	1575

And here begins a new form:

Object	Property	Setting
Form2	Caption	Edit a structure
	Height	2715
	Left	5760
	Top	3405
	Width	3750
Label1	Caption	Array element:
	Height	255
	Left	360
	Top	240
	Width	1095
Label2	Caption	Name:
	Height	255
	Left	360
	Top	600
	Width	1095
Label3	Caption	Age:
	Height	255
	Left	360
	Top	960
	Width	1095

Object	Property	Setting
Text1	Height	285
	Left	1680
	Text	(Empty)
	Top	240
	Width	495
Text2	Height	285
	Left	1680
	Text	(Empty)
	Top	600
	Width	1575
Text3	Height	285
	Left	1680
	Text	(Empty)
	Top	960
	Width	495
Command1	Caption	&Close
	Height	375
	Left	1080
	Top	1680
	Width	1575

Type the following in the *(General) (Declarations)* part of the Code window in Module1:

```
Type PersonRecord
  Name As String
  Age As String
End Type

Public FunArray(1 To 3) As PersonRecord
```

Type the following in the Form1 Code window:

```
Private Sub Command1_Click()
  Load Form2
  Form2!Text1.Text = ""
```

(continued)

(continued)

```
    Form2!Text2.Text = ""
    Form2!Text3.Text = ""
    Form2.Show
End Sub

Private Sub Command2_Click()
    Unload Form2
    Unload Me
End Sub
```

Type the following in the Form2 Code window:

```
Private Sub Command1_Click()  Dim I As Integer
    If Text1.Text <> "" Then
        I = Int(CSng(Text1.Text))
    End If
    FunArray(I).Name = Text2.Text
    FunArray(I).Age = Text3.Text
    Select Case I    Case 1Form1!Label2.Caption =
            FunArray(I).NameForm1!Label3.Caption =
            FunArray(I).Age
        Case 2
            Form1!Label5.Caption = FunArray(I).Name
            Form1!Label6.Caption = FunArray(I).Age
        Case 3
            Form1!Label8.Caption = FunArray(I).Name
            Form1!Label9.Caption = FunArray(I).Age
    End Select
    Form2.Hide
End Sub
```

Part III
Making Noise and Drawing Pictures

In this part . . .

Put any little kid in a room alone and within seconds
that kid will likely find something to bang on, throw
around, scribble on, or smear across the walls. Now take
this innate desire to make noise and draw pictures,
transfer it to the electronic landscape of Visual Basic, and
you understand what this part of the book is all about.

The chapters in Part III explain how to play sound files,
display business graphics (so you can visually explain
why your company has lost billions of dollars), or even
display video clips on your computer screen. So if you've
always wanted to make your program flashier, noisier, and
just downright more entertaining than a silent, dull word
processor, browse through Part III and make your own
programs sing and shout on the computer screen.

Chapter 12
Making Noise and Playing Music

*M*ost computers now come equipped with built-in speakers, a sound card, and a CD-ROM drive (which most likely still don't work together correctly with your software). As a result, more programs now offer fancy music, sound effects, and recorded voices in addition to a slick user interface.

Visual Basic can help you add noise to your own programs — from simple beeps to recorded sounds. Of course, if you don't have a sound card and speakers, you can still add sound to your Visual Basic programs, you just won't be able to hear them.

Beeping for Attention

At the simplest level, Visual Basic can make a beeping noise to call attention to itself. If you want to make simple beeps, you can use the Visual Basic Beep command:

```
Private Sub Command1_Click()
    Beep
End Sub
```

Beeps can warn users if they press the wrong key ("Beep. Do you really want to launch your nuclear missiles?") or to validate that the user did something right, such as entering the correct data.

Whichever way you decide to use a beep, make sure you're consistent so one part of your program doesn't beep as a warning and another part of your program beeps to verify that the user typed something correctly. Such inconsistency can cause your users much confusion, and can help cement in their head the idea that computers are too difficult to use.

For a bit more variety in the types of beeps your program can generate, you can dig into the Windows API (Application Program Interface) and use the MessageBeep procedure. (Chapter 20 goes into the gory details on using the Windows API.)

To use the MessageBeep procedure, you must first create a module (.BAS) file and put the following declaration in it:

```
Declare Function MessageBeep Lib "user32" (ByVal wType As
        Long) As Long
```

After you place this function declaration in a module (.BAS) file, you can use one or more of the following six constants, as shown in Table 12-1, to define the type of beep to use:

Table 12-1   Constants to use with the MessageBeep procedure

Constant	Value
MB_ICONHAND	&H10&
MB_ICONSTOP	&H10&
MB_ICONQUESTION	&H20&
MB_ICONEXCLAMATION	&H30&
MB_ICONASTERISK	&H40&
MB_ICONINFORMATION	&H40&

Depending on which constant you use, the MessageBeep procedure plays a different sounding beep. Code like this will call up the MessageBeep procedure:

```
Private Sub Command1_Click()
   MessageBeep MB_ICONQUESTION
End Sub
```

Playing WAV and MIDI Files

Although beeps are easy to use, they are boring and unmusical. You may want to play music or recorded voices instead. Playing sounds other than beeps in your Visual Basic program requires specific code (just like everything else in this book, right?).

Two of the most popular ways to play sound is through WAV or MIDI files. WAV files are actual digital recordings which you can store on disk, which means they sound realistic but gobble up huge amounts of disk space. MIDI files contain instructions for making sound, kind of like a digital version of a player piano — the MIDI file works like a piano roll and your sound card works like the piano. MIDI files take up much less space than WAV files, but can soften sound synthetic — like listening to a robot trying to sing.

WAV files are what you need if you want to play recorded sounds such as voices or special effects (for example, thunder, gun fire, or applause). MIDI files are best for simple music and melodies. Most sound cards can play a variety of "instruments," and MIDI files can access the sound card instruments — you don't hear a symphony orchestra, but you might at least say the sound is pretty good.

The Windows API provides many functions that enable you to play WAV and MIDI sound files. The two most straightforward functions are:

```
sndPlaySound

mciExecute
```

This chapter sticks with these simpler Windows API functions, but be aware that you have other options. However, If you want to use any of the various functions other than the ones I cover in this chapter, you must understand the structure of WAV and MIDI files.

Using the sndPlaySound function

To play WAV files, you can use the sndPlaySound function, which is in the Windows API. To use the sndPlaySound function, you must first create a module (.BAS) file and type the following declaration:

```
Declare Function sndPlaySound Lib "winmm.dll" Alias
        "sndPlaySoundA" (ByVal lpszSoundName As String,
        ByVal uFlags As Long) As Long
```

This declaration tells Visual Basic, "There's a function called sndPlaySound which lets you define a WAV file and how you want the WAV file to play."

After you create the preceding function declaration, you can use one or more of the six constants, shown in Table 12-2, that define how the WAV file plays:

Table 12-2   Constants to use with the sndPlaySound function

Constant	Value	What it does
SND_SYNC	&H0	tells Visual Basic to play the WAV file and then return control back to your program only after the WAV file has finished playing
SND_ASYNC	&H1	tells Visual Basic to play the WAV file and then immediately return control back to your program, even before the WAV file finishes playing
SND_NODEFAULT	&H2	tells Visual Basic not to use the default WAV file in the event the specified WAV file is missing
SND_MEMORY	&H4	tells Visual Basic to play the WAV file previously loaded into memory
SND_LOOP	&H8	tells Visual Basic to keep playing the WAV file over and over again. This constant is almost always used with the SND_ASYNC constant; otherwise your program would never let you do anything after the WAV file started playing
SND_NOSTOP	&H10	tells Visual Basic to finish playing the WAV file before starting to play another WAV file

To use the sndPlaySound function, you must specify

- The name of the WAV file you want to play
- How you want to play the WAV file (using one or more of the six constants listed in Table 12-2)

For example, if you want to play a WAV file called TADA.WAV in the C:\WINDOWS\MEDIA directory, use the sndPlaySound function as follows:

```
Dim MakeSound As Long
MakeSound = sndPlaySound("C:\WINDOWS\MEDIA\TADA.WAV",
        SND_ASYNC Or SND_NOSTOP)
```

If you want to use two or more constants at the same time, separate them with the Or keyword as in the above example that uses both the SND_ASYNC and the SND_NOSTOP constants.

Using the mciExecute function

To play either WAV or MIDI files using the `mciExecute` function, you must first create a module (.BAS) file and type the following declaration:

```
Declare Function mciExecute Lib "winmm.dll" Alias
          "mciExecute" (ByVal lpstrCommand As String) As
          Long
```

To play a WAV file called TADA.WAV located in the C:\WINDOWS\MEDIA directory, you would use the `mciExecute` function as follows:

```
Dim MakeSound As Long
MakeSound = mciExecute("play C:\WINDOWS\MEDIA\tada.wav")
```

To play a MIDI file called CANYON.MID located in the C:\WINDOWS\MEDIA directory, you would use the `mciExecute` function as follows:

```
Dim MakeSound As Long
MakeSound = mciExecute("play C:\WINDOWS\MEDIA\canyon.mid")
```

At this point, you may be wondering what's the difference between the `sndPlaySound` and the `mciExecute` functions? Good question. The two main differences between the `sndPlaySound` and the `mciExecute` functions are that the `mciExecute` function can

✔ Play both WAV and MIDI files (the `sndPlaySound` function can play only WAV files)

✔ Be coded to play only portions of WAV or MIDI files

Take a look at this example of playing a portion of a sound file with the `mciExecute` function:

```
Dim MakeSound As Long
MakeSound = mciExecute("play C:\WINDOWS\MEDIA\canyon.mid
          from 100 to 500")
```

The preceding `mciExecute` command tells Visual Basic to start playing the CANYON.MID file 100 milliseconds (1/10th of a second) from the beginning, continue to 500 milliseconds from the beginning, and then stop.

Using the Multimedia Control

The sndPlaySound and mciExecute functions from the Windows API are fairly simple ways to play WAV and MIDI files. You may want to avoid the Windows API, however, and give your users control over making the computer sing. In that case, use the Visual Basic Multimedia control instead. The Multimedia control both isolates you from the complexities of the Windows API and provides a slick and simple VCR-like control on your form.

The Multimedia control can be used to record sound as well as play videos, depending on the type of hardware (sound cards, video cards, CD-ROM drive) that the user has installed in his/her computer. But this chapter concentrates only on using the Multimedia control to play WAV and MIDI files. If you'd like to read how to use the Multimedia control for video stuff, skip ahead to Chapter 14.

Installing the Multimedia control

The Multimedia control comes in the MCI32.OCX file that you must load in the Visual Basic Toolbox before you can use it. To load the Multimedia control, follow these steps:

1. Choose Project⇨Components, or press Ctrl+T. The Components dialog box appears.

2. Click the check box next to Microsoft Multimedia Control .5.0. Make sure that an X appears in the check box.

3. Click OK. Visual Basic displays the Multimedia icon in the Toolbox.

4. Click the Multimedia control and draw it on your form, as shown in Figure 12-1.

Playing WAV and MIDI Files with the Multimedia Control

To play WAV or MIDI files, you must specify the following properties:

- Wait
- DeviceType
- FileName
- Command

Next Pause Step Record

Previous | Play | Back | Stop | Eject

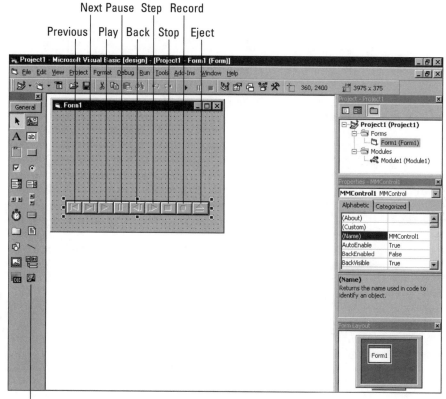

Figure 12-1:
The
Multimedia
control and
its buttons.

Multimedia control tool icon

The Wait property determines whether the Multimedia control waits for the next command to complete before returning control back to your program. To play WAV and MIDI files, set the Wait property to True. (*Note:* The Wait property can be defined only by using BASIC code.)

The DeviceType property determines what type of file you want to play. To play WAV files, set the DeviceType property to WaveAudio. To play MIDI files, set the DeviceType property to Sequencer.

The FileName property determines the WAV or MIDI file you want to play.

The Command property tells the Multimedia control what to do. For playing WAV or MIDI files, the two choices for the Command property are Open and Close. (*Note:* The Command property can be defined only by using BASIC code.)

The following program shows you a working example:

```
Private Sub Form_Load()
  MMControl1.Wait = True
  MMControl1.DeviceType = "WaveAudio"
  MMControl1.FileName = "C:\WINDOWS\MEDIA\tada.wav"
  MMControl1.Command = "Open"
End Sub

Private Sub Form_Unload(Cancel As Integer)
  MMControl1.Command = "Close"
End Sub
```

1. The first line defines the start of the Form_Load event procedure that runs the moment the form is loaded.

2. The second line sets the Wait property to True, which means that the Multimedia control accepts a command and waits until that command finishes before returning control back to the program.

3. The third line sets the DeviceType property to WaveAudio, which means that the Multimedia control can now play WAV files. If the DeviceType property is set to Sequencer, the control can play MIDI files instead.

4. The fourth line sets the FileName property to identify the exact WAV file to play.

5. The fifth line sets the Command property to Open, which means that the Multimedia control plays the WAV file defined by the FileName property. Notice that the WAV file starts playing only after the user clicks the Play button displayed on the Multimedia control.

6. The sixth line defines the end of the Form_Load event procedure.

7. The seventh line defines the start of the Form_Unload event procedure that runs the moment the form is unloaded.

8. The eighth line closes the Multimedia control.

9. The ninth line defines the end of the Form_Unload event procedure.

When you place the Multimedia control on a form and run this program, the Multimedia control displays buttons that the user can press to play the C:\WINDOWS\MEDIA\tada.wav.

You can have your program play MIDI or WAV files without displaying a Multimedia control by setting the control's Visible property to False. To play a file when the Multimedia control is invisible, use BASIC code to define the following:

   ✔ DeviceType

   ✔ FileName

   ✔ Command

To use BASIC code to play a WAV or MIDI file, you must use the Command property twice. The first time you must set the Command property to Open. The second time you must set the Command property to Play. For example:

```
Private Sub Command1_Click()
  MMControl1.DeviceType = "WaveAudio"
  MMControl1.FileName = "C:\WINDOWS\MEDIA\tada.wav"
  MMControl1.Command = "Open"
  MMControl1.Command = "Play"
End Sub
```

This code plays the TADA.WAV file whenever the user clicks the Command1 command button. This assumes that the Multimedia control is drawn on the same form as the Command1 command button.

You might want to disable one or more buttons on the Multimedia control. For example, it doesn't make any sense to have an Eject button if you're playing a WAV sound file since the Eject button is only useful for loading and ejecting a compact disc. You can disable a Multimedia control button through the Properties window or through BASIC code. To disable a Multimedia control button, set one or more of the following properties to False:

Property	Set to	Disables this button
PrevEnabled	False	Prev
NextEnabled	False	Next
PlayEnabled	False	Play
PauseEnabled	False	Pause
BackEnabled	False	Back
StepEnabled	False	Step
StopEnabled	False	Stop
RecordEnabled	False	Record
EjectEnabled	False	Eject

Test your newfound knowledge

1. What is the difference between WAV and MIDI files?

   a. WAV files are sounds you make when you wave good-bye to someone. MIDI files are sounds you make when that same person is out of earshot.

   b. WAV files are those natural recordings of the ocean that you can play to relax yourself while listening to your Walkman on the beach. MIDI files are completely unnatural recordings that you can use to stress yourself out while driving through rush hour.

   c. WAV files contain the actual recording of a noise stored on disk. MIDI files contain instructions for recreating a sound. As a result, MIDI files are much smaller than similar WAV files, but WAV files sound more realistic and are good for sound effects like thunder or applause.

   d. WAV files and MIDI files are two types of files that never work when you need them.

2. Name three ways to play WAV files.

   a. Use the `sndPlaySound` function, use the `mciExecute` function, or use the Multimedia control stored as an OCX file.

   b. Smack the computer with your hand, kick the computer with your foot, or punch the computer with your fist. This still won't play WAV files, but it can make you feel better after your computer messes up.

   c. You cannot play WAV files using Visual Basic unless you first invest another $3,000 to order the Microsoft Multimedia Programmer's Toolkit, Reference Set, and Software Development Kit.

   d. The three ways to play WAV files are with a trumpet, with a saxophone, and with an electronic synthesizer.

Try It Yourself

To show you how to use the Multimedia control, create the following program. This program, shown in Figure 12-2, enables you to play audio CDs in your computer CD-ROM drive.

Object	Property	Setting
Form	Caption	A Simple and Cheap CD player
	Height	3540
	Left	1665
	Top	1110
	Width	6510
Label1	Caption	Total Tracks:
	Height	255

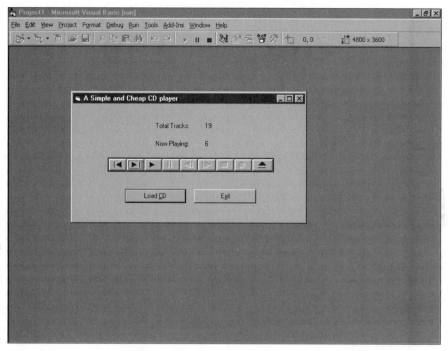

Figure 12-2:
What the
sample
program
looks like.

Object	Property	Setting
	Left	2280
	Top	480
	Width	1215
Label2	Caption	(Empty)
	Height	255
	Left	3600
	Top	480
	Width	375
Label3	Caption	(Empty)
	Height	255
	Left	3600
	Top	960
	Width	375

Object	Property	Setting
Label4	Caption	Now Playing:
	Height	255
	Left	2280
	Top	960
	Width	1215
MMControl1	Height	375
	Left	960
	Top	1440
	Width	4575
Command1	Caption	Load &CD
	Height	375
	Left	1440
	Top	2280
	Width	1695
Command2	Caption	E&xit
	Height	375
	Left	3360
	Top	2280
	Width	1695

Type the following in the Code window:

```
Private Sub Command1_Click()
  MMControl1.Command = "Open"
  Label2.Caption = Str(MMControl1.Tracks)
End Sub

Private Sub Command2_Click()
  Unload Me
End Sub

Private Sub Form_Load()
  MMControl1.Wait = True
  MMControl1.UpdateInterval = 0
  MMControl1.DeviceType = "CDAudio"
  Label2.Caption = "0"
  Label3.Caption = "0"
```

```
End Sub

Private Sub MMControl1_Ejectclick(Cancel As Integer)
  MMControl1.Command = "Eject"
  MMControl1.Command = "Close"
  Label2.Caption = "0"
  Label3.Caption = "0"
End Sub

Private Sub MMControl1_NextCompleted(Errorcode As Long)
  Label3.Caption = Str(MMControl1.Track)
End Sub

Private Sub MMControl1_PlayClick(Cancel As Integer)
  MMControl1.UpdateInterval = 1000
  Label3.Caption = Str(MMControl1.Track)
End Sub

Private Sub MMControl1_PrevCompleted(Errorcode As Long)
  Label3.Caption = Str(MMControl1.Track)
End Sub

Private Sub MMControl1_StopClick(Cancel As Integer)
  MMControl1.UpdateInterval = 0
  MMControl1.To = MMControl1.Start
  MMControl1.Track = 1
  Label3.Caption = "1"
End Sub
```

Chapter 13
Creating Business Charts

A picture is worth a thousand words, which is why business presentations often have a lot to say, though few people pay attention to any of it. If you need your program to display charts of any type, you're in luck. Visual Basic comes with a special Microsoft Chart ActiveX control called MSCHART.OCX.

Loading the Microsoft Chart ActiveX Control

Before you can use the Microsoft Chart ActiveX control, you must load it in the Visual Basic Toolbox. To load the Microsoft Chart control, follow these steps:

1. Choose Project⇨Components, or press Ctrl+T. The Components dialog box appears.

2. Click the check box next to Microsoft Chart Control. Make sure a check mark appears in the check box.

3. Click OK. Visual Basic displays the Microsoft Chart icon in the Toolbox.

4. Click the Chart control and draw it on your form, as shown in Figure 13-1.

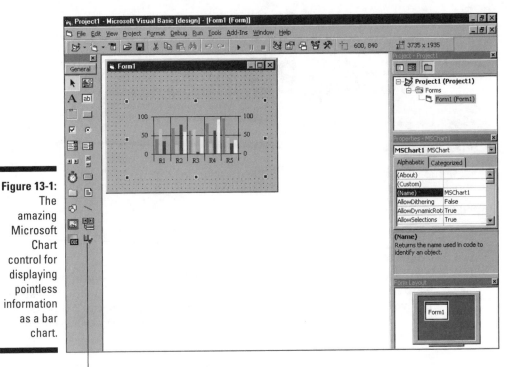

Figure 13-1:
The amazing Microsoft Chart control for displaying pointless information as a bar chart.

Microsoft Chart icon in the toolbox

Choosing Your Chart

Once you draw the Microsoft Chart control on a form, you need to decide what type of chart you want to create. You can create your chart at design-time (using the Properties window) or run-time (using BASIC code).

To choose a specific chart type, you need to change the ChartType property, which can draw twelve types of charts (as shown in Figure 13-2):

- 0 – VtChChartType3dBar
- 1 – VtChChartType2dBar
- 2 – VtChChartType3dLine
- 3 – VtChChartType2dLine
- 4 – VtChChartType3dArea
- 5 – VtChChartType2dArea
- 6 – VtChChartType3dStep
- 7 – VtChChartType2dStep
- 8 – VtChChartType3dCombination

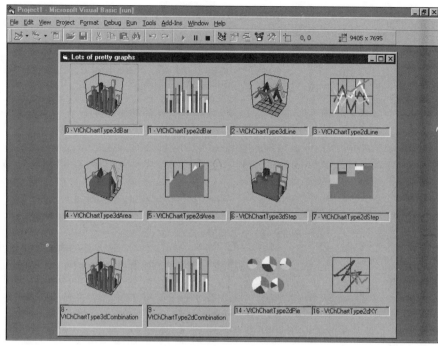

Figure 13-2:
The twelve
types of
charts you
can create.

✔ 9 – VtChChartType2dCombination

✔ 14 – VtChChartType2dPie

✔ 16 – VtChChartType2dXY

In addition to the ChartType property, you might want to define the following properties for your chart as well:

✔ FootnoteText – displays text that appears at the bottom of your chart

✔ ShowLegend – displays a legend on the chart that identifies what the different colors represent

✔ TitleText – displays a title at the top of your chart

You can modify the preceding properties directly in the Properties window or you can use the Property Pages dialog box by following these steps:

1. Click the chart control and open the Properties window (by pressing F4, choosing View⇨Properties Window, or clicking the Properties window icon on the toolbar).

2. Double-click the *(Custom)* property and the Property Pages dialog box appears.

3. Make any changes and click OK when you're finished.

TIP

If you need to change only one or two properties, you might find it easier to change the properties directly in the Property window rather than display the cumbersome Property Pages dialog box.

To change chart properties using BASIC code, just define the chart control name and the property you want to change. For example:

```
MSChart1.ChartType = VtChChartType3dLine
```

will give you a 3d Line Chart (VtChChartType3dLine) as per the list of ChartType properties at the beginning of this section and as shown in Figure 13-2.

Creating Pie Charts

Pie charts display proportional relationships, such as how much each salesperson has really contributed to the company profits. To create a two-dimensional pie chart, you need to define the following properties:

- ChartType – set this property value to 14
- RowCount – determines the number of different pie charts to display
- ColumnCount – defines the number of different "slices" that make up a complete pie chart

To stuff your pie chart with data, you need to define the following properties:

- RowLabel – provides a label for each pie chart displayed
- Row – identifies the pie chart to modify (The value of Row can never be greater than the value of RowCount.)
- Column – identifies the pie slice to modify
- Data – defines the size of the pie slice identified by the Column property

To help you understand how all these properties work, the following code, used to modify a Chart control with the properties listed in Table 13-1, creates the chart shown in Figure 13-3:

Table 13-1		Properties for Creating Chart in Figure 13-3
Property	*Value*	*What It Means*
ChartType	14	Displays a pie chart
RowCount	2	Displays two pie charts
ColumnCount	3	Divides each pie chart into three slices

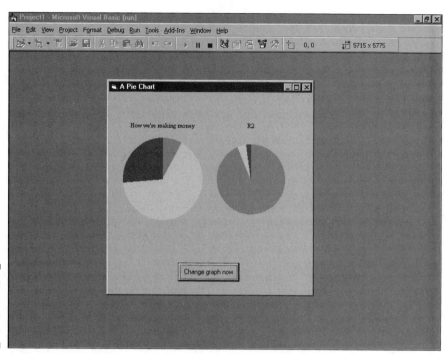

Figure 13-3:
Creating a
real-life pie
chart.

```
MSChart1.RowLabel = "How we're making money"
MSChart1.Row = 1
MSChart1.Column = 1
MSChart1.Data = 9

MSChart1.Row = 1
MSChart1.Column = 2
MSChart1.Data = 75

MSChart1.Row = 1
MSChart1.Column = 3
MSChart1.Data = 30
```

1. The first line displays the first pie chart with the label "How we're making money."

2. The second line tells Visual Basic to modify the first pie chart.

3. The third line tells Visual Basic to use the first pie slice.

4. The fourth line tells Visual Basic to stuff the number 9 into this first pie slice.

5. The fifth line reminds Visual Basic to modify the first pie chart.

6. The sixth line tells Visual Basic to use the second pie slice.

7. The seventh line tells Visual Basic to stuff the number 75 into this second pie slice.

8. The eighth line keeps reminding Visual Basic to stick with the first pie chart.

9. The ninth line tells Visual Basic to use the third pie slice.

10. The tenth line tells Visual Basic to stuff the number 30 into the third pie slice.

If you want to create a pie chart and stuff it with data, you can use the following code:

```
Private Sub Form_Load()
  MSChart1.ChartType = VtChChartType2dPie
  MSChart1.RowCount = 2
  MSChart1.ColumnCount = 3

  MSChart1.RowLabel = "How we're making money"
  MSChart1.Row = 1
  MSChart1.Column = 1
  MSChart1.Data = 9

  MSChart1.Row = 1
  MSChart1.Column = 2
  MSChart1.Data = 75

  MSChart1.Row = 1
  MSChart1.Column = 3
  MSChart1.Data = 30
End Sub
```

Assuming you draw the Chart control on a form, your chart is going to look similar to the one in Figure 13-4.

Creating Bar Charts

Bar charts let you compare one or more sets of data such as the amount of sales made for each month. You can create a two-dimensional (2D) or three-dimensional (3D) bar chart by setting the ChartType property to 0 (3D pie chart) or 1 (2D pie chart).

To create a bar chart, you need to define the following properties:

- ✔ ChartType – set this property value to 0 (3D) or 1 (2D)
- ✔ RowCount – determines the number of different bar charts to display
- ✔ ColumnCount – defines the number of different "bars" that appear within each chart

To fill your bar chart with data, you need to define the following properties:

- ✔ RowLabel – provides a label for each bar chart displayed
- ✔ Row – identifies the bar chart to modify (The value of Row can never be greater than the value of RowCount.)
- ✔ Column – identifies the bar to modify
- ✔ Data – defines the height of the bar identified by the Column property

To help you understand how all these properties work, the following code, used to modify a Chart control with the properties in Table 13-2, creates a bar chart shown in Figure 13-4:

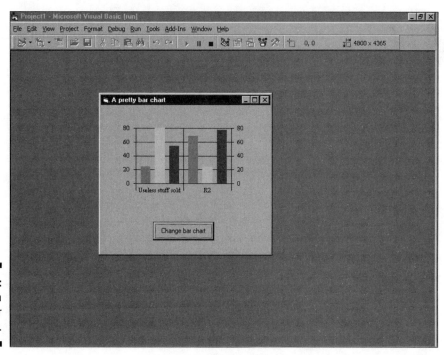

Figure 13-4:
Creating a
real-life bar
chart.

Table 13-2		Properties for Creating Chart in Figure 13-4
Property	*Value*	*What It Means*
ChartType	1	Displays a 2-D bar chart
RowCount	2	Displays two bar charts
ColumnCount	3	Divides each bar chart into three bars

```
MSChart1.RowLabel = "Useless stuff sold"
MSChart1.Row = 1
MSChart1.Column = 1
MSChart1.Data = 24

MSChart1.Row = 1
MSChart1.Column = 2
MSChart1.Data = 80

MSChart1.Row = 1
MSChart1.Column = 3
MSChart1.Data = 54
```

1. The first line displays the first bar chart with the label "Useless stuff sold."

2. The second line tells Visual Basic to modify the first bar chart.

3. The third line tells Visual Basic to use the first bar.

4. The fourth line tells Visual Basic to stuff the number 24 into this first bar.

5. The fifth line reminds Visual Basic to modify the first bar chart.

6. The sixth line tells Visual Basic to use the second bar.

7. The seventh line tells Visual Basic to stuff the number 80 into this second bar.

8. The eighth line keeps reminding Visual Basic to stick with the first bar chart.

9. The ninth line tells Visual Basic to use the third bar.

10. The tenth line tells Visual Basic to stuff the number 54 into the third bar.

Creating Area Charts

Area charts are simply line charts with the area under the line filled in with lovely colors. That way you can better see what the chart is trying show, such as how little you make in comparison to your boss who doesn't do a thing.

To create an area chart, you need to define the following properties:

- ChartType – set this property value to 4 (3D) or 5 (2D)
- RowCount – determines the number of points to plot
- ColumnCount – defines the number of different "areas" that appear within the chart

To stuff your area chart with data, you need to define the following properties:

- RowLabel – provides a label for each point plotted on the area chart
- Row – identifies the point to modify (The value of Row can never be greater than the value of RowCount.)
- Column – identifies the area to modify
- Data – defines the height of the area identified by the Column property

To help you understand how all these properties work, the following code, used to modify a Chart control with the properties in Table 13-4, creates the area chart shown in Figure 13-5:

Table 13-4	Properties Used to Create Chart in Figure 13-5	
Property	*Value*	*What It Means*
ChartType	5	Displays a 2-D area chart
RowCount	3	Plots three points
ColumnCount	3	Displays three areas

```
MSChart1.Row = 1
MSChart1.RowLabel = "Jan."
MSChart1.Column = 1
MSChart1.Data = 25
MSChart1.Column = 2
MSChart1.Data = 78
```

(continued)

(continued)

```
MSChart1.Column = 3
MSChart1.Data = 98

MSChart1.Row = 2
MSChart1.RowLabel = "Feb."
MSChart1.Column = 1
MSChart1.Data = 8
MSChart1.Column = 2
MSChart1.Data = 12
MSChart1.Column = 3
MSChart1.Data = 47

MSChart1.Row = 3
MSChart1.RowLabel = "Mar."
MSChart1.Column = 1
MSChart1.Data = 16
MSChart1.Column = 2
MSChart1.Data = 47
MSChart1.Column = 3
MSChart1.Data = 35
```

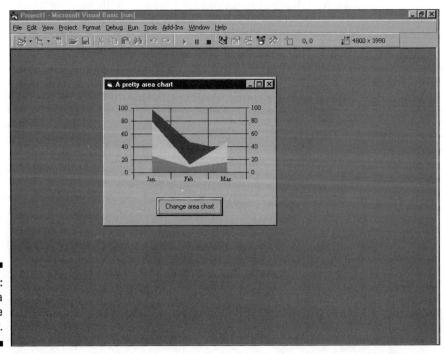

Figure 13-5:
Creating a
real-life
area chart.

1. The first line tells Visual Basic to plot the first point on the area chart.

2. The second line tells Visual Basic to label this first point as "Jan."

3. The third line tells Visual Basic to plot the first area of the chart.

4. The fourth line tells Visual Basic to use the number 25 as the first point for the first area on the chart.

5. The fifth line tells Visual Basic to plot the second area of the chart.

6. The sixth line tells Visual Basic to use the number 78 as the first point for the second area on the chart.

7. The seventh line tells Visual Basic to plot the third area of the chart.

8. The eighth line tells Visual Basic to use the number 98 as the first point for the third area on the chart.

9. The ninth line tells Visual Basic to move on to the second point.

10. The tenth line tells Visual Basic to label this second point as "Feb."

11. The eleventh line tells Visual Basic to plot the first area of the chart.

12. The twelfth line tells Visual Basic to use the number 8 as the second point for the first area on the chart.

13. The thirteenth line tells Visual Basic to use the second area of the chart.

14. The fourteenth line tells Visual Basic to use the number 12 as the second point for the second area on the chart.

15. The fifteenth line tells Visual Basic to plot the third line of the chart.

16. The sixteenth line tells Visual Basic to use the number 47 as the second point for the third area on the chart.

17. The seventeenth line tells Visual Basic to move on to the third point.

18. The eighteenth line tells Visual Basic to label this third point as "Mar."

19. The nineteenth line tells Visual Basic to plot the first area of the chart.

20. The twentieth line tells Visual Basic to use the number 16 as the third point for the first area on the chart.

21. The twenty-first line tells Visual Basic to plot the second area of the chart.

22. The twenty-second line tells Visual Basic to use the number 47 as the third point for the second area on the chart.

23. The twenty-third line tells Visual Basic to plot the third area of the chart.

24. The twenty-fourth line tells Visual Basic to use the number 35 as the third point for the third area on the chart.

Test your newfound knowledge

1. What is the difference between the RowCount property and the ColumnCount property in a pie chart?

   a. The RowCount property doesn't work, so you have to use the ColumnCount property instead.

   b. The RowCount property defines the number of pie charts to create. The ColumnCount defines how many "slices" make up each pie chart.

   c. Both the RowCount and the ColumnCount properties are designed to confuse you even further with more options than you ever dreamed were possible with a computer program.

   d. You mean there's a difference? No wonder my Visual Basic programs aren't working correctly.

2. What does the following code do to a line chart?

   ```
   MSChart1.Row = 1
   MSChart1.RowLabel = "Jan."
   MSChart1.Column = 2
   MSChart1.Data = 25
   ```

   a. I didn't know Visual Basic code had to do anything.

   b. This code contains the secret five-number combination that will get you into Fort Knox.

   c. This code labels the first point as "Jan." Then it plots the second point of the line chart at point 25.

   d. Warning! This code contains a deadly computer virus that will bring the Internet to its knees, crash your computer, and destroy all electrical appliances in your household. Do not use under penalty of law.

Chapter 14

Animation and Video

· ·

In This Chapter

▶ Simple animation made easy

▶ Moving pictures with your cursor keys

▶ Seeing video on your PC

· ·

*M*ost people would rather look at graphics than read text, which explains the popularity of television and movies along with the resultant illiteracy problems of each succeeding generation. Pictures make information easier to understand and moving pictures are often more enjoyable than still pictures.

So, if you're looking for another way to spice up your programs, look no further. With Visual Basic, you can animate your graphics or display actual video on your screen. Animation can simply entertain users, or it can be used as an integral part of your program to make your programs prettier, easier to use, and more attractive than ever.

Simple Animation Made Easy

To create simple animation, you can display a picture (stored in either a PictureBox or an Image) and move it around the screen. To move a PictureBox or Image, you can use the following:

✔ Left property

✔ Top property

✔ Move method

Moving pictures around

The Left property defines the location of the PictureBox or Image in relation to the left side of the form it is on (not the left side of the screen). If an object appears flush against the left side of a form, the Left property is 0. To change the Left property of an object, you can use BASIC code like this:

```
Image1.Left = Image1.Left + 10
```

This command tells Visual Basic to move the Image1 image box 10 twips (one inch is equal to 1440 twips; one centimeter is equal to 567 twips) to the right. Increasing the Left property moves an object to the right. Decreasing the Left property moves an object to the left.

The Top property defines the location of the PictureBox or Image in relation to the top of the form it is on (not the top of the screen). If an object appears flush against the top of a form, the Top property is 0. To change the Top property of an object, you can use BASIC code like this:

```
Image1.Top = Image1.Top + 10
```

This command tells Visual Basic to move the Image1 image box 10 twips down. Increasing the Top property moves an object down. Decreasing the Top property moves an object up.

The Move command lets you modify the Left and Top properties of an object in one command (which works faster than changing the Left and Top properties separately). To use the Move command, you can use BASIC code like this:

```
Image1.Move (Image1.Left + 10), (Image1.Top + 15)
```

This command tells Visual Basic to move the Image1 image box 10 twips to the right (by adding 10 to the Left property) and move the Image1 image box 15 twips down (by adding 15 to the Top property).

The illusion of animation

Moving a static graphic image can be interesting for about three seconds. Okay, five seconds if you're 10 months old or you are a cat. To make animation really come alive (and really freak out your cat), you need to rapidly change the image so that it appears to be moving. For example, a movie actually consists of still frames rapidly displayed one after the other.

To create a similar effect with computer animation, you need several graphic images that are slightly different, like a flip book. You can either create these graphic images (using a program such as Microsoft Paint) or use the limited graphic image collection that comes with Visual Basic.

When you have two or more images that you want to use to create your animation, you need to display one image, then the other image, and then another image, over and over again so that it looks like your picture is moving. By switching between two or more images, Visual Basic can create the illusion of animation.

Using the Timer control

After you have two or more images that you want to display, the next step is getting Visual Basic to rapidly display one after the other. The simplest way to do this is by using the Timer control.

To use the Timer control, draw the Timer control anywhere on your form and modify the following two properties:

- ✔ Enabled
- ✔ Interval

The Enabled property activates the Timer control and must be set to True.

The Interval property defines the number of milliseconds that Visual Basic waits between following any instructions stored in the Timer control's event procedure. It can be any value from 1 to 65,535. (Note that 10,000 milliseconds equals 10 seconds.)

The Timer control event procedure needs to do the following:

- ✔ Move the PictureBox or Image
- ✔ Change the picture displayed in the PictureBox or Image

To move the PictureBox or Image, you can use the Move method or specify the Left and Top properties separately. Both methods are described earlier in this chapter.

To change the displayed picture, draw one PictureBox or Image to display your animation plus one PictureBox or Image for each picture that makes up your animation, as shown in Figure 14-1.

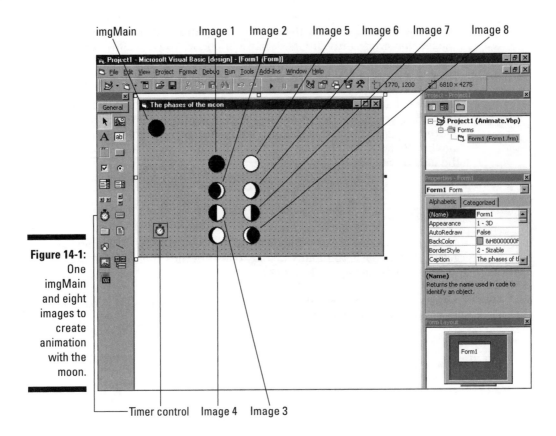

Figure 14-1:
One imgMain and eight images to create animation with the moon.

A typical `Timer` event procedure used to create animation might look like this:

```
Private Sub Timer1_Timer()
  Static Counter As Integer
  imgMain.Move imgMain.Left + 25
  Counter = Counter + 1
  If Counter = 9 Then Counter = 0
  Select Case Counter
    Case 1
      imgMain.Picture = Image1.Picture
    Case 2
      imgMain.Picture = Image2.Picture
    Case 3
      imgMain.Picture = Image3.Picture
    Case 4
      imgMain.Picture = Image4.Picture
```

```
      Case 5
        imgMain.Picture = Image5.Picture
      Case 6
        imgMain.Picture = Image6.Picture
      Case 7
        imgMain.Picture = Image7.Picture
      Case 8
        imgMain.Picture = Image8.Picture
    End Select
End Sub
```

1. The first line defines the start of the `Timer` event procedure, which runs, then waits the number of milliseconds defined by the Timer's Interval property, then runs again, and so on. So if the Interval property were set to 1,000, the `Timer` event procedure would run every 1,000 milliseconds (which is the same as running every second).

2. The second line declares a variable called `Counter` as an integer. The magic word `Static` tells Visual Basic to remember the value of `Counter` each time the `Timer` event procedure runs. The first time the `Timer` event procedure runs, `Counter` is equal to 0.

3. The third line moves an Image, called `imgMain`, to the right by 25 twips.

4. The fourth line adds one to the value of `Counter`.

5. The fifth line checks to see if the value of `Counter` is 9. If so, it resets the value of `Counter` to 0.

6. The sixth line defines the start of a `Select-Case` statement that determines which picture to display based on the value of the `Counter` variable.

7. The seventh line checks if the value of `Counter` is 1.

8. The eighth line takes the picture stored in the `Image1` box and displays it in the `imgMain` box.

9. The ninth through twenty-second lines check the value of `Counter` and display the appropriate picture in the `imgMain` box.

10. The twenty-third line defines the end of the `Select-Case` statement that started on the sixth line.

11. The twenty-fourth line defines the end of the `Timer` event procedure.

Putting it all together

To give you a real-life example to study, create the following program and run it for yourself:

Object	Property	Setting
Form	Caption	The phases of the moon
	Height	4275
	Left	1770
	Top	1200
	Width	6810
Image1	Height	480
	Left	1920
	Picture	Moon01
	Top	1200
	Width	480
Image2	Height	480
	Left	1920
	Picture	Moon02
	Top	1920
	Width	480
Image3	Height	480
	Left	1920
	Picture	Moon03
	Top	2520
	Width	480
Image4	Height	480
	Left	1920
	Picture	Moon04
	Top	3120
	Width	480
Image5	Height	480
	Left	2880
	Picture	Moon05
	Top	1200
	Width	480

Object	Property	Setting
Image6	Height	480
	Left	2880
	Picture	Moon06
	Top	1920
	Width	480
Image7	Height	480
	Left	2880
	Picture	Moon07
	Top	2520
	Width	480
Image8	Height	480
	Left	2880
	Picture	Moon08
	Top	3120
	Width	480
Image9	Height	480
	Left	240
	Name	imgMain
	Picture	Moon01
	Top	240
	Width	480
Timer1	Enabled	True
	Interval	200
	Left	360
	Top	3000

The Moon icons are stored in the GRAPHICS\ICONS\ELEMENTS directory inside your Visual Basic directory.

Type the following in the Code window:

```
Private Sub Timer1_Timer()
  Static Counter As Integer
  imgMain.Move imgMain.Left + 25
```

(continued)

(continued)

```
   Counter = Counter + 1
   If Counter = 9 Then Counter = 0
   Select Case Counter
     Case 1
       imgMain.Picture = Image1.Picture
     Case 2
       imgMain.Picture = Image2.Picture
     Case 3
       imgMain.Picture = Image3.Picture
     Case 4
       imgMain.Picture = Image4.Picture
     Case 5
       imgMain.Picture = Image5.Picture
     Case 6
       imgMain.Picture = Image6.Picture
     Case 7
       imgMain.Picture = Image7.Picture
     Case 8
       imgMain.Picture = Image8.Picture
   End Select
End Sub
```

Moving Pictures with Your Cursor Keys

Although the Timer control can create animation without the user doing a thing, you might want to display animation that the user can control through the keyboard.

To move a PictureBox or Image using the keyboard, your program needs to check whether the user presses certain keys, such as the up or right arrow key. To check for keystrokes, you must do the following:

- ✔ Set the form's KeyPreview property to True using the Properties window.

- ✔ Use the following constants, listed in Table 14-1, to define the keys the user presses.

- ✔ Create a Form_KeyDown event procedure to move your PictureBox or Image and create animation. For example:

Table 14-1		Visual Basic's keyboard constants
Constant	*Value*	*Key pressed*
vbKeyLeft	0x25	Left arrow key
vbKeyUp	0x26	Up arrow key
vbKeyRight	0x27	Right arrow key
vbKeyDown	0x28	Down arrow key

```
Private Sub Form_KeyDown(KeyCode As Integer, Shift As
          Integer)
  Select Case KeyCode
    Case vbKeyLeft
      If Picture1.Left > 0 Then
        Picture1.Move (Picture1.Left - 25)
      End If
    Case vbKeyUp
      If Picture1.Top > 0 Then
        Picture1.Top = Picture1.Top - 25
      End If
    Case vbKeyRight
      If Picture1.Left < (Form1.ScaleWidth -
          Picture1.Width) Then
        Picture1.Move (Picture1.Left + 25)
      End If
    Case vbKeyDown
      If Picture1.Top < (Form1.ScaleHeight -
          Picture1.Height) Then
        Picture1.Top = Picture1.Top + 25
      End If
  End Select
End Sub
```

1. The first line defines the start of the Form_KeyDown event procedure.

2. The second line defines the start of the Select-Case statement that checks to see which key the user pressed.

3. The third line checks whether the user pressed the left arrow key. If so, follow the fourth, fifth, and sixth lines. Otherwise, skip to the seventh line.

4. The fourth line makes sure the Picture1 PictureBox is away from the left side of the form. If so, follow the fifth line.

5. The fifth line moves the `Picture1` PictureBox 25 twips to the left.

6. The sixth line marks the end of the `If-Then` statement that started on line four.

7. The seventh line checks whether the user pressed the up arrow key. If so, follow the eighth, ninth, and tenth lines.

8. The eighth line makes sure the `Picture1` PictureBox is away from the top of the form. If so, follow the ninth line.

9. The ninth line moves the `Picture1` PictureBox up 25 twips.

10. The tenth line marks the end of the `If-Then` statement that started on line eight.

11. The eleventh line checks whether the user pressed the right arrow key. If so, follow the twelfth, thirteenth, and fourteenth lines.

12. The twelfth line makes sure the `Picture1` PictureBox is away from the right side of the form. If so, follow the thirteenth line.

13. The thirteenth line moves the `Picture1` PictureBox 25 twips to the right.

14. The fourteenth line marks the end of the `If-Then` statement that started on line twelve.

15. The fifteenth line checks whether the user pressed the down arrow key. If so, follow the sixteenth, seventeenth, and eighteenth lines.

16. The sixteenth line makes sure the `Picture1` PictureBox is away from the bottom of the form. If so, follow the seventeenth line.

17. The seventeenth line moves the `Picture1` PictureBox down 25 twips.

18. The eighteenth line marks the end of the `If-Then` statement that started on line sixteen.

19. The nineteenth line marks the end of the `Select-Case` statement that began on line two.

20. The twentieth line marks the end of the `Form_KeyDown` event procedure.

Seeing Video on Your PC

Believe it or not, you can actually display real-life video images on your lowly computer screen. Although this may seem only marginally useful, someone (maybe you) might be able to find a legitimate business use for such technology that doesn't require the disclaimer, "Adult entertainment only."

To display video through Visual Basic, you have to store video images in a special file format called Audio-Video Interleave format, or AVI. An AVI file is essentially a collection of compressed video images stored in a single file that ends with the AVI file extension such as MYDOG.AVI, VACATION.AVI, or XXX.AVI. (***Note:*** Visual Basic comes loaded with several AVI files stored in the Visual Basic folder such as the Graphics\AVIs directory.)

Unfortunately, AVI files tend to gobble up huge amounts of disk space, which means you will find it impractical for an AVI file to run for more than a few seconds, let alone a few minutes. Still, displaying real live video on the screen can give your program an element of futuristic appeal that can make the user forget that your program doesn't do much else.

To display AVI files, you must use the Microsoft Multimedia control, which you can load into the Visual Basic Toolbox by following these steps:

1. Choose Project⇨Components, or press Ctrl+T. The Components dialog box appears.

2. Click the check box next to Microsoft Multimedia Control 5.0. Make sure that an X appears in the check box.

3. Click OK. Visual Basic displays the Multimedia icon in the Toolbox.

4. Click the Multimedia control and draw it on your form.

Microsoft also offers a free ActiveX control (available on their web site `http://www.microsoft.com`) called the Microsoft ActiveMovie Control. This ActiveX control lets you display video as well.

To show you how to display a real-life AVI file, create the following program, shown at run-time in Figure 14-2.

Faster graphics with the Windows Game SDK

Moving a PictureBox or Image around the screen may work for simple animation, but if you're trying to create the next flight simulator, computer-aided design tool, or virtual reality interface, you need faster, more flexible graphics.

To encourage programmers to develop video games in Windows 95, Microsoft offers a toolkit called the Windows Game Software Development Kit (SDK). This SDK lets you create graphics that directly access the computer screen rather than go through the layers of Windows 95 operating system routines that would slow the graphics down.

To use the SDK, however, you must access routines written in a language other than Visual Basic. Fortunately, you can use these graphics routines without knowing how they work — you just have to hope that they really do work because you won't be able to correct them if they don't.

As another alternative, many companies sell ActiveX controls that isolate the Windows Game SDK features so you can use them easily from within Visual Basic.

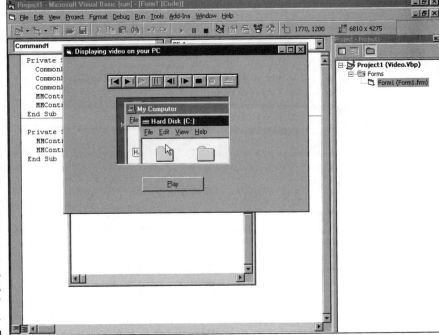

Figure 14-2:
The sample program playing the Whatson.AVI file stored in the C:\ WINDOWS\ HELP directory.

Test your newfound knowledge

1. What is the difference between the following two lines of code:

   ```
   imgMain.Move imgMain.Left + 25
   imgMain.Left = imgMain.Left + 25
   ```

   a. Both commands are used by only left-wing liberals who write Visual Basic programs to promote their political causes.

   b. The two lines are identical and move an Image box named imgMain to the right by 25 twips.

   c. Both commands are harmless, but they're useful to put in your program because then it looks like you know what you're doing.

   d. Both lines are the same length. An optical illusion makes them look different.

2. What do AVI files contain and why should you use them sparingly?

   a. AVI files contain saturated fats and artificial preservatives that may be dangerous to your health.

   b. AVI files contain habitats for endangered species that you should protect at all costs.

   c. AVI files contain video images that gobble up lots of hard disk space, so if you use too many of them, your AVI files may overwhelm a small hard disk.

   d. AVI files contain computer viruses that can wreck your hard disk. You should use them only when crashing your computer can get you the day off.

Object	Property	Setting
Form	Caption	Displaying video on your PC
	Height	4545
	Left	1545
	Top	1200
	Width	6810
CommonDialog1	Left	600
	Top	3000
MMControl1	Height	375
	Left	1200
	Top	480
	Width	3615
Picture1	Height	1815
	Left	1440
	Top	1080
	Width	3135
Command1	Caption	&Load
	Height	375
	Left	2160
	Top	3240
	Width	1695

Type the following in the Code window:

```
Private Sub Form_Load()
  MMControl1.DeviceType = "AVIVideo"
  MMControl1.hWndDisplay = Picture1.hWnd
End Sub

Private Sub Command1_Click()
  CommonDialog1.Filter = "AVI Files (*.AVI)|*.AVI"
  CommonDialog1.FilterIndex = 1
  CommonDialog1.ShowOpen
  MMControl1.filename = CommonDialog1.filename
  MMControl1.Command = "Open"
End Sub
```

Part IV

Saving Stuff in and Retrieving Stuff from Files

In this part . . .

Almost every program needs to save data to disk, whether the data is a word processor document, a list of foreign political contributor names and addresses, or the high score to a video game. This part of the book explains how to save and retrieve data in text files, random access files, and database files.

In addition, Part IV explains how to print your database information to create reports that even a complete moron like (plug in any of your favorite coworkers' names here) can understand and use.

Chapter 15

Saving and Retrieving
Plain Ol' Text Files

● ●

In This Chapter

▶ Getting to know text files

▶ Creating a text file

▶ Opening an existing text file

▶ Stuffing data into a text file

● ●

Can you imagine a word processor that won't let you save your documents to a disk? Or a database program that forced you to type all your data every time you turned on your computer? Obviously such programs would be either completely worthless or best-sellers if they were sold by a major software publishing giant.

To make your programs more useful, they may need to save data to a disk file and then retrieve it. For storing strings of text, the easiest method is to store data in a text file, which is also called an ASCII file.

What Is a Text (ASCII) File?

A text, or ASCII (American Standard Code for Information Interchange), file contains letters, numbers, and any other symbols you can type from the keyboard. What text files cannot contain are underlines, boldface, italics, fonts, type sizes, or any fancy formatting.

You can think of text files as a universal standard for exchanging data between computers. You can share a text file with any computer in the world. Even a lowly Apple IIe can store data in a text file, copy it to a Cray supercomputer, and let the Cray work its supercomputing magic on it.

The advantage of text files is that they are simple to create and easy to share with other programs or other computers. The disadvantage is that they store data inefficiently and are clumsy when you try to retrieve specific information. The reason is that when a program loads a text file, it starts at the beginning and loads it one character at a time. When it reaches the end of the text file, it stops — that's why text files are sometimes called sequential files.

Text files are like cassette tapes. Recording music on a cassette tape is easy, but retrieving a specific song is next to impossible. ("Fast forward, play. No, that's not it. Rewind, stop, play. Almost. Rewind some more, stop, play. There it is!")

Finding the start of your favorite song on a cassette tape is as difficult as finding specific data stored somewhere in a text file. For that reason, text files are best used for storing plain ol' text. That's why they call them *text files* (as opposed to *useless files*, *universal data exchange files*, or *those boring character files over there*).

Creating a Text File

Before you can store data in a text file, you have to create the text file. To create a text file, use the following syntax:

```
Open "Filename" For Output As #FileNumber
```

The keyword `Open` tells Visual Basic to create a new text file. The `"Filename"` tells Visual Basic the name of your new text file. This name can be any valid file name.

The keywords `For Output` tell Visual Basic that you want your newly created text file to get ready to accept some data or output from the program.

The `FileNumber` is any number between 0 and 511. Even though you just defined a name for your text file, Visual Basic is too stupid to understand English, so you have to identify the file by a number as well.

For example, you might tell Visual Basic, "Okay, stupid. I want to create a file called EATA.DOG. But instead of calling it by name, you can call it file number 1."

Use different file numbers to identify your files. If you're suddenly struck with severe amnesia and can't remember what file numbers you've already used, you can wimp out and let Visual Basic choose an unused file number for you by using the FreeFile keyword. For example:

```
Dim FreeNumber
FreeNumber = FreeFile
Open "DONT.CRY" For Output As FreeNumber
```

This tells Visual Basic to create a text file called DONT.CRY and assign it to the next available file number. This value may not always be the same, depending on any other files you may have opened.

If you want to use your own file numbers, you can. For example:

```
Open "GOAL.DAT" For Output As #1
```

This tells Visual Basic to create a text file called GOAL.DAT and assign it file number 1.

```
Open "C:\FILES\STEPONA.CAT" For Output As #200
```

This tells Visual Basic to create a text file in the C:\FILES directory, call the file STEPONA.CAT, and assign it file number 200.

Theoretically, you can open up to 512 text files. Realistically, if you try opening that many files, your computer could choke and run out of memory.

Opening an Existing Text File

Visual Basic gives you three ways to open an existing text file, depending on what you want to do with it:

- ✔ Read data from it
- ✔ Erase everything stored in the text file and replace its entire contents with new text
- ✔ Preserve the contents of the text file and add new text at the end of the file

Reading data from a text file

To read data from a file, use this syntax:

```
Open "Filename" For Input As #FileNumber
```

The previous code tells Visual Basic, "Open an existing text file called 'Filename,' get ready to read data or input from it, and assign it a file number."

Note that if a text file called Filename does not exist, Visual Basic will scream, wring its hands in agonized frustration, and create a run-time error.

Opening and erasing the contents of a text file

To open an existing text file, erase everything stored in it, and add new text, use this syntax:

```
Open "Filename" For Output As #FileNumber
```

This tells Visual Basic, "Open an existing text file called Filename, get ready to stuff new data into it regardless of what it may already contain, and assign it a file number." (For those sharp readers out there, this is the same syntax used to create a new text file.)

Adding new data to a text file

To open an existing text file, save its contents, and add new text at the end of the file, use this syntax:

```
Open "Filename" For Append As #FileNumber
```

This tells Visual Basic, "Open an existing text file called Filename, get ready to add or append data to it, and assign it a file number."

If you try to Append to a text file that doesn't exist, Visual Basic politely creates a new text file for you. Isn't that nice?

Stuffing Data into a Text File

Once you create a text file, the next obvious step is to stuff something into it. Visual Basic provides two ways to stuff data into a text file, depending on how you opened the text file:

✔ To store data at the beginning of the text file and overwrite anything already there, use this command:

```
Open "Filename" For Output As #FileNumber
```

✔ To store data at the end of the text file and preserve anything already there, use this command:

```
Open "Filename" For Append As #FileNumber
```

To stuff text into a text file, use the following syntax:

```
Print #FileNumber, "Text string"
```

This command says, "Take the text string and shove it into the file represented by the #FileNumber."

The following commands create a new text file called SECRET.TXT and stuff it with the strings, This is the first line, This is the second line, and This is the third line, as shown in Figure 15-1.

Figure 15-1:
The contents of the SECRET.TXT file.

```
This is the first line
This is the second line
This is the third line
```

```
Open "SECRET.TXT" For Output As #1
Print #1, "This is the first line"
Print #1, "This is the second line"
Print #1, "This is the third line"
```

The following commands add the strings This is a new line and Do you understand this yet? into the text file called SECRET.TXT, as shown in Figure 15-2.

```
Open "SECRET.TXT" For Append As #1
Print #1, "This is a new line"
Print #1, "Do you understand this yet?"
```

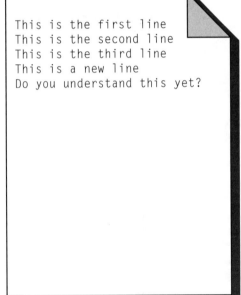

```
This is the first line
This is the second line
This is the third line
This is a new line
Do you understand this yet?
```

Figure 15-2:
The contents of the SECRET.TXT file after appending new text.

Closing a File

Whenever you create a text file or open an existing text file, you must close it before your program ends. If you don't, Visual Basic may get confused and mess up the contents of your text files by mistake.

Because you can have more than one file open at a time, the following command closes all open files:

```
Close
```

If you want to close a specific file, use the following syntax:

```
Close #FileNumber
```

For example, the following command closes a text file assigned a file number of 1:

```
Close #1
```

Reading Data from a Text File

To read data from a text file, you have to open the text file with the following command:

```
Open "Filename" For Input As #FileNumber
```

Once you open a text file, you can load the file contents into a variable. For example:

```
Dim FileContents As String
Open "FileName" For Input As #FileNumber
FileContents = Input$(LOF(#FileNumber), #FileNumber)
```

1. The first line says, "Create a variable called FileContents and make it hold only string values."

2. The second line says, "Open the FileName and assign it a number specified by #FileNumber."

3. The third line says, "Determine the Length of the File (LOF) identified by the FileNumber and take this entire length of the file identified by #FileNumber and stuff it into the variable called FileContents."

To see how this works, suppose you had a text file called GOALS.LST that contains these two strings:

```
"My first goal is to bring peace to the world."

"My second goal is to get my own apartment."
```

The following code would read the data stored in the GOALS.LST text file:

```
Dim FileContents As String
Open "GOALS.LST" For Input As #1
FileContents = Input$(LOF(#1), #1)
```

The preceding code example will stuff the entire contents of the GOALS.LST file into the variable called FileContents.

Changing Data Stored in a Text File

You can't directly manipulate any data stored in a text file. Instead, you have to store the text file data in a variable, manipulate that variable, and then store the variable's contents back into the text file.

Essentially, to change any data in a text file, you have to follow these steps:

1. Open the text file using the following syntax:

   ```
   Open "Filename" For Input As #FileNumber
   ```

2. Copy the contents of the text file into a variable:

   ```
   FileContents = Input$(LOF(#FileNumber), #FileNumber)
   ```

3. Close the file:

   ```
   Close #FileNumber
   ```

   or:

   ```
   Close
   ```

4. Edit the contents of the variable.

5. Open the text file to write over the existing contents:

   ```
   Open "Filename" For Output As #FileNumber
   ```

6. Store the newly edited text into the text file:

   ```
   Print #FileNumber, FileContents
   ```

7. Close the file again:

```
Close #FileNumber
```

or:

```
Close
```

Try It Yourself

To see how to read, write to, and edit a text file, create the following program. This program loads a text file and displays its contents in a text box, where you can edit its contents. The program looks like the one displayed in Figure 15-3.

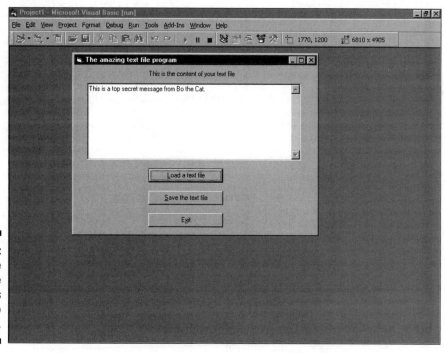

Figure 15-3:
What the sample program is supposed to look like.

Test your newfound knowledge

1. What kind of information can text files contain?

   a. Text files can contain text, or ASCII, data, which is nothing more than letters, numbers, punctuation marks, and anything else you can type from the keyboard.

   b. Text files contain information proving that the United States government really did recover a crashed flying saucer in Roswell, New Mexico back in 1947.

   c. Text files contain all of your hard disk data in encrypted form so that nobody can ever use it again.

   d. Text files never contain anything useful because computers never do anything worthwhile.

2. What does the following code do?

   ```
   Open "C:\TEST.TXT" For Input
      As #1
      Text1.Text =
   ```
   ```
   Input$(LOF(#1),#1)
      Close #1
   ```

   a. This code tests whether Visual Basic is working correctly. If so, it messes something else up so you don't get your expectations up too high.

   b. The first two lines erase all the text files on your computer. The third line shuts down your computer for good.

   c. The first line opens a text file called C:\TEST.TXT and assigns it a file number of 1. The second line stores the contents of the C:\TEST.TXT file into the Text property of a text box called Text1. The third line closes the C:\TEST.TXT file.

   d. The first line displays a dialog box, screaming for input from the user. The second and third lines take that input and throw it away to prove once and for all that computers are superior to human beings.

Object	Property	Setting
Form	Caption	The amazing text file program
	Height	4905
	Left	1770
	Top	1200
	Width	6810
Label1	Caption	This is the content of your text file
	Height	255
	Left	2040
	Top	120
	Width	2535
Text1	Height	2055

Object	Property	Setting
	Left	360
	MultiLine	True
	ScrollBars	2 – Vertical
	Text	(Empty)
	Top	480
	Width	5895
CommonDialog1	Left	360
	Top	3000
Command1	Caption	&Load a text file
	Height	375
	Left	2040
	Top	2760
	Width	2055
Command2	Caption	&Save the text file
	Height	375
	Left	2040
	Top	3360
	Width	2055
Command3	Caption	E&xit
	Height	375
	Left	2040
	Top	3960
	Width	2055

Type the following in the Code window:

```
Private Sub Command1_Click()
  Dim ThisFile As String
  CommonDialog1.Filter = "Text Files (*.TXT)|*.TXT"
  CommonDialog1.FilterIndex = 1
  CommonDialog1.ShowOpen
  ThisFile = CommonDialog1.filename
  Open ThisFile For Input As #1
```

(continued)

(continued)

```
  Text1.Text = Input$(LOF(#1), #1)
  Close #1
End Sub

Private Sub Command2_Click()
  If CommonDialog1.filename = "" Then
    CommonDialog1.Filter = "Text Files (*.TXT)|*.TXT"
    CommonDialog1.FilterIndex = 1
    CommonDialog1.ShowSave
  End If
  Open CommonDialog1.filename For Output As #1
  Print #1, Text1.Text
  Close #1
  Text1.Text = ""
End Sub

Private Sub Command3_Click()
  Unload Me
End Sub
```

Chapter 16

Random Access Files for Storing Structured Information

In This Chapter

▶ Learning about random access files

▶ Important variables every random access file needs

▶ Creating and opening a random access file

*I*n Visual Basic, you are best off storing fixed amounts of information such as names, addresses, or phone numbers in a *structure*. (See Chapter 11 for more on structures.) For example:

```
Type FriendStructure
    Name As String * 25
    Address As String * 30
    Phone As String * 15
End Type
```

Although structures store your data in memory, you may also want to save the data in a file on your disk. You could store it in an Access database file, but when you use the Access database feature (known in Visual Basic as the Jet Engine), your program experiences unsightly bloating. If you'd rather create your own more streamlined files to store data structures, the best way is to use a random access file.

If you want to store structures in a random access file, all string variables in the structures must be a fixed size. In the previous example of the structure called FriendStructure, all of the string variables are fixed — the Name variable is a string of 25 characters, the Address variable is a string of 30 characters, and the Phone variable is a string of 15 characters. If you forget to define a string length for a variable in a structure, you won't be able to save the structure in a random access file.

What Is a Random Access File?

A random access file is like a collection of 3-by-5 index cards stuffed in a shoe box. Each card contains information organized by a structure (such as by name, address, and phone number), and the entire collection of cards makes up the random access file.

The random access file gets its name because you can quickly select or store a card (structure) in the beginning of the file, at the end of the file, or anywhere in between.

Think of your favorite album. If it is recorded on a cassette tape, you have to play the whole tape before you got to the last song (this is how ASCII or text files work, as I describe in the previous chapter). But if it is recorded on a CD, you can jump right away to the last song, the fifth song, and then to the second-to-last song in that order — that's random access.

Random access files can hold only one type of structure, as shown in Figure 16-1. This would be like having one shoe box to hold only 3-by-5 index cards, another shoe box to hold only 4-by-6 index cards, and a third shoe box to hold only $8^1/_2$-by-11 sheets of paper.

```
Type
  Name As String * 5
  Phone As String * 8
End Type
```

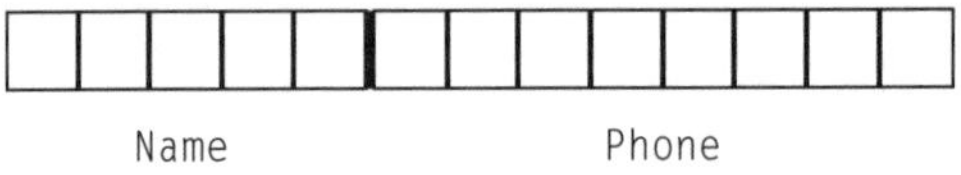

Name   Phone

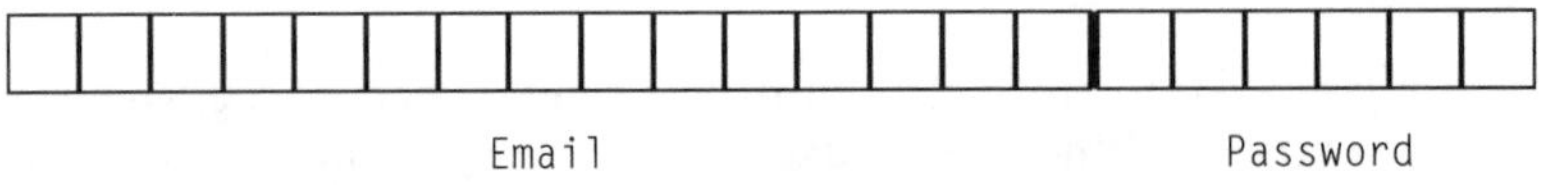

Figure 16-1: How Visual Basic stores structures in a random access file.

```
Type
  Email As String * 15
  Password As String * 6
End Type
```

Email   Password

Important Variables That Random Access Files Can Use

Once you define your structure, declare three public variables to help you save your structure's data to a random access file. The three variables are:

- ✔ A variable to represent your defined structure, such as:

```
Dim Friends As FriendStructure
```

- ✔ A variable to keep track of the current position, such as:

```
Dim Position As Long
```

- ✔ A variable to keep track of the last structure's position, such as:

```
Dim LastOne As Long
```

You need a variable to represent your structure so that it can hold the data. The Position variable points to the current record being used in the random access file. The LastOne variable keeps track of the last record in the file.

The only crucial variable that you absolutely must have is the variable, in this case FriendStructure, that represents your structure.

Creating and Opening a Random Access File

If you try to open a random access file that doesn't already exist, Visual Basic kindly creates one for you. But before you can open a random access file, you must specify the length of the structure. Suppose that you have defined the following structure:

```
Type Pet
   Name As String *10
   Age As Integer
End Type
```

You can determine its length using the magical Len command as follows:

```
Dim SLength As Long
Dim PetList As Pet
SLength = Len(PetList)
```

Once you determine the length of the structure, you can open a random access file:

```
Open "Filename" For Random As #FileNumber Len = SLength
```

The "Filename" tells Visual Basic the name of your random access file. This name can be any valid file name.

The keywords `For Random` tell Visual Basic that you want to open or create a random access file.

The `FileNumber` is any number between 0 and 511. Even though you just defined a name for your random access file, Visual Basic needs to identify it by a number. This number tells Visual Basic, "Okay, stupid. I want to create a file called ANIMALS.PET. But instead of calling it by name, just call it file number 1."

Use different file numbers to identify your files. If you can't remember what file numbers you've already used and don't want to examine your code to find the answer, Visual Basic can choose an unused file number for you by using the FreeFile keyword. For example:

```
Dim FreeNumber
FreeNumber = FreeFile
Open "DONT.CRY" For Random As FreeNumber Len = SLength
```

The previous code tells Visual Basic to open a random access file called DONT.CRY and assign it to the next available file number. The file number may not always be the same, depending on any other files you may have opened.

If you want to use your own file numbers, you can. For example:

```
Open "GOAL.DAT" For Random As #1
```

This tells Visual Basic to create a random access file called GOAL.DAT and assign it file number 1.

You don't have to specify your own file numbers if you don't want to, but they can make your code look a lot cleaner and simpler to read than if you use the FreeFile keyword:

```
Open "C:\FILES\NO.CAT" For Random As #200
```

The previous code tells Visual Basic to create a random access file in the C:\FILES directory, call the file NO.CAT, and assign it file number 200.

Theoretically, you can open up to 512 random access files. Realistically, opening that many files will gobble up memory and most likely crash your computer.

Stuffing Data into a Random Access File

Once you open a random access file, the next step is to stuff some structures into it. To stuff a structure into a random access file, use this syntax:

```
Put #FileNumber, Position, DataName
```

The `Put` command tells Visual Basic, "Put some information into the random access file identified by the FileNumber."

The `Position` tells Visual Basic the exact location to put the data. The first structure in a random access file is at position 1, the second is at position 2, and so on.

The `DataName` is the variable containing the structure data you want to store in the random access file.

Visual Basic provides two ways to stuff data into a random access file:

- ✔ Add a new structure to the end of the file
- ✔ Replace an existing structure with a new one

Stuffing data at the end of a random access file

Before you can add a structure to the end of a random access file, you need to know how many structures already exist in the file. To find this value, use this formula:

```
LastOne = LOF(FileNumber) \ Len(StructureName)
```

This tells Visual Basic, "Find the length of a random access file identified by this FileNumber, and divide it by the length of the structures it contains. This number will be the number of structures contained in the random access file. Store this value in the variable called LastRecord."

To add a new structure at the end of a random access file, follow these steps:

1. Identify the structure you want to add to the random access file:

```
Type StructureType
   Name As String *10
End Type
```

2. Define a variable to represent your structure:

```
Dim StructureName As StructureType
```

3. Determine the length of the structure:

```
Dim SLength As Long
SLength = Len(StructureName)
```

4. Open a random access file to store this information:

```
Open "Filename" For Random As #FileNumber Len = Slength
```

5. Determine the total number of structures stored in the random access file you just opened:

```
LastOne = LOF(FileNumber) \ Len(StructureName)
```

6. Tell Visual Basic to store this new structure in the position one greater than the current number of structures:

```
LastOne = LastOne + 1
```

7. Stuff the structure into the random access file:

```
Put #FileNumber, LastOne, StructureName
```

Replacing a specific structure in a random access file

If you wanted to replace an existing structure with a new one, follow these steps:

1. Identify the structure you want to add to the random access file:

```
Type StructureType
   Name As String * 10
End Type
```

2. Define a variable to represent your structure:

```
Dim StructureName As StructureType
```

3. Determine the length of the structure:

```
Dim SLength As Long
SLength = Len(StructureName)
```

4. Open a random access file to store this information:

```
Open "Filename" For Random As #FileNumber Len = Slength
```

5. Determine the position of the structure you want to replace. (Calculating this value requires your own code. For example, if you want to replace the second structure, you can store the value of 2 in a variable called Position.)

6. Stuff a new structure into the position of the structure that you want to replace:

```
Put #FileNumber, Position, StructureName
```

Reading Data from a Random Access File

Once you open a random access file, you can then read data from that random access file with the following commands:

```
Dim GetData As StructureType
Get FileNumber, Position, GetData
```

1. The first line says, "Define a variable (called GetData) as the same StructureType stored in the random access file you want to open."

2. The second line says, "From the random access file identified by FileNumber, go to a certain Position in this file, and store its contents in the GetData variable."

Deleting Data in a Random Access File

Sad to say, Visual Basic offers no simple command to delete data from a random access file in one clean stroke. Instead, you have to replace the structure you want to delete with the next structure in the file, as shown in Figure 16-2.

A random access file before deleting a structure

Bo	555-1234	Scraps	555-6789	Tasha	555-5555

Figure 16-2:
How Visual
Basic
clumsily
deletes
structures
one at a
time.

The same random access file with the second structure deleted
by copying the third structure in the second stucture's location

Bo	555-1234	Tasha	555-5555	Tasha	555-5555

Keep repeating this process until you've copied all the structures from their previous location and moved them to a new location. This process will leave two copies of the last structure at the end of the random access file. Oh well, that's how it works.

The following code copies each structure from a random access file and moves it to another position:

```
Dim Temp As StructureType
Dim Location As Integer
Open "Filename" For Random As #FileNumber Len = Slength
LastOne = LOF(FileNumber) \ Len(Temp)
For Location = DeletedPosition To LastOne - 1
  Get FileNumber, Location + 1, Temp
  Put FileNumber, Location, Temp
Next Location
```

1. The first line says, "Create a variable called Temp, and define it as the structure type defined by the StructureType variable (in this case, the structure simply contains **Name As String * 10**)."

2. The second line says, "Create a variable called Location and define it as an integer."

3. The third line opens the file specified by Filename and assigns it the number specified by `#FileNumber`.

4. The fourth line calculates the number of structures stored in the random access file and stuffs this value into a variable called `LastOne`.

5. The fifth line says, "Start a For-Next loop starting from the position of the structure that you want to delete (`DeletedPosition`) to the second-to-last position in the random access file."

6. The sixth line says, "Grab the structure stored in the next position and copy its contents to the Temp variable."

7. The seventh line says, "Put the value of the Temp variable into the current position."

8. The eighth line says, "Keep repeating this until you get to the last structure in the random access file."

To eliminate the duplicate structures at the end of a random access file, you need to write code that does the following:

1. Creates a new random access file.

2. Copies all the structures, except for the duplicate at the very end, to this new file.

3. Closes both files.

4. Deletes the original file using the Kill command, such as:

```
Dim Filename As String
Kill Filename
```

5. Rename the new file to the name of the original file using the Name command, such as:

```
Dim OriginalName As String
Name OriginalName
```

Complicated and confusing? You bet. But that's how clumsy programming can be sometimes. Now aren't you glad you don't have to do this for a living?

Closing a File

Whenever you open a random access file, you must close it before your program ends. If you don't, Visual Basic may get confused and mess up the contents of your random access files by mistake (or on purpose just to spite you — you never know).

Because you can have more than one file open at a time, the following command closes all open files:

```
Close
```

If you want to close a specific file, use the following syntax:

```
Close #FileNumber
```

For example, the following command closes a random access file assigned a file number of 1:

```
Close #1
```

Test your newfound knowledge

1. When do you use a random access file instead of a text file?

   a. Flip a coin. If it's heads, you use a random access file. If it's tails, you use a text file.

   b. You use a random access file when you want to store information that you don't want to find again. You use a text file when you want to store important business papers inside your computer.

   c. Random access files are bigger, slower, smaller, and faster than text files, so you never have to use a text file unless you don't know what you're doing.

   d. Random access files are best for storing information in structures. Text files are better for storing text or sequential information.

2. What are two ways that you can add data to a random access file?

   a. You can replace an existing structure or you can add a structure to the end of the random access file.

   b. There is no way to add data to a random access file, which means that random access files are always empty and totally useless for any type of programming.

   c. Like most parts of a computer, random access files periodically fail to work. This ensures that you don't become complacent with your computer and start thinking that you can actually use it for something productive.

   d. You can add data to a random access file only if you're lucky. Why else do you think they call them random access files?

Try It Yourself

To see how to read, write to, and edit a random access file, create the following program. When you run this program, you can type the names of three people and their ages in a form. If you want to save the data you enter, click on the Save File command button.

After you save your data in a random access file, try erasing the data displayed in the form and then click the Load File command button to load the file you created using the Save File command button. The Load File command button loads a random access file off the hard (or floppy) disk and displays its contents back in the form again.

Finally, click the Delete structures command button to delete the second structure displayed on the form. This deletes the second structure in the random access file by copying over it with the next structure stored in the file. (In a real-life program, you should also write code to eliminate duplicate structures in your random access file, but for the purposes of this example, it's more important that you see how to save, load, and delete structures in a random access file.)

The program, consisting of one .FRM file (Form1) and one .BAS file (Module1), is shown at run-time in Figure 16-3.

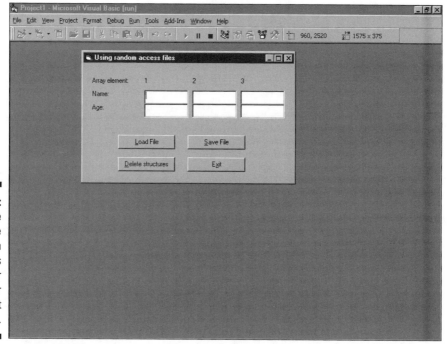

Figure 16-3:
What the sample program looks like as long as your computer doesn't crash.

Object	Property	Setting
Form	Caption	Using random access files
	Height	3570
	Left	1995
	Top	1260
	Width	5910
Label1	Caption	Array element:
	Height	255
	Left	240
	Top	360
	Width	1215
Label2	Caption	Name:
	Height	255
	Left	240
	Top	720
	Width	1215
Label3	Caption	Age:
	Height	255
	Left	240
	Top	1080
	Width	1215
Label4	Caption	1
	Height	375
	Left	1680
	Width	1215
Label5	Caption	2
	Height	375
	Left	3000
	Width	1215
Label6	Caption	3
	Height	375
	Left	4320

Object	Property	Setting
	Width	1215
Text1	Height	375
	Left	1680
	Text	(Empty)
	Top	720
	Width	1215
Text2	Height	375
	Left	1680
	Text	(Empty)
	Top	1080
	Width	1215
Text3	Height	375
	Left	3000
	Text	(Empty)
	Top	720
	Width	1215
Text4	Height	375
	Left	3000
	Text	(Empty)
	Top	1080
	Width	1215
Text5	Height	375
	Left	4320
	Text	(Empty)
	Top	720
	Width	1215
Text6	Height	375
	Left	4320
	Text	(Empty)
	Top	1080
	Width	1215

Object	Property	Setting
CommonDialog1	Left	120
	Top	1440
Command1	Caption	&Load File
	Height	375
	Left	960
	Top	1920
	Width	1575
Object	Property	Setting
Command2	Caption	&Delete structure 2
	Height	375
	Left	960
	Top	2520
	Width	1575
Command3	Caption	&Save File
	Height	375
	Left	2880
	Top	1920
	Width	1575
Command4	Caption	E&xit
	Height	375
	Left	2880
	Top	2520
	Width	1575

Type the following in the Module1 Code window:

```
Type FriendStructure
  Name As String * 20
  Age As Integer
End Type

Public Slength, LastOne As Long
Public ThisFile As String
```

Type the following in the Form1 Code window:

```
Private Form_Load()
  CommonDialog1.Filter = "Random Files *.*|*.*"
  CommonDialog1.FilterIndex = 1
End Sub

Private Sub Command1_Click()
  Dim GetData As FriendStructure
  CommonDialog1.ShowOpen
  ThisFile = CommonDialog1.filename
  SLength = Len(GetData)
  Open ThisFile For Random As #1 Len = SLength

  Get 1, 1, GetData
  Text1.Text = GetData.Name
  Text2.Text = GetData.Age

  Get 1, 2, GetData
  Text3.Text = GetData.Name
  Text4.Text = GetData.Age

  Get 1, 3, GetData
  Text5.Text = GetData.Name
  Text6.Text = GetData.Age

  Close #1
End Sub

Private Sub Command2_Click()
  Dim GetData As FriendStructure
  Dim I As Integer
  CommonDialog1.ShowOpen
  ThisFile = CommonDialog1.filename
  SLength = Len(GetData)
  Open ThisFile For Random As #2 Len = SLength
  LastOne = LOF(2) \ Len(GetData)
  For I = 2 To LastOne - 1
    Get 2, I + 1, GetData
    Put 2, I, GetData
  Next I
Close #2
End Sub
```

(continued)

(continued)

```
Private Sub Command3_Click()
  Dim GetData As FriendStructure
  CommonDialog1.ShowSave
  ThisFile = CommonDialog1.filename
  SLength = Len(GetData)
  Open ThisFile For Random As #1 Len = SLength

  GetData.Name = Text1.Text
  GetData.Age = Text2.Text
  Put #1, 1, GetData
  Text1.Text = ""
  Text2.Text = ""

  GetData.Name = Text3.Text
  GetData.Age = Text4.Text
  Put #1, 2, GetData
  Text3.Text = ""
  Text4.Text = ""

  GetData.Name = Text5.Text
  GetData.Age = Text6.Text
  Put #1, 3, GetData
  Text5.Text = ""
  Text6.Text = ""
  Close #1
End Sub

Private Sub Command4_Click()
  Unload Me
End Sub
```

Chapter 17

Connecting and Printing Database Files

In This Chapter

▶ Creating a database grid

▶ Picking out data with a combo box

▶ Showing database information in a list box

▶ Printing with Crystal Reports

*B*ecause many people use Visual Basic to create programs that store information in databases, Microsoft decided that they might as well make it easy for everyone (and help promote another Microsoft product) by linking Visual Basic with Microsoft Access.

Through this odd marriage between Visual Basic and Microsoft Access, you can create Visual Basic programs that can read, modify, and store data in a variety of database file formats such as Access (.MDB), dBASE (.DBF), or Paradox (.DB) database files.

 Accessing database files requires that you know a little bit about the database file format and the structure of the information stored inside. If you have no clue what a database is, then you might want to refresh your knowledge of databases by reading *Visual Basic 5 For Dummies.*

To help your programs use database files, Visual Basic provides an assortment of controls to access database information. Some of the more common types of database controls are:

- ✔ Database grids
- ✔ Database combo boxes
- ✔ Database list boxes
- ✔ A database printing utility called Crystal Reports
- ✔ Text boxes
- ✔ Labels

Database grids can yank data out of a database and display it in rows and columns so you can see multiple database records at a glance, as shown in Figure 17-1.

Database combo boxes let users choose data stored in a particular database field, as shown in Figure 17-2.

Database list boxes display data stored from a particular database field, as shown in Figure 17-3.

Text boxes and labels can display information stored in a database field. A text box gives users the option of editing the data while a label just displays the data without giving users a chance to modify it in any way.

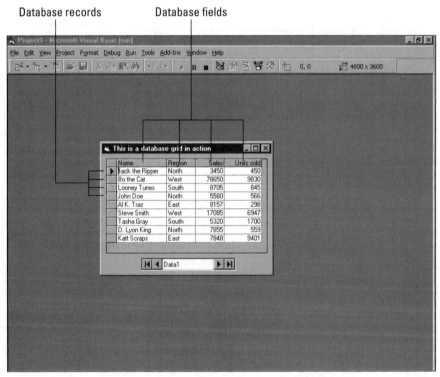

Database records   Database fields

Figure 17-1:
A typical
database
grid.

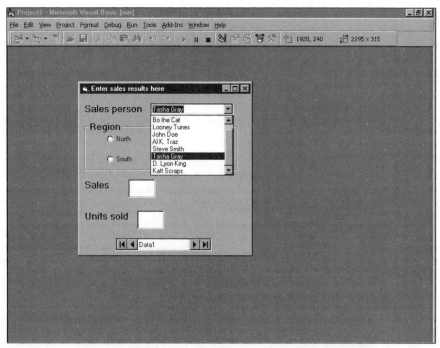

Figure 17-2:
A typical
database
combo box.

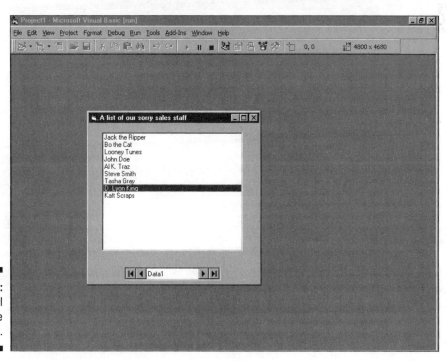

Figure 17-3:
A typical
database
list box.

The Database grid, Database combo box, and the Database list box are all ActiveX controls that must be added to your Visual Basic project before you can use them. To add these ActiveX controls to your program, follow these steps:

1. Choose Project➪Components (or press Ctrl+T). A Components dialog box appears.

2. Place an X (click the box) in the Microsoft Data Bound Grid Control check box to add the Database Grid to the Toolbox.

3. Place an X (click the Microsoft Data Bound List Controls 5.0 check box) and click OK. (This adds the Database combo box and the Database list box to the Toolbox.) Visual Basic displays the Database grid, the Database combo box, and the Database list box icons in the Toolbox as shown in Figure 17-4.

To help you connect your programs to a database easily, Visual Basic offers the VB Data Form Wizard, which you can activate by choosing Project➪Add Form and then clicking the VB Data Form Wizard.

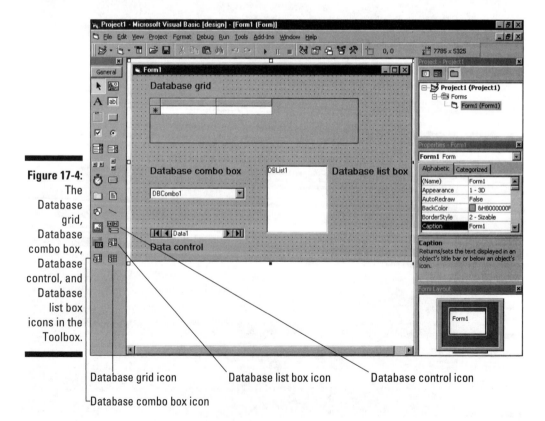

Figure 17-4: The Database grid, Database combo box, Database control, and Database list box icons in the Toolbox.

As a special bonus treat, Microsoft has thrown in a new database grid called the Microsoft FlexGrid Control 5.0. This database grid works similar to an ordinary database grid, but with the exception that it can merge cells containing identical data together. If you don't like the database controls that Microsoft Visual Basic 5 gives you, rest assured that plenty of third party software companies sell their own ActiveX controls that you can buy and use instead.

Connecting to a Database

To help you connect your programs to a database file, Visual Basic provides a special Data control. To use the Data control, follow these steps:

1. Click the Data icon in the Visual Basic Toolbox and draw the Data control on the form. Figure 17-4 shows the Data control icon.

2. Click the Data control and open the Properties window (by pressing F4, choosing View⇨Properties Window, or clicking the Properties window icon on the toolbar).

3. Double-click the DatabaseName property to display the DatabaseName dialog box.

4. Click the Access (.MDB) file that you want to use, and then click Open.

5. Click the RecordSource property and choose the database table or query you want to use.

At this point you're ready to connect a database grid, list box, or combo box to a real-life Microsoft Access database file.

Making your own databases

You have two ways to create databases for your Visual Basic programs. If you have a copy of a separate database program such as Microsoft Access or Lotus Approach, you can use it to create a database and fill it with information. If you don't own a separate database program, you can use the Visual Data Manager, an add-in program that comes with Visual Basic.

To use the Visual Data Manager, choose Add-Ins⇨Visual Data Manager. The Data Manager will let you define your database fields and add data as well. Although the Data Manager is not as powerful as separate database programs like Microsoft Access, it can do the job if you don't want to invest in Microsoft Access.

Creating a Database Grid

The main purpose of the database grid is to display multiple records in rows and columns in a way that resembles a spreadsheet. Each row in the grid displays a single record. Each column displays all the entries in a given field, and each cell in the grid displays a specific record's data stored in the given single field.

To create a database grid, follow these steps:

1. Click the Database grid icon in the Visual Basic Toolbox, as shown in Figure 17-4, and then draw the database grid the form.

2. Click the database grid and open the Properties window (by pressing F4, choosing View⇨Properties Window, or clicking the Properties window icon on the toolbar).

3. Click the DataSource property, and then click the data control that you want to use (such as Data1).

Once you create a database grid and link it to a data control, your database grid automatically displays your selected data records — you don't have to write any BASIC code.

The data control, defined by the database grid's DataSource property, determines which records appear in the grid. If you want the database grid to display different records, you have to change the RecordSource property of the data control as described in the previous section.

Modifying data displayed in a grid

Once you connect a database grid to a data control to display records, you can edit any of the data displayed in the database grid. Three properties let you alter the way the database grid works, as shown in Table 17-1.

Table 17-1		Three Properties That Change the Way the Database Grid Works
Property	*Value*	*What It Does*
AllowUpdate	True	Lets the user edit any data displayed in the database grid
	False	Displays data in the database grid but won't let the user edit any of it

Property	Value	What It Does
AllowDelete	True	Lets the user delete entire records
	False	Does not allow the user to delete records
AllowAddNew	True	Lets the user add new records
	False	Does not allow the user to add new records

To change any of these properties at design time, follow these steps:

1. Click the database grid open the Properties window (by pressing F4, choosing View⇨Properties Window, or clicking the Properties window icon on the toolbar).

2. Click the AllowAddNew, AllowDelete, or AllowUpdate property and set its value to True or False.

Changing colors and fonts

Once you connect a database grid to a data control to display records, you can work on the rest of your program. However, for those who like to customize their program to the utmost, take heart — you can also modify the color and fonts of the database grid.

To change the colors displayed in the database grid, follow these steps:

1. Click the database grid and open the Properties window (by pressing F4, choosing View⇨Properties Window, or clicking the Properties window icon on the toolbar).

2. Double-click the BackColor (or ForeColor) property and click the Palette tab. A color palette appears.

To change the fonts displayed in the database grid, follow these steps:

1. Click the database grid and open the Properties window (by pressing F4, choosing View⇨Properties Window, or clicking the Properties window icon on the toolbar).

2. Double-click the Font property. A font dialog box appears.

3. Click the font you want from the Font list box, choose a style from the Font Style combo box, and choose the type size from the Size combo box and click OK.

Choosing Data with a Combo Box

The database combo box can be used to enter new data in a database. By using a database combo box, the user can choose from a list of data already stored in a particular field or type a new value.

For example, a program might ask the user to type his or her state (in the Union that is, not mental state). Instead of displaying an empty text box, the database combo box can list several state abbreviations already stored in the database. If the user needs to type in a different abbreviation (such as for another country), the user can type the unlisted abbreviation in the combo box.

Four properties determine how the database combo box works:

- DataSource
- DataField
- RowSource
- ListField

The DataSource property determines which data control to use. Remember, the data control defines which database to use.

The DataField property determines which field to display in the database combo box. If you want the database combo box to display a default value, set the DataField property to a specific database field. If you don't want to display a default value, leave the DataField property blank.

The RowSource property determines the source of data to appear in the list portion of the combo box.

The ListField property determines the type of data that appears in the list portion of the database combo box.

To create a data combo box, follow these steps:

1. Click the Database combo box icon in the Visual Basic Toolbox and then draw the database combo box on the form. (See Figure 17-4.)

2. Click the database combo box and open the Properties window (by pressing F4, choosing View➪Properties Window, or clicking the Properties window icon on the toolbar).

3. Click the DataSource property, and then click the data control that you want to use (such as Data1).

4. Click the RowSource property, and then click the data control that you want to use (such as Data1).

5. Click the ListField property, and then click the field that you want to appear in the database combo box.

6. Click the DataField property, and then click the field that you want to appear as the default choice in the database combo box. (Usually the default field is the same field you choose in Step 5.)

The value the user chooses or types in a database combo box is stored in the database combo box's Text property. For example, the following code stores the value of a user's selection or typed entry in a variable called `Choice`:

```
Choice = DBCombo1.Text
```

Showing Database Information in a List Box

The database list box can display a list of data stored in a database field. Although you can see the information, you can't edit, delete, or add to it. Think of the database list box as a picture window into your database; you can look but you can't touch.

Four properties determine how the database list box works:

✔ DataSource
✔ DataField
✔ RowSource
✔ ListField

The DataSource property determines which data control to use. Remember, the data control defines which database to use.

The DataField property determines what type of information to display in the database list box. Usually, the DataField and the ListField properties are identical.

The RowSource property determines the source of data to appear in the list portion of the list box.

The ListField property determines the type of data that appears in the list box.

To create a data list box, follow these steps:

1. Click the Database list box icon in the Visual Basic Toolbox and then draw the database list box on the form. (See Figure 17-4.)

2. Click the database list box and open the Properties window (by pressing F4, choosing <u>V</u>iew⇨Properties <u>W</u>indow, or clicking the Properties window icon on the toolbar).

3. Click the DataSource property, then click the data control that you want to use (such as Data1).

4. Click the RowSource property, then click the data control that you want to use (such as Data1).

5. Click the ListField property, then click the field that you want to appear in the database list box.

6. Click the DataField property, then click the field that you want to appear highlighted. (Usually this field is the same field you choose in Step 5.)

The value the user chooses in a database list box is stored in the database list box's Text property. For example, the following code stores the value of the user's choice in a variable called Choice:

```
Choice = DBList1.Text
```

Crystal Reports

Once you have a bunch of data stored in a file and displayed in your Visual Basic program, your next question might be how to print all the information out. To print reports and not have to go through the laborious process of writing additional BASIC code, Microsoft has generously given you a special add-on called Crystal Reports.

Microsoft gives you a watered-down version of Crystal Reports in Visual Basic. If you need the absolute latest features of Crystal Reports, you have to buy a separate copy from Seagate Software at http://img.seagatesoftware.com.

Crystal Reports simply lets Visual Basic print database information in pretty reports that can impress your boss. To use the Crystal Reports program, you have to add the Crystal Reports ActiveX control to your Visual Basic program first.

The Crystal Report control is always invisible when your program is running.

To add the Crystal Report custom control to your program, follow these steps:

1. Open the project that you want to use with the Crystal Reports program.

2. Choose Project⇨Components, or press Ctrl+T. The Components dialog box appears.

3. Click the Crystal Report Control 4.6 (make sure a check mark appears in the box) and then click OK.

4. Click the Crystal Report control and draw it on your form as shown in Figure 17-5. Don't worry about the location of the Crystal Reports control on your form since it isn't visible when your programming is running.

Designing a report

Once you place the Crystal Reports custom control on your form, the next step is to design your report. A report contains three basic elements:

✔ Text

✔ Fields from specific database records

✔ Formulas for calculating results

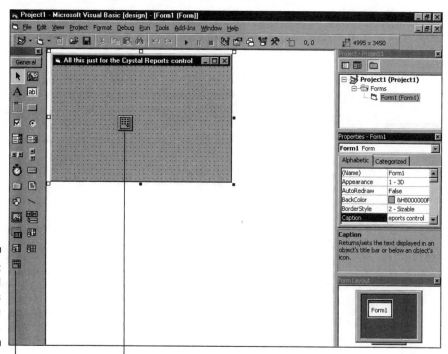

Figure 17-5:
The Crystal Reports icon in the Toolbox.

Crystal Reports icon   Crystal Reports control

Text is included simply to make your report look good, such as by displaying a title or a page number. The data on your report comes from database fields, such as people's names, addresses, or zip codes. Formulas help you make sense out of your data, such as by calculating sales from several salespeople so you can see who's selling the most and who needs to be fired, as shown in Figure 17-6.

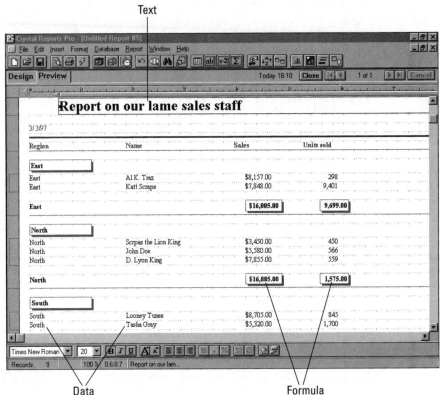

Figure 17-6:
A typical
Crystal
Reports.

To design your report, you must use the Report Designer program which you can get to by following these steps:

1. Choose <u>A</u>dd-Ins➪<u>R</u>eport Designer. The Crystal Reports window appears.

2. Choose <u>F</u>ile➪<u>N</u>ew. A Create New Report dialog box appears.

3. Click the type of report you want to create (such as a Summary or Graph). A Create Report Expert dialog box appears.

4. Click the Data File button and click OK. A Choose Database File dialog box appears.

5. Select the database file you want to use and click Add.

6. Repeat Step 5 for each database file you want to include on your report. Then click Done. Crystal Reports displays all the tables in your chosen database files as shown in Figure 17-7. (You may want to delete any database table that your program doesn't need.)

7. Click Next. Another dialog box appears, letting you choose which fields you want to display on your report.

8. Click a field that you want to display on your report and click Add. Repeat this step for each field you want to display.

9. Click Next. Another dialog box appears, asking you to pick a field to use to group and sort your data on your report.

10. Click a field that you want to group and sort on your report and click Add. Repeat this step for each field you want to use.

11. Click Next. Still another dialog box appears, asking if you want to display subtotals.

12. Click a field that you want to subtotal and click Add. Repeat this step for each field that you want to display subtotals such as sum, average, or maximum.

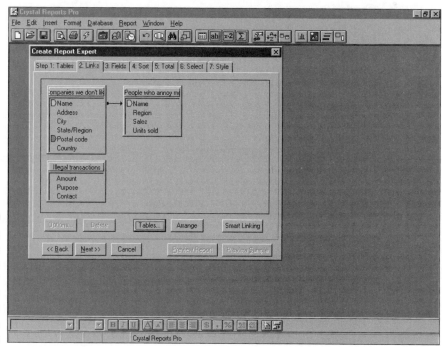

Figure 17-7:
Database tables from your chosen database files.

13. Click <u>N</u>ext. Still another dialog box appears, asking which fields you want to use as a filter for your report. A filter can help your program load only the database information it actually needs, thus making the database load faster.

14. Click <u>N</u>ext. One final dialog box appears, asking you to pick a style for your report.

15. Type a title for your report in the Title text box and click a style from the Style list box.

16. Click Preview <u>S</u>ample. A Preview Sample dialog box appears as shown in Figure 17-8.

17. Click the All records radio button and click OK. Crystal Reports displays your report. (*Note:* You may have to choose <u>R</u>eport⇨<u>Z</u>oom to see your report displayed in a larger size.)

18. Choose <u>F</u>ile⇨<u>S</u>ave. A File Save As dialog box appears.

19. Type a name for your report and click OK.

After you design a report, you can always go back later and revise it.

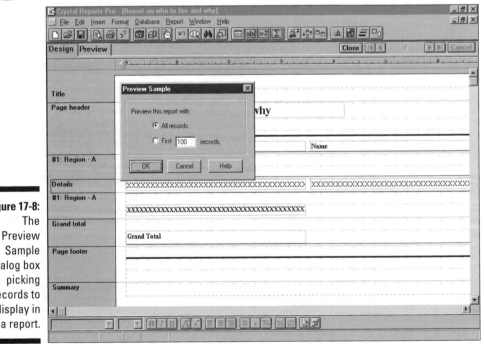

Figure 17-8:
The Preview Sample dialog box picking records to display in a report.

Adding text to your report

Once you create a report, you may want to add additional text such as a title or other information. Titles can be as simple as "Fourth Quarter Sales Results" or as long-winded as "Our Company Is Going Bankrupt and This is Why It's Not My Fault."

To add text to your report, make sure the Crystal Reports window appears (as described in Steps 1 through 5 in the Printing with Crystal Reports section) and then follow these steps:

1. Choose File➪Open. A File Open dialog box appears.

2. Click the Crystal Report file that you want to use and click OK. Crystal Reports displays your report on the screen.

3. Click the Design tab.

4. Choose Insert➪Text Field. An Edit Text Field dialog box appears.

5. Type the text you want to appear on your report and then click Accept. The cursor turns into a text box.

6. Move the cursor where you want to place your text and click the left mouse button. Crystal Reports displays your text on the report.

7. Choose Format➪Font, or use the Font list box that appears on the toolbar at the bottom of the screen. A Font dialog box appears.

8. Make any changes to the font, type size, and type style for your title, and then click OK.

Adding fields from a database to your report

A database field acts like a container for specific information, such as names, addresses, ages, or telephone numbers. You don't tell Crystal Reports the specific data you want to appear; instead, you specify the fields you want to appear. Then when you run your program, Crystal Reports plugs in the specific data, such as "John Doe," "123 Main Street," "24," or "555-1234."

To add database fields to a report, follow these steps:

1. Choose Insert➪Database field. An Insert Database Field dialog box appears as shown in Figure 17-9.

2. Click the database field that you want to add to your report and then click Insert. The cursor turns into a box.

3. Move the cursor where you want the database field to appear and click the left mouse button.

4. Repeat Steps 2 and 3 for each database field that you want to add to your report.

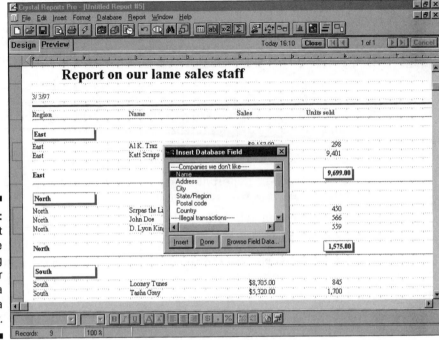

Figure 17-9:
The Insert
Database
Field dialog
box for
adding a
field to a
report.

5. Click <u>D</u>one when you're done.

As a shortcut, you can click a field in the Insert Database Field dialog box and simply drag the field where you want it to appear on your report.

If you click the Design tab of your report, Crystal Reports displays database field information as a box filled with characters such as XXX (for text), 555 (for numbers), $555 (for currency values), YYYYM (for dates), or True/False (for Boolean). The number of characters in the box indicates the maximum number of characters that can appear. You can always change the size of a database field to show more or less information — for instance, you can size a box to show only the first ten characters in a field even though the field may allow up to 25 characters.

Moving, resizing, and formatting fields

After placing database or text fields on your form, you may want to move, resize, or format them so your report looks pretty.

To modify a field, follow these steps:

1. Click the field that you want to modify. Black handles appear on the right and left sides of the selected field.

2. To move the field, press the up, down, left, and right arrow keys, or point to the selected field and drag the mouse.

3. To change the width of a selected field, press Shift+right arrow or Shift+left arrow, or drag the right or left handle with the mouse.

4. To change the font of a selected field, choose Format⇨Font. The Font dialog box appears.

5. Make any changes to the font, font style, or size and click OK.

 To select multiple fields at once, hold down the Shift key and click all the fields you want to select. To change the font or format quickly, just click the field you want to change, then click the Format Bar located at the bottom of the screen. Or point to the field you want to change and press the right mouse button to display a shortcut menu.

Adding formulas to your report

After you decide what type of data you want to appear, you may want to create formulas that will calculate a result such as by adding the total expenses of each salesperson. The three simplest types of formulas you can add to your report are

✔ Subtotals

✔ Grand totals

✔ Summaries

The Subtotals formula calculates a sum based on certain conditions. For example, suppose your report lists sales results for different salespeople. A subtotal could calculate how much each person sold in January, February, March, and so on.

To add a subtotal to a report, follow these steps:

1. Click the numeric field that you want to subtotal.

2. Choose Insert⇨Subtotal. An Insert Subtotal dialog box appears, as shown in Figure 17-10.

3. Click the list box labeled "When the report is printed, the records will be sorted and grouped by:" and choose a criterion.

4. Click OK. Crystal Reports displays a subtotal field on the report.

The Grand totals formula calculates a sum for a specific field. For example, suppose your report displays sales results for different salespeople. A grand total could calculate the total amount of sales from every salesperson.

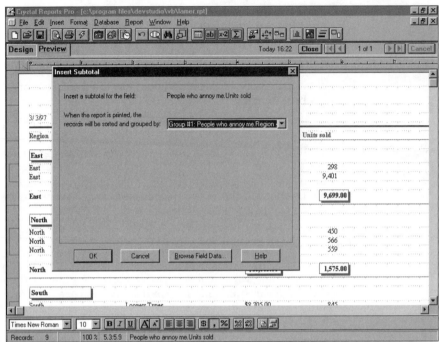

Figure 17-10:
The Insert
Subtotal
dialog box.

To insert a grand total, follow these steps:

1. Click the numeric field that you want to total.

2. Choose Insert⇨Grand Total. An Insert Grand Total dialog box appears.

3. Click OK. Crystal Reports displays a grand total field on the report.

Some of the more common Summaries formula can calculate the following:

- ✔ Sums – totals the values in a group
- ✔ Averages – calculates the average value of a group
- ✔ Maximum – identifies the highest value of a group
- ✔ Minimum – identifies the lowest value of a group
- ✔ Count – counts the total number of values in a group

To insert a summary, follow these steps:

1. Click the numeric or text field that you want to summarize.

2. Choose Insert⇨Summary. An Insert Summary dialog box appears.

3. Click the list box labeled "Insert a field which calculates the" and choose a summary such as one of the following:

- sum

- average

- maximum

- minimum

- count

4. Click the list box labeled "When the report is printed, the records will be sorted and grouped by:" and choose a criterion for grouping.

5. Click OK. Crystal Reports displays a summary field on the report.

Subtotals, Grand totals, and Summaries work only with numerical information.

Adding page numbers, dates, and record numbers to your report

To help make life easier for you, Crystal Reports already knows how to display page numbers, dates, and record numbers. All you have to do is tell Crystal Reports where you want the information to appear.

To display page numbers, dates, or record numbers, follow these steps:

1. Choose Insert⇨Special Field and then choose one of the following:

- Page Number Field

- Record Number Field

- Group Number Field

- Print Date Field

The cursor then appears as a box.

2. Move the cursor where you want to place your page number, date, or record number and click the left mouse button.

Saving your report

To see how your report will look, follow these steps:

1. Choose File⇨Print Preview, or click the Preview tab. Visual Basic displays your report on the screen.

2. Click the Close button (near the top of the screen) to exit the print preview.

Once you're happy with the way your report looks, save it to a file so your Visual Basic program will know where to find it again. To save a report, follow these steps:

1. From the File menu, choose Save. A File Save As dialog box appears.

2. Type your report's name in the File name box. If necessary, choose the drive and directory where you want to save your report.

3. Click Save.

4. From the File menu, choose Exit. The familiar Visual Basic screen appears again.

If you want to save hard disk space, don't save the data along with your report. To prevent Crystal Reports from saving data with your report, pull down the Report menu and look for the Save Data with Closed Report command. If a check mark appears next to this command, Crystal Reports saves the data with your report (and possibly gobbles up lots of hard disk space in the process). Choose the Save Data with Closed Report to remove the check mark.

If you want your reports to load quickly, then save your data along with your report. That way your program won't have to waste time loading the report and then loading the data that belongs in the report in two separate (and slow) steps.

Displaying a Report

Once you define the type of data you want to appear in your report and saved the report as a file on your hard disk, you need to specify one of three places for your report to appear:

✔ Displayed in a window on the screen

✔ Saved to a file on a disk

✔ Printed on paper through your printer

To tell Crystal Reports which database file to yank information from, you can write BASIC code such as:

```
Report1.DataFiles = "C:\MyApplication\Data\STUFF.MDB"
```

The previous command tells Crystal Reports to use the STUFF.MDB database file stored in the C:\MyApplication\Data directory.

Displaying a report in a window

To save paper, you may want to display a report in a window on the screen. By displaying a report on the screen, your program can give the user a preview of what type of data the report contains and how it will look if the user decides to print it.

To display a report in a window, you need to define four properties:

- ✔ ReportFileName – tells your program which report to display
- ✔ WindowTitle – defines a title bar for the window
- ✔ Destination – tells your program where to send the report
- ✔ Action – tells your program to display the report now

You can define these four properties using BASIC code such as the following:

```
CrystalReport1.ReportFileName = "C:\TEST\SURVEY.RPT"
CrystalReport1.WindowTitle = "Why We're Going Bankrupt"
CrystalReport1.Destination = crptToWindow
CrystalReport1.Action = 1
```

1. The first line tells Visual Basic to use the Crystal Report file called SURVEY.RPT, stored in the C:\TEST directory.
2. The second line tells Visual Basic to display the string "Why We're Going Bankrupt" in the report window.
3. The third line tells Visual Basic to get ready to send the report to a window.
4. The fourth line tells Visual Basic to display the report in a window.

You can also specify the location of the window on the screen by defining the following four properties:

- ✔ WindowHeight
- ✔ WindowLeft
- ✔ WindowTop
- ✔ WindowWidth

Printing a report

Displaying a report on the screen can be convenient, but eventually your program may need to print a copy so users can get a convenient print out of the report information.

To print a report, you need to define four properties:

- ✔ ReportFileName – tells your program which report to print
- ✔ Destination – tells your program where to send the report

✔ CopiesToPrinter – tells your program how many copies of the report to print

✔ Action – tells your program to print the report now

To print a report, you can use BASIC code such as the following commands:

```
CrystalReport1.ReportFileName = "C:\TEST\lamer.rpt"
CrystalReport1.Destination = crptToPrinter
CrystalReport1.CopiesToPrinter = 1
CrystalReport1.Action = 1
```

1. The first line tells Visual Basic to use the Crystal Report file called LAMER.RPT, stored in the C:\TEST directory.

2. The second line tells Visual Basic to get ready to send the report to the printer.

3. The third line tells Visual Basic to print one copy of the report.

4. The fourth line tells Visual Basic to start printing now.

Saving a report to disk

Since reports often display interesting or useful information, you may want to transfer report data to another program, such as a spreadsheet or database. To transfer report data to another program, you have to save the report as a file on a floppy or hard disk.

To save a report to disk, you need to define three properties:

✔ PrintFilename – specifies the drive, directory and filename to store the report

✔ PrintFileType – specifies the file format to save the report

✔ Action – tells your program to save the report now

The PrintFileType specifies one of following file types:

✔ crpt123WK1 – Lotus 1-2-3 *.WK1 format

✔ crpt123WK3 – Lotus 1-2-3 *.WK3 format

✔ crpt123WKS – Lotus 1-2-3 *.WKS format

✔ crptCharSep – ASCII text format with data separated by a single character

✔ crptCrystal – Crystal Reports format

✔ crptCSV – Comma-delimited ASCII text format

✔ crptDIF – DIF (data interchange format) format, often used to transfer data between different spreadsheet programs

✔ crptExcel21 – Excel version 2.1 format

✔ crptExcel30 – Excel version 3.0 format

✔ crptExcel40 – Excel version 4.0 format

✔ crptExcel50 – Excel version 5.0 format

✔ crptHTML30 – HyperText Markup Language version 3.0 format

✔ crptIntExpl – Internet Explorer format

✔ crptNetscape – Netscape Navigator format

✔ crptRecord – ASCII text format with one record per line

✔ crptRTF – Rich Text File format

✔ crptTabSep – Tab-separated ASCII text format

Test your newfound knowledge

1. Name two differences between the database grid and the database list box.

   a. The database grid doesn't work at all, so you always have to use the database list box instead.

   b. Microsoft simply included the database grid and the database list box as a way to add more features and justify charging a higher price. Other than that, neither the database grid nor the database list box do much of anything except look nice on the screen.

   c. The database grid can display information in every which way except the way you want it to work. The database list box is something Santa Claus uses to keep track of naughty children.

   d. The database grid lets you display multiple records that you can edit. The

   database list box simply displays a list of information stored in a specific database field; you can't edit any of it.

2. What can you do with Crystal Reports?

   a. Crystal Reports is a special program designed to make Visual Basic obsolete and completely useless as a programming tool.

   b. Crystal Reports lets your Visual Basic programs print information stored in a database file.

   c. Crystal Reports can help you report bugs in your programs caused by Microsoft's shoddy workmanship.

   d. Crystal Reports erases any rival programming tools on your hard disk, such as Borland's Delphi or PowerSoft's PowerBuilder.

   ✔ crptTabSepText – Tab-separated ASCII text format with carriage returns

   ✔ crptText – ASCII text format

   ✔ crptWinWord – Microsoft Word format

To save a Crystal Report as a file, you need to type the following BASIC code in the Code window of your Visual Basic program:

```
CrystalReport1.ReportFileName = "C:\TEST\lamer.rpt"
CrystalReport1.PrintFileType = crptText
CrystalReport1.Destination = crptToFile
CrystalReport1.PrintFileName = "C:\TEMP\KATZ.TXT"
CrystalReport1.Action = 1
```

1. The first line tells Visual Basic to use the Crystal Report file called LAMER.RPT, stored in the C:\TEST directory.

2. The second line tells Visual Basic save the report in the ASCII text format.

3. The third line tells Visual Basic to send the report to a file.

4. The fourth line tells Visual Basic to store the report in a file called KATZ.TXT in the C:\TEMP directory.

5. The fifth line tells Visual Basic to get to work saving the report in a file now.

Part V
Using ActiveX Controls, OLE, DLL, API, and Other Confusing Acronyms

The 5th Wave   By Rich Tennant

Re'al Pro'gram·mers

Real Programmers don't look stylish. To do so would indicate a belief in society.

In this part . . .

*B*y itself, Visual Basic is a powerful programming tool, but it can't do everything. To give Visual Basic more power (and also prevent you from creating everything from scratch), this part of the book explains how to use and create ActiveX controls that you can plug into your programs, and how to combine your program with other languages such as C++ (ugh), Delphi, or even languages as obscure as LISP, Prolog, or Modula-3. You also find out how to use built-in Windows functions that allow you to use components of Windows itself to help you write better programs.

If you ever feel that Visual Basic's limitations restrict your creativity, dig into Part V to find ways to let your imagination soar (just as long as you don't crash your computer in the process).

Chapter 18

Using ActiveX Controls

*I*n the world of computer programming, you often find it easier to copy somebody else's work rather than do it yourself. Within seconds of taking a programming class, your teacher is likely to tell you about all the benefits of creating reusable code — using parts of a program that you know already work. (Of course if you copy somebody else's homework, it's called plagiarism.)

Many programmers write their own programs, dissect the parts that can be used in another program, and paste the excised part in the new program to create something different. The main advantage of using prewritten code is that you don't have to write it yourself and debug it. Others have already done that for you (you hope), so you can just enjoy the benefit of their labor.

A collection of prewritten code is called a *library*. Programmers love collecting code libraries and sharing them with one another. Each time you need to write a new program, just look in your code library first. If you have some code that already performs the function that you need, you can copy it and paste it into your new program in much less time than if you had to write the entire program from scratch.

Unfortunately, program libraries have one serious drawback. A code library contains the actual source code for the program. So if you write some top secret programs for breaking into the Pentagon or the Kremlin, and you don't want anyone to see how you did it, don't store it in a program library.

Of course, if you keep your most valuable code out of a program library, no one else can use it but you, which partially defeats the purpose of reusable code in the first place.

To enable you to share your programming genius without revealing your source code, Microsoft has created the ActiveX control standards. Essentially, ActiveX controls act like a black box. You don't care how it works and you never see its source code, but you can plug it into your programs and use it anyway.

The History of ActiveX Controls

Essentially, an *ActiveX control* is nothing more than a program somebody else has written that you can include in your own Visual Basic programs. Just in case you want to know where ActiveX controls come from, keep reading.

The VBX standard

When Microsoft first released Visual Basic and didn't quite know what they were doing, Visual Basic used miniature programs called VBXs, which stood for Visual Basic eXtensions. Much to Microsoft's surprise, the VBX standard quickly caught on and many companies released VBXs to do practically everything from sending and receiving faxes to loading and editing Microsoft Excel spreadsheet files.

VBXs quickly made life easier for Visual Basic programmers. On the other hand, C++ and Pascal programmers had to struggle with source code libraries and the mess that would inevitably result when trying to insert somebody else's code into their own program. By contrast, Visual Basic programmers just had to buy a VBX, plug it into their programs, set a few properties, write a little bit of BASIC code, and within minutes they had a professional program that worked.

Noticing a good thing when they saw it, other languages quickly adopted the VBX standard. Soon you could plug VBX programs in Visual C++, Borland C++, Symantec C++, Delphi, PowerBuilder, dBASE, and a host of other programming tools that most Visual Basic programmers don't care about.

Microsoft created the VBX standard for Windows 3.1, which is a 16-bit operating system. As more powerful computers arrived (80486, Pentium, Pentium Pro), Microsoft eventually released a 32-bit operating system (Windows 95 and Windows NT) to take advantage of the faster microprocessors.

Because the VBX standard grew out of the 16-bit programming world of Windows 3.1, VBX custom controls aren't designed for writing 32-bit programs in Windows 95/NT. Using the VBX controls in either of the 32-bit operating systems is like putting a 4-cylinder Pinto engine into what used to be your 8-cylinder, high-performance roadster.

The OCX standard

To take advantage of the new 32-bit environment of Windows 95/NT, Microsoft created a new standard called OCX, which stands for OLE Custom eXtensions. (OLE itself is another acronym which stands for Object Linking and Embedding, and is a standard that allows programs to work together.)

Since OCX sounds like a typical computer science acronym, Microsoft decided to make the name sexier by relabeling them as *ActiveX controls*. Besides the different name, Microsoft hopes that people will eventually use ActiveX controls to create interactive web pages. So when you flip through a programming magazine, you may still see references to OCX or ActiveX controls, even though they're essentially different names for the same type of miniature programs that you can plug into Visual Basic.

Problems with ActiveX Controls

ActiveX controls let you create powerful programs quickly and easily, but be careful. Because you don't have the source code to an ActiveX control, you may run into one of the following problems:

- Bugs in the ActiveX control
- Different ActiveX control versions
- Dependence on the ActiveX control publisher

Bugs in the ActiveX control

Because ActiveX controls are nothing more than programs, they're likely to have bugs in them just like any other program. If a bug occurs in your own program, you can track it down and kill it (see Chapters 21 through 23). But if a bug occurs in an ActiveX control that your program uses, you have no way to correct it.

All you can do is write or call (or yell at, cry to) the company that makes the ActiveX control and tell them what the bug is. Then you can do nothing but wait until that company corrects the bug and sends you the corrected version of the ActiveX control.

Of course, while you wait for the debugged version of the ActiveX control for your program, your program isn't working correctly. So be prepared to deal with angry, upset, confused, or irritated customers and know that there's not a thing you can do to correct your program until you get the corrected version of the ActiveX control.

If you thought relying on your relatives to get anything accomplished was annoying, wait until you have to rely on programmers you've never met to get your own program working correctly.

Different ActiveX control versions

Like ordinary programs, ActiveX controls go through several versions as the company irons out bugs, adds new features, or makes the ActiveX control smaller and more efficient. Unfortunately, that means your program might be using version 1.5 of a particular ActiveX control and someone else might be using version 1.1 of that same ActiveX control.

For example, suppose a customer installs your program, which uses version 1.5 of a ActiveX control called STINKS.OCX. Then that same customer installs a second program that uses version 1.1 of the same STINKS.OCX ActiveX control.

For some odd reason, Windows likes to store VBX and OCX ActiveX controls in the \WINDOWS\SYSTEM directory. So if you're not careful, the installation of this second program might copy version 1.1 of the STINKS.OCX over version 1.5 of the STINKS.OCX that your program needs. The next time someone runs your program, instead of finding version 1.5 of the STINKS.OCX ActiveX control, it finds version 1.1 of the STINKS.OCX ActiveX control. Because your program really needs version 1.5 of the STINKS.OCX ActiveX control, your program may not work, or even worse, it may crash Windows 95 or Windows NT completely.

In this case, your program no longer works and neither you nor your customer may have a clue why. Until you replace version 1.1 of the STINKS.OCX ActiveX control with the one your program needs, your program may never work again. Isn't programming fun? Still want to be a programmer?

Dependence on the ActiveX control publisher

Although many ActiveX control publishers are established companies, others come from small companies that may have no clue how to handle their finances, or from unknown programmers who have created a highly useful freeware or shareware ActiveX control and have no intention of upgrading or enhancing it.

If your program uses a unique ActiveX control and the company that created it goes out of business, you're plain out of luck. You aren't able to upgrade or enhance the ActiveX control yourself, and you also have to find an equivalent custom control from another company and rewrite your program to use the replacement.

So the first big thing to remember when using ActiveX controls is to buy them from companies that you trust (or hope) will be around in the future to support them. The second big thing to remember is that when using ActiveX controls, no matter who you buy them from, you're essentially allowing your own program to be held hostage to the whims of the company that created the ActiveX controls.

ActiveX controls can be extremely useful, but because of these drawbacks, most hard-core programmers prefer to write everything from scratch (and take ten times as long to do it, as well).

Loading ActiveX Controls

Once you decide to use a particular ActiveX control, you need to do the following:

✔ Load the ActiveX control into the Visual Basic Toolbox

✔ Draw the ActiveX control on your form

✔ Set any necessary properties for the ActiveX control

✔ Write any necessary BASIC code to make the ActiveX control work with the rest of your program

To load an ActiveX control into the Visual Basic Toolbox, follow these steps:

1. Choose Project⇨Components, or press Ctrl+T. A Components dialog box appears.

2. Find the ActiveX control you want to add to the Visual Basic Toolbox and click its check box so that an X appears. (You may have to click the Browse button in case the custom control you want to use doesn't appear in the Components dialog box.)

3. Click OK. Visual Basic displays your newly added ActiveX control in the Visual Basic Toolbox.

To remove any unused ActiveX controls from your Visual Basic program, follow these steps:

1. Choose Project⇨Components, or press Ctrl+T. A Components dialog box appears.

2. Hold down the Shift key and click OK. Visual Basic removes any unused ActiveX controls from the Toolbox.

Writing Your Own ActiveX Controls

You have two ways in which you can write your own ActiveX controls:

- ✔ Use another language such as C++ or Delphi
- ✔ Use Visual Basic

If you don't mind the idea of learning another programming language, go ahead and spend the next few months of your life teaching yourself C++ or Delphi. C++ and Delphi are both powerful programming languages and with them you can create ActiveX controls that can do practically anything. Unfortunately, the trade-off for power is that you have to waste your time buying and learning a different language compiler such as Visual C++ or Delphi.

As a simpler alternative, you can now create your own ActiveX controls in Visual Basic. Essentially, writing an ActiveX control in Visual Basic is no different than writing an ordinary program in Visual Basic. The main difference is that when you compile an ActiveX control, you can then sell or give away your ActiveX control for other people to use in their own programs (including your C++ or Delphi programming friends).

An ActiveX control typically provides a useful feature that others would want to plug into their own programs, such as an Excel-compatible spreadsheet, a word processor, send and receive fax features, or a pop-up calendar.

Creating an ActiveX control

Creating an ActiveX control is easy. The hard part is making it do something useful. If you want to create an ActiveX control, follow these steps:

1. Choose File⇨New Project, or press Ctrl+N. A New Project dialog box appears.

2. Click the ActiveX Control icon and click OK. A borderless form appears as shown in Figure 18-1. Notice that the Project Explorer window displays a UserControl instead of a Form. At this point you're ready to start designing your ActiveX control.

Giving your ActiveX control a name and icon

The most important properties to define for your ActiveX control are:

✔ The Project Name

✔ The ToolboxBitmap

✔ The Name of your ActiveX control's main form

The Project Name property defines the name of your ActiveX control. When using an ActiveX control in Visual Basic, the Project Name appears in the Components dialog box.

To define your ActiveX control's Property Name, follow these steps:

1. Choose Project⇨Properties. A Project Properties dialog box appears.

2. Type your project name in the Project Name text box and click OK.

The ToolboxBitmap property defines the icon used to represent your ActiveX control. When using an ActiveX control in Visual Basic, the ToolboxBitmap appears in the Visual Basic Toolbox as an icon, as shown in Figure 18-2.

The Name property of your ActiveX control appears as a tooltip in the Toolbox, as shown in Figure 18-2.

To define the Name and ToolboxBitmap property of your ActiveX control, follow these steps:

1. Choose View⇨Project Explorer, press Ctrl+R, or click the Project Explorer icon.

2. Click the main user control form of your ActiveX control.

3. Open the Properties window (by pressing F4, choosing View⇨Properties Window, or clicking the Properties window icon on the toolbar).

4. Double-click the (Name) property and type a name for your ActiveX control.

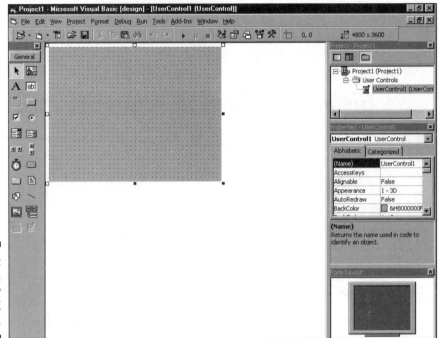

Figure 18-1:
Creating a new ActiveX control.

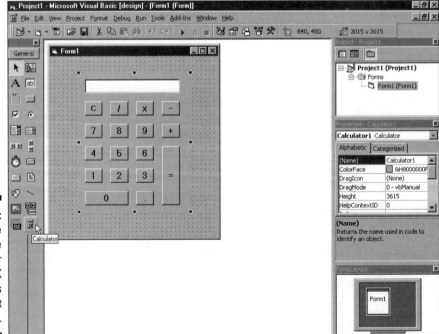

Figure 18-2:
The purpose of your ActiveX control's project name.

Toolbox bitmap icon

5. Double-click the ToolboxBitmap property. A Load Bitmap dialog box appears.

6. Click the graphic image that you want to represent your ActiveX control and click Open.

If you don't define a graphic image for the ToolboxBitmap property, Visual Basic gives your ActiveX control a generic graphic image. You can design your own icons (assuming you're a good artist) using the Microsoft Paint program that comes with Windows 95.

Defining properties for your ActiveX control

Properties allow the user of your ActiveX control to modify the appearance or behavior of the ActiveX control so they can customize it to use in their own programs. To define properties for your ActiveX control, you have to write BASIC code in the *(General)(Declarations)* portion of the Code window such as:

```
Private m_ColorFace As OLE_COLOR
```

This code tells Visual Basic, "Define a variable called m_ColorFace as a data type defined by OLE_COLOR." *Note:* OLE_COLOR is a data type that Visual Basic has already defined for storing color values.

To help identify your property variables, Visual Basic suggests that you give them an 'm_' prefix as shown above. So instead of calling your variable 'ColorFace,' call it 'm_ColorFace.' That way you can quickly glance through your code and identify your property variables.

Once you define one or more properties, you can define a default value by writing an Initialize procedure such as:

```
Private Sub UserControl_InitProperties()
  m_ColorFace = &H8000000F
End Sub
```

This code tells Visual Basic, "As soon as someone plugs this ActiveX control into their own program, set the m_ColorFace property variable to &H8000000F."

Creating properties

When defining properties, you can save yourself some typing if you just choose Tools⇨Add Procedure. This pops up a dialog box where you can define a property, and Visual Basic takes care of typing everything but your actual code.

To give users the ability to change properties for your ActiveX control, you have to write more BASIC code to make your properties available to the user, such as:

```
Public Property Get ColorFace() As OLE_COLOR
  ColorFace = m_ColorFace
End Property
```

This code tells Visual Basic, "ColorFace is a new property for your ActiveX control and it gets its value from the m_ColorFace variable."

To actually change a property for your ActiveX control, you have to write additional code using the Let keyword that tells Visual Basic, "Change the ColorFace property with a new value" like this:

```
Public Property Let ColorFace(ByVal vNewValue As OLE_COLOR)
  m_ColorFace = vNewValue
  UserControl.BackColor = vNewValue
  PropertyChanged "ColorFace"
End Property
```

1. The first line tells Visual Basic, "Get ready to change the value of the ColorFace property by the value stored in the vNewValue variable."

2. The second line tells Visual Basic, "Stuff the value of the vNewValue variable into the m_ColorFace variable."

3. The third line tells Visual Basic, "Take the value of the vNewValue variable and use it to change the BackColor property of the ActiveX control."

4. The fourth line tells Visual Basic, "Okay, stupid, change the ColorFace property now."

5. The fifth line tells Visual Basic, "This is the end of the BASIC code for changing the value of the ColorFace property."

The previous two chunks of code let you change the value of the ColorFace property, but you still need to write additional code to make your ActiveX control display the property changes:

```
Private Sub UserControl_WriteProperties(PropBag As
           PropertyBag)
  With PropBag
    .WriteProperty "ColorFace", m_ColorFace
  End With
End Sub
```

PropertyBag is a pre-defined Visual Basic data type that stores information about the properties of an object. Although the previous example only changes a single property, you are more likely to need to change multiple properties at once. Rather than type multiple PropBag.WriteProperty commands, it's easier to use a With statement as shown in the previous code example.

This code tells Visual Basic, "Take the value stored in the m_ColorFace variable and stuff it into the ColorFace property."

To read the value of the BackColor property and display it in the ColorFace property, you need additional BASIC code as shown in the next code example:

```
Private Sub UserControl_ReadProperties(PropBag As
           PropertyBag)
  Me.ColorFace = PropBag.ReadProperty("ColorFace",
           UserControl.BackColor)
End Sub
```

Testing and compiling your ActiveX control

To test an ordinary Visual Basic program, all you have to do is press F5 to start it running. But to test your ActiveX control, you have to compile it and then plug it into a normal Visual Basic program.

To compile an ActiveX control, follow these steps:

1. Choose File⇨Save Project.
2. Choose File⇨Make. A Make Project dialog box appears.
3. Click OK.

After you compile an ActiveX control into an .OCX file, you can create a separate program to test your ActiveX control. To test your compiled ActiveX control, follow these steps:

1. Click the close box of the Code window and the Design window of your ActiveX control.

2. Choose <u>W</u>indow and click the window name of your ActiveX control.

3. Choose <u>F</u>ile⇨A<u>d</u>d Project. The Add Project dialog box appears.

4. Click the Standard EXE icon and click <u>O</u>pen. Visual Basic displays a blank form with your ActiveX control in the Toolbox.

5. Click the ActiveX control in the Toolbox and draw it on your form. At this point, you can test your ActiveX control.

To go back and work on your ActiveX control, choose <u>F</u>ile⇨<u>R</u>emove Project.

Try It Yourself

To help you understand how a real ActiveX control works, try creating and compiling the following ActiveX control:

Object	*Property*	*Setting*
UserControl	(Name)	Calculator
	Height	3600

Test your newfound knowledge

1. What is the purpose of ActiveX controls?

   a. To provide ever-changing standards that nobody can keep up with, just to make the computer industry exciting once again.

   b. ActiveX controls help you convert C++ programs into Visual Basic so they run more slowly and less efficiently, which is a goal that all good software companies strive for with each new version of their program.

   c. ActiveX controls are small programs that somebody else wrote which you can add to your own programs.

   d. There is no purpose to ActiveX controls or anything else for that matter. Life is meaningless, and then you die.

2. How can you create your own ActiveX controls?

   a. You can't, so don't even bother trying.

   b. Put two ActiveX controls in the same room together, turn off the lights, play romantic music, and nine months later you may have a new ActiveX control to play with.

   c. You must erase your co-worker's entire hard disk first. (Although this isn't necessary, it can be lots of fun on the last day of the two-week notice you gave when quitting your job.)

   d. You can write them in another language such as C++, or you can use Visual Basic to create your own ActiveX controls.

Object	Property	Setting
	Width	2910
Text1	(Name)	txtResults
	Font	MS Sans Serif
	Font style	Bold
	Font size	12
	Height	375
	Left	120
	Top	120
	Width	2655
Command1	(Name)	cmdClear
	Caption	C
	Font	MS Sans Serif
	Font style	Bold
	Font size	10
	Height	375
	Left	120
	Top	720
	Width	495
Command2	(Name)	cmdOperator (0)
	Caption	+
	Font	MS Sans Serif
	Font style	Bold
	Font size	12
	Height	375
	Index	0
	Left	2280
	Top	1320
	Width	495
Command3	(Name)	cmdOperator (1)
	Caption	-
	Font	MS Sans Serif
	Font style	Bold
	Font size	12

Object	Property	Setting
	Height	375
	Index	1
	Left	2280
	Top	720
	Width	495
Command4	(Name)	cmdOperator (2)
	Caption	x
	Font	MS Sans Serif
	Font style	Bold
	Font size	12
	Height	375
	Index	2
	Left	1560
	Top	720
	Width	495
Command5	(Name)	cmdOperator (3)
	Caption	/
	Font	MS Sans Serif
	Font style	Bold
	Font size	12
	Height	375
	Index	3
	Left	840
	Top	720
	Width	495
Command6	(Name)	cmdOperator (4)
	Caption	=
	Font	MS Sans Serif
	Font style	Bold
	Font size	12
	Height	1575
	Index	4
	Left	2280
	Top	1920

Object	Property	Setting
	Width	495
Command7	(Name)	cmdDecimal
	Caption	. (*This is a period*)
	Font	MS Sans Serif
	Font style	Bold
	Font size	12
	Height	375
	Left	1560
	Top	3120
	Width	495
Command8	(Name)	cmdNumber (0)
	Caption	0
	Font	MS Sans Serif
	Font style	Bold
	Font size	12
	Height	375
	Index	0
	Left	120
	Top	3120
	Width	1215
Command9	(Name)	cmdNumber (1)
	Caption	1
	Font	MS Sans Serif
	Font style	Bold
	Font size	12
	Height	375
	Index	1
	Left	120
	Top	2520
	Width	495
Command10	(Name)	cmdNumber (2)
	Caption	2
	Font	MS Sans Serif
	Font style	Bold

Object	Property	Setting
	Font size	12
	Height	375
	Index	2
	Left	840
	Top	2520
	Width	495
Command11	(Name)	cmdNumber (3)
	Caption	3
	Font	MS Sans Serif
	Font style	Bold
	Font size	12
	Height	375
	Index	3
	Left	1560
	Top	2520
	Width	495
Command12	(Name)	cmdNumber (4)
	Caption	4
	Font	MS Sans Serif
	Font style	Bold
	Font size	12
	Height	375
	Index	4
	Left	120
	Top	1920
	Width	495
Command13	(Name)	cmdNumber (5)
	Caption	5
	Font	MS Sans Serif
	Font style	Bold
	Font size	12
	Height	375
	Index	5

Object	*Property*	*Setting*
	Left	840
	Top	1920
	Width	495
Command14	(Name)	cmdNumber (6)
	Caption	6
	Font	MS Sans Serif
	Font style	Bold
	Font size	12
	Height	375
	Index	6
	Left	1560
	Top	1920
	Width	495
Command15	(Name)	cmdNumber (7)
	Caption	7
	Font	MS Sans Serif
	Font style	Bold
	Font size	12
	Height	375
	Index	7
	Left	120
	Top	1320
	Width	495
Command16	(Name)	cmdNumber (8)
	Caption	8
	Font	MS Sans Serif
	Font style	Bold
	Font size	12
	Height	375
	Index	8
	Left	840
	Top	1320
	Width	495

Object	Property	Setting
Command17	(Name)	cmdNumber (9)
	Caption	9
	Font	MS Sans Serif
	Font style	Bold
	Font size	12
	Height	375
	Index	9
	Left	1560
	Top	1320
	Width	495

Type the following in the *(General) (Declarations)* part of the Code window:

```
Dim Number1 As String
Dim Number2 As String
Dim Operation As String
Dim ClearMe As Boolean
Dim Result As Single
Private m_ColorFace As OLE_COLOR
```

Type the following in the Code window:

```
Private Sub cmdClear_Click()
  Number1 = ""
  Number2 = ""
  Operation = ""
  Result = 0
  txtResults.Text = ""
End Sub

Private Sub cmdDecimal_Click()
  If Number1 = "" Then
    Number1 = "0"
  End If
  txtResults.Text = Number1 & "."
  Number1 = ""
End Sub

Private Sub cmdNumber_Click(Index As Integer)
  If ClearMe Then
```

```
          ClearMe = False
          Number2 = txtResults.Text
          txtResults.Text = ""
        End If
        Select Case Index
          Case 0
            Number1 = "0"
          Case 1
            Number1 = "1"
          Case 2
            Number1 = "2"
          Case 3
            Number1 = "3"
          Case 4
            Number1 = "4"
          Case 5
            Number1 = "5"
          Case 6
            Number1 = "6"
          Case 7
            Number1 = "7"
          Case 8
            Number1 = "8"
          Case 9
            Number1 = "9"
        End Select
        txtResults.Text = txtResults.Text & Number1
        Number1 = txtResults.Text
      End Sub

      Private Sub cmdOperator_Click(Index As Integer)
        ClearMe = True
        Select Case Index
          Case 0 ' + sign
            Operation = "+"
          Case 1 ' - sign
            Operation = "-"
          Case 2 ' x sign
            Operation = "x"
          Case 3 ' / sign
            Operation = "/"
          Case 4 ' = sign
            Select Case Operation
              Case "+"
```

(continued)

(continued)

```vb
            Result = CSng(Number2) + CSng(Number1)
        Case "-"
            Result = CSng(Number2) - CSng(Number1)
        Case "/"
            Result = CSng(Number2) / CSng(Number1)
        Case "x"
            Result = CSng(Number2) * CSng(Number1)
      End Select
      txtResults.Text = CStr(Result)
      Operation = ""
  End Select
End Sub


Public Property Get ColorFace() As OLE_COLOR
  ColorFace = m_ColorFace
End Property


Public Property Let ColorFace(ByVal vNewValue As OLE_COLOR)
  m_ColorFace = vNewValue
  UserControl.BackColor = vNewValue
  PropertyChanged "ColorFace"
End Property


Private Sub UserControl_InitProperties()
  m_ColorFace = &H8000000F
End Sub


Private Sub UserControl_ReadProperties(PropBag As _
          PropertyBag)
  Me.ColorFace = PropBag.ReadProperty("ColorFace", _
          UserControl.BackColor)
End Sub


Private Sub UserControl_WriteProperties(PropBag As _
          PropertyBag)
  With PropBag
    .WriteProperty "ColorFace", m_ColorFace
  End With
End Sub
```

Chapter 19

Creating OLE Programs

● ●

In This Chapter

▶ The basics of OLE

▶ Using the Insert Object dialog box

▶ Using the Paste Special dialog box

▶ Adding in-place activation

▶ Creating OLE servers

● ●

*O*LE (which is an acronym for the long-winded term *Object Linking and Embedding*) is Microsoft's attempt to create yet another standard that everyone else doesn't want to follow but does because they want to make a lot of money. The idea behind OLE is that you create small, simple programs and then combine them to create a larger, more complicated program (that probably still doesn't work).

For more information about OLE, buy a copy of *OLE For Dummies*. Order today! Operators are standing by.

The Basics of OLE

OLE can work in two ways:

✔ Linking

✔ Embedding

Linking lets you store multiple files in separate locations, but display them within a single program. For example, OLE can link a file created by Harvard Graphics, another file created by Lotus 1-2-3, and a third file created by Microsoft Access and display all three separate files within a WordPerfect document. The moment you modify the data in one file (such as the Lotus 1-2-3 file), your changes immediately appear in the WordPerfect document.

Because the software industry likes to reward individuality, not all programs handle OLE links the same way. Some programs, such as Excel 97, give you the option of updating OLE links automatically or only when you ask to update OLE links. Other programs always update OLE links automatically without giving you a choice.

Embedding lets you cram multiple files, created by other programs, into a single file. For example, you could cram a Freelance Graphics file, a Microsoft Excel file, and a dBASE file all into a single Microsoft Word file.

Microsoft Office 97 offers a feature called binders, which lets you store multiple documents (such as a Word, Excel, and PowerPoint file) in a single file. A Microsoft Office 97 binder is nothing more than a fancy use of OLE embedding.

The main difference between linking and embedding is that linking stores files in separate locations while embedding stores multiple files in one file.

When you use OLE, one program is known as the client and the other is known as the server. The *OLE client* is the program that holds OLE data created by another program. The *OLE server* is the program that creates OLE data to store in the OLE client. For example, if you create a graphic in CorelDRAW! and then embed it in or link it to a Word document, Word is the client and CorelDRAW! is the server.

If you want your Visual Basic programs to remain compatible with the rest of the world, you may need to create programs that can act as both OLE clients and servers (which this chapter tells you how to do). You have two ways of creating an OLE client:

- ✔ Use the Insert Object dialog box.
- ✔ Use the Paste Special dialog box.

Using the Insert Object Dialog Box

The Insert Object dialog box lets you embed or link whole files into an OLE client Visual Basic program. To use the Insert Object dialog box, you just need to place an OLE control on a form and then use the InsertObjDlg command. For example:

```
OLE1.InsertObjDlg
```

To show how the InsertObjDlg command works, the following steps show how to create a program that uses the Insert Object dialog box:

1. Click the OLE icon in the Toolbox and draw the OLE container on the form. An Insert Object dialog box automatically appears, as shown in Figure 19-1.

OLE control on the form

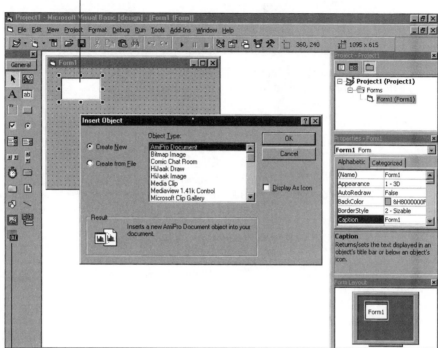

Figure 19-1:
The Insert
Object
dialog box.

OLE icon in the Toolbox

2. Click Cancel to remove the Insert Object dialog box. (This dialog box lets you, as the programmer, link or embed OLE objects into your program at design time.)

3. Click the CommandButton icon in the Toolbox and draw two buttons on the form.

4. Click the Command1 command button and open the Properties window (by pressing F4, choosing <u>V</u>iew⇨Properties <u>W</u>indow, or clicking on the Properties window icon on the toolbar).

5. Change the caption of Command1 to **Use OLE**.

6. Click the Command2 command button and switch to the Properties window (by pressing F4, choosing <u>V</u>iew⇨Properties <u>W</u>indow, or clicking on the Properties window icon on the toolbar).

7. Change the caption of Command2 to **Exit**.

8. Double-click the Exit button to open the Code window, or press F7.

9. Type **Unload Me** in the Private Sub Command2_Click() procedure as follows:

```
Private Sub Command2_Click();
   Unload Me
End Sub
```

10. Click in the Object list box of the Code window and choose Command1.

11. Type **OLE1.InsertObjDlg** in the `Private Sub Command1_Click()` procedure as follows:

```
Private Sub Command1_Click()
   OLE1.InsertObjDlg
End Sub
```

This Visual Basic code looks deceptively simple. It actually tells your Visual Basic program how to use the Insert Object dialog box to link or embed files.

Testing OLE embedding

Once you create your Visual Basic program, you can test its OLE embedding capabilities by following these steps:

1. Press F5 to run your program.

2. Click the Use OLE button. The Insert Object dialog box appears.

3. Click the Create New radio button.

4. Choose Bitmap Image or Paintbrush Picture from the Object Type list box and click OK. The pull-down menus of Microsoft Paint appears at the top of your form and a box appears in your OLE container.

5. Draw a picture inside this box inside the OLE container. Your Visual Basic program displays your drawing in the OLE container as shown in Figure 19-2.

6. Click the Exit button to exit your program.

Testing OLE linking

Once you create your Visual Basic program, you can test its OLE linking capabilities by following these steps:

1. Click the Start button on the Windows 95 taskbar, choose Programs➪ Accessories➪Paint. When the Microsoft Paint window appears, draw a picture.

2. Choose File➪Save (or press Ctrl+S). A Save As dialog box appears.

3. Type a file name for your drawing and click Save.

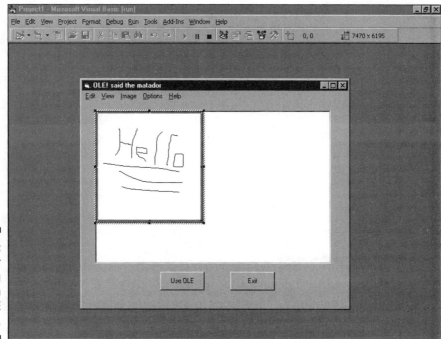

Figure 19-2:
Your
drawing
displayed in
the OLE
container.

4. Switch to Visual Basic and run your program by pressing F5.

5. Click the Use OLE button. The Insert Object dialog box appears (see Figure 19-1).

6. Click the Create from File radio button. The Insert Object dialog box changes its appearance.

7. Click the Link check box.

8. Click the Browse button. A Browse dialog box appears.

9. Choose the file name (such as a Paint file) that you want to link to your Visual Basic program and click Insert.

10. Click OK. Your Visual Basic program displays the linked file within the OLE container as shown in Figure 19-3.

11. Click the Exit button to exit your program.

Using the Paste Special Dialog Box

The Insert Object dialog box embeds or links whole files into an OLE client Visual Basic program. If you just want to use part of a file as an OLE object,

Figure 19-3:
A Microsoft
Paint file
displayed
within
an OLE
container.

you can use the Paste Special dialog box instead. By using the Paste Special dialog box, you can copy an OLE object to the clipboard and then embed or link the object in your Visual Basic program.

To use the Paste Special dialog box, you just need to place an OLE control on a form and then type the following PasteSpecialDlg BASIC code in the Code window. For example:

```
OLE1.PasteSpecialDlg
```

To create a sample program that uses the Paste Special dialog box, you can modify the previous program you created in this chapter or just follow these steps to create a new program from scratch:

1. Choose File⇨New Project and double-click the Standard EXE icon in the New Project dialog box.

2. Click the OLE icon in the Toolbox and draw the OLE container on the form. An Insert Object dialog box automatically appears (see Figure 19-1).

3. Click Cancel to remove the Insert Object dialog box. (This dialog box lets you, as the programmer, link or embed OLE objects into your program at design-time.)

4. Click the CommandButton icon in the Toolbox and draw two buttons on the form.

5. Click the `Command1` command button and open the Properties window (by pressing F4, choosing <u>V</u>iew⇨Properties <u>W</u>indow, or clicking on the Properties window icon on the toolbar).

6. Change the caption of `Command1` to **Use OLE**.

7. Click the `Command2` command button and switch to the Properties window (by pressing F4, choosing <u>V</u>iew⇨Properties <u>W</u>indow, or clicking on the Properties window icon on the toolbar).

8. Change the caption of `Command2` to **Exit**.

9. Double-click the Exit button to open the Code window.

10. Type **Unload Me** in the `Private Sub Command2_Click()` procedure as follows:

```
Private Sub Command2_Click();
  Unload Me
End Sub
```

11. Click in the Object list box of the Code window and choose Command1.

12. Type the following in the `Private Sub Command1_Click()` procedure. (Note that you don't have to type the first and last lines because Visual Basic will do that for you automatically.)

```
Private Sub Command1_Click()
  If OLE1.PasteOK = True Then
    OLE1.PasteSpecialDlg
  End If
  ' Display a message if there is nothing on the clip-
      board
  If OLE1.OLEType = vbOLENone Then
    MsgBox "Nothing has been copied or cut to the clip-
      board."
  End If
End Sub
```

The previous simple Visual Basic procedure tells your Visual Basic program how to paste an OLE object stored on the clipboard. If nothing has been copied or cut to the clipboard, a message box appears and says, "Nothing has been copied or cut to the clipboard."

Testing OLE embedding

Once you create a Visual Basic program that uses the Paste Special dialog box, you can test its OLE embedding capabilities by following these steps:

1. Click the Start button on the Windows 95 taskbar, choose <u>P</u>rograms⇨ Accessories⇨Paint to load Microsoft Paint and draw a picture.

2. Use the Selection tool to select part or all of your drawing.

3. Choose Edit⇨Copy (or press Ctrl+C).

4. Switch to Visual Basic and press F5 to run your program.

5. Click the Use OLE button. The Paste Special dialog box appears.

6. In the Object Type list box, choose Bitmap Image and click OK. Your Visual Basic program displays the embedded OLE data.

7. Click the Exit button to exit your program.

Testing OLE linking

Once you create your Visual Basic program, you can test its OLE linking capabilities by following these steps:

1. Load a program such as Microsoft Word or Microsoft Excel and type some text or numbers.

2. Choose File⇨Save from the menu bar (or press Ctrl+S). A Save As dialog box appears.

3. Type a file name for your file (such as your Word document or Excel spreadsheet) and click Save.

4. Highlight your text or numbers.

5. Choose Edit⇨Copy (or press Ctrl+C).

6. Switch to Visual Basic and run your program by pressing F5.

7. Click the Use OLE button. (Just remember that most programs you use, such as Excel 97, won't have a Use OLE button.) The Paste Special dialog box appears.

8. Click the Paste Link radio button.

9. Click OK. Your Visual Basic program displays the linked OLE data.

10. Switch to the program in which you created the file you saved in Step 3, edit the file, and then save the file (the file must be saved for OLE to work).

11. Switch back to your Visual Basic program to verify that the OLE link displays the changed file in your Visual Basic program.

12. Click the Exit button to exit your program.

A program can use both the Insert Object and the Paste Special dialog boxes. The previous examples simply isolate the minimum amount of code necessary for using either type of dialog box.

Adding In-Place Activation

For an OLE client program to follow the complete OLE standard, it needs to offer *in-place activation*. In-place activation is a fancy term which means that when you double-click an embedded OLE object so you can edit it, the client program's menus are replaced with the OLE server's menus.

For example, if you have an OLE object created by Microsoft Excel and embedded in Microsoft Word, the Microsoft Word menus appear at the top of the screen. But if you double-click on the Microsoft Excel embedded OLE object, Excel's menus suddenly appear on the screen and the Word menus disappear. When you click an embedded OLE object, the pull-down menus of the OLE server (such as Microsoft Excel) appear.

The OLE server can display its pull-down menus within a Visual Basic program in two ways:

 ✔ By replacing one or more titles on the Visual Basic program menu bar

 ✔ By adding its own menu titles to the Visual Basic program menu bar

---

Test your newfound knowledge

1. What is the difference between using the Insert Object and the Paste Special dialog boxes?

   a. The Insert Object dialog box can link or embed only entire files. The Paste Special dialog box can link or embed any object copied or cut from another program.

   b. The Insert Object dialog box is used by the medical profession to insert objects into places where people normally don't insert objects. The Paste Special dialog box is used to trap cockroaches in glue.

   c. The Insert Object and Paste Special dialog boxes both use OLE to create programs that refuse to use OLE.

   d. There is no difference because hardly anybody knows how to use OLE anyway.

2. What is the difference between an OLE client and an OLE server?

   a. The OLE server infects the OLE client like a virus and destroys it before it can damage your computer.

   b. An OLE client is a person who has suffered severe psychological distress trying to understand why anyone would want to use OLE.

   c. An OLE client stores and displays data created by an OLE server.

   d. An OLE client and an OLE server are two types of programs that refuse to work together.

Figure 19-4 shows a typical pull-down menu within a Visual Basic program. If an OLE server (such as Microsoft Excel) replaces the menu titles in the menu bar, the Visual Basic program menu title changes as shown in Figure 19-5.

In many cases, you may want to keep portions of your Visual Basic menu bar intact and just include the menu bar of the OLE server, as shown in Figure 19-6. For example, you probably don't want an OLE server (such as Microsoft Excel) to wipe out your Visual Basic program's File menu title; otherwise, your Visual Basic program won't be able to save, print, or exit until the OLE server's menu bar goes away.

To keep your Visual Basic program's menu titles intact when the OLE server's menus appear, you have to use the Menu Editor to change the NegotiatePosition property of your menu titles.

For a menu title that you want to keep intact, give it a NegotiatePosition from the following list, as shown in Figure 19-7:

  ✔ 0 – None

  ✔ 1 – Left

  ✔ 2 – Middle

  ✔ 3 – Right

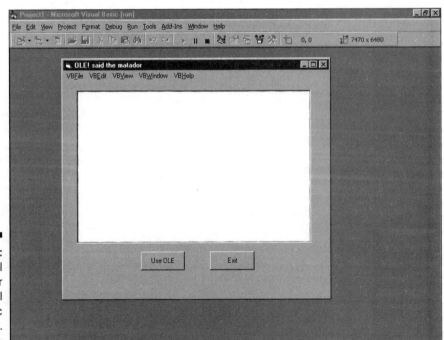

Figure 19-4:
A typical menu bar in a Visual Basic program.

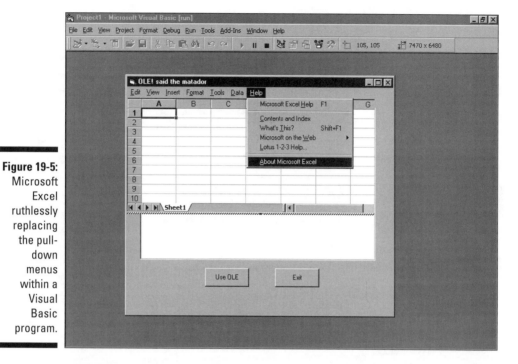

Figure 19-5:
Microsoft Excel ruthlessly replacing the pull-down menus within a Visual Basic program.

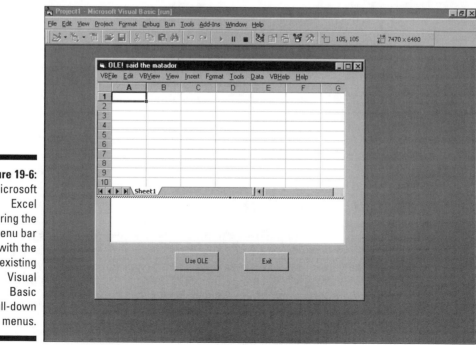

Figure 19-6:
Microsoft Excel sharing the menu bar with the existing Visual Basic pull-down menus.

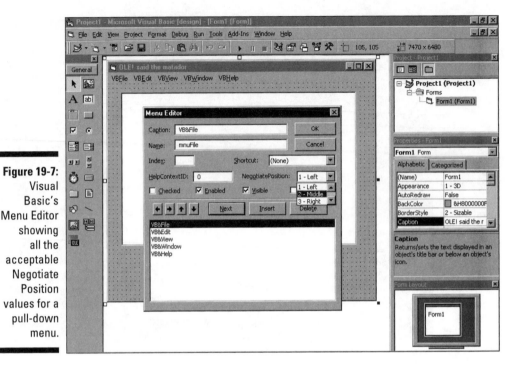

Figure 19-7:
Visual
Basic's
Menu Editor
showing
all the
acceptable
Negotiate
Position
values for a
pull-down
menu.

Set the NegotiatePosition property to 0 – None for any menu titles that you want replaced with the OLE server's menu titles.

In Figure 19-6, the VBFile menu title has a NegotiatePosition value of 1 – Left, so it appears to the far left of the menu bar. The VBView menu has a NegotiatePosition value of 2 – Middle. The VBHelp menu title has a NegotiatePosition value of 3 – Right, so it appears on the right end of the menu bar.

Two or more menu titles can have the same NegotiatePosition values.

Creating OLE Servers

OLE servers are nothing more than programs that provide objects for another program to use. Many OLE servers are complete programs that provide their own user interface (such as Microsoft Excel). However, OLE servers don't have to have a user interface and can exist solely to provide objects for another program to use and display.

The following example shows how to create a simple OLE server so that you can understand the bare minimum of code necessary for creating an OLE server in Visual Basic.

Visual Basic can create two types of OLE servers: *in-process* and *out-of-process* servers. An in-process server is actually a dynamic link library (DLL); an out-of-process server is an executable (EXE) file. The example in this chapter shows how to create an out-of-process (EXE) OLE server.

An OLE server provides objects for other programs to use. In Visual Basic, objects are defined by a special file called a *class module*. A class module defines an object and contains methods and properties. Methods perform actions on the object (class), and properties describe the characteristics of an object (class).

Writing an OLE server

To create a simple OLE server, follow these steps:

1. Choose File⇨New Project and double-click the ActiveX DLL icon in the New Project dialog box.

2. Choose Project⇨Project1 Properties A Project Properties dialog box appears.

3. Click in the Startup Object list box and choose Sub Main.

4. Type **OLEObject** in the Project Name box.

5. Type **OLE Test** in the Project Description box and click OK.

6. Type the following in the Class1 code window:

```
Public TextString As String
Dim IntegerData As Integer
```

7. Choose Tools⇨Add Procedure. An Add Procedure dialog box appears.

8. Type **Cubed** in the Name box, click the Function radio button, and click OK.

9. Modify the function as follows:

```
Public Function Cubed (X As Integer) As Integer
    Cubed = X * X * X
End Function
```

10. Choose Tools⇨Add Procedure. An Add Procedure dialog box appears.

11. Type **Quantity** in the Name box, click the Property radio button, and click OK.

12. Modify the Property Get Quantity definition as follows:

```
Public Property Get Quantity () as Variant
   Quantity = IntegerData
End Property
```

13. Modify the Property Let Quantity definition as follows:

```
Public Property Let Quantity(ByVal vNewValue As Variant)
   IntegerData = vNewValue
End Property
```

14. Choose Project➪Add Module and double-click on the Module icon within the Add Module dialog box. The Module1 code window appears.

15. Choose Tools➪Add Procedure. An Add Procedure dialog box appears.

16. Type **Main** in the Name box, click the Sub radio button, click the Public radio button, and click OK.

17. Press F5 to run your OLE server. (*Note:* It's important that you run the OLE server program before following the instructions in the "Testing your OLE server" section below.)

Testing your OLE server

Once you create and successfully compile your OLE server, you have to create a test program to verify that the OLE server actually works. The following example shows how to create this simple test program.

1. Load a second copy of Visual Basic. A New Project dialog box appears.

2. Click on the Standard EXE icon and click Open.

3. Draw a command button on the form.

4. Double-click the command button to open the code window.

5. Modify the event procedure as follows:

```
Private Sub Command1_Click()
   ' Declare a variable object
   Dim OLEObject As Object

   ' Create that object
   Set OLEObject = CreateObject("OLEObject.Class1")
```

```
' Use the object's Cubed method
MsgBox CStr(OLEObject.Cubed(3))
MsgBox CStr(OLEObject.Cubed(4))
MsgBox CStr(OLEObject.Cubed(5))

' Change the object's properties
OLEOBject.Quantity = 99
MsgBox CStr (OLEObject.Quantity)

OLEObject.TextString = "See? OLE actually works!"
MsgBox OLEObject.TextString
End Sub
```

6. Press F5 to run the OLE test program.

7. Click the Command1 button. A Project1 dialog box appears, displaying the cube of 3, which is 27.

8. Click OK. A Project1 dialog box appears, displaying the cube of 4, which is 64.

9. Click OK. A Project1 dialog box appears, displaying the cube of 5, which is 125.

10. Click OK. A Project1 dialog box appears, displaying the number 99.

11. Click OK. A Project1 dialog box appears, displaying the message, "See? OLE actually works!"

12. Click OK.

13. Choose Run⇨End to stop the OLE test program.

14. Switch to the copy of Visual Basic running your OLE server.

15. Choose Run⇨End from the menu bar to stop the OLE server program.

OLE may define a new standard for getting programs to share data with one another, but that doesn't mean that everyone who uses a computer will even know what OLE is, let alone how to use it. Most likely, OLE will languish as a standard for another few years until some breakthrough makes OLE literacy nearly as important as computer literacy.

But until that time, most users probably have no clue what OLE is, how to use it, or why they should even bother learning about it. If you decide to add OLE capabilities to your Visual Basic programs, the only people most likely to use it are power users. Still, it's a good idea to use OLE in your programs just so they can remain compatible with the majority of Windows 95 programs floating around in the marketplace.

Chapter 20

Linking to DLL Files and Using the Windows API

• •

In This Chapter

▶ What the heck are DLL files?

▶ How to create a DLL file

▶ Linking your program to a DLL file

▶ Understanding the Windows API

• •

*V*isual Basic thankfully isolates you from having to know how the guts of your computer works, but at the same time it sacrifices flexibility. To get back some of this flexibility, you can use:

  ✔ DLL files

  ✔ Windows API functions

When using DLL files or the Windows API functions, you can completely crash your computer, so be sure to save your work often. Using the Windows API is especially dangerous and unstable if you make a mistake because API functions let you fiddle around with the internal guts of Windows 95 or Windows NT. Using the API functions is like giving you complete access to alter someone's internal organs.

What the Heck Are DLL Files?

Face it. Visual Basic is great at creating user interfaces but not necessarily always the best language to use for intensive number-crunching or for manipulating the bits and bytes of your microprocessor's registers. Rather than force Visual Basic to do everything, many programmers use Visual Basic to create their user interface and then use another programming language to create the algorithms that make the program do something useful.

Of course, you can't suddenly start typing C++ code in the Visual Basic Code window and expect it to work. Instead, you have to write your initial Visual Basic code and save it in a Visual Basic file. Then you have to write code using another compiler (such as for C++, Pascal, LISP, FORTRAN, or assembly language) and save it in a special file called a dynamic link library (DLL). Finally, you have to write additional Visual Basic code to tell Visual Basic how to use the code trapped inside the DLL file.

The purpose of using a DLL file is to write faster, more efficient code in another language and then link it with the lovely interface of your Visual Basic program. That way, you get the best of both worlds — the simplicity of Visual Basic with the efficiency of another language such as C++.

Three great reasons to use a DLL file instead of Visual Basic are:

- ✔ For speed
- ✔ To use a more appropriate programming language to solve a problem
- ✔ To isolate algorithms in separate files so you can reuse them

DLL files essentially act as black boxes for Visual Basic, meaning that someone else can write a DLL file for you and you can use it without knowing exactly how the DLL file works or in what language it's written — what's important is that you know what it does.

How to Create a DLL File

Once you decide to use a DLL file with your Visual Basic program, you have two choices. You can use an existing DLL file (and pray that it works correctly) or you can write your own DLL file. Four popular languages for creating DLL files are:

- ✔ Visual Basic (surprise!)
- ✔ PowerBASIC
- ✔ Delphi
- ✔ C or C++

If you're a complete nonconformist, you could write DLL files in any language, even obscure ones like COBOL, Modula-2, or Ada. The programming language you use isn't important. What matters is whether your language compiler lets you create DLL files and whether your DLL files work the way they should.

Visual Basic DLL files

Believe it or not, Visual Basic can create DLL files that you can use in your Visual Basic programs or in other types of programs. So why would you want to create a DLL file in Visual Basic?

First, writing DLL files in Visual Basic is easy because you already know how to use Visual Basic, so you don't have to learn another programming language or buy another compiler. Creating your DLL files in Visual Basic is probably the easiest solution.

The drawback is that Visual Basic may not always be the most appropriate or fastest language for solving a particular problem. Essentially, a Visual Basic DLL file is an ActiveX DLL file (OLE server) that gives you the convenience of isolating your code in a DLL file, but doesn't give you the speed or flexibility advantage of creating a DLL file using a more powerful language such as C++. For more information on creating OLE servers in Visual Basic, see Chapter 19.

PowerBASIC DLL files

At one time, Borland International sold PowerBASIC as a QuickBasic compatible compiler called Turbo Basic. After Borland realized that Turbo Basic wasn't terribly profitable, they gave it back to its original developer, who renamed it PowerBASIC.

PowerBASIC lets you write small and fast DLL files that can rival similar DLL files created with C++. Because PowerBASIC uses the BASIC programming language, you won't have to learn the cryptic commands of C++ just to create a DLL file. If you love BASIC but want the speed advantages that a non-Visual Basic DLL file can give you, consider PowerBASIC instead of C++.

For more information about PowerBASIC, contact:

PowerBASIC, Inc.
316 Mid Valley Center
Carmel, CA 93923
Internet: http://www.powerbasic.com

Delphi DLL files

Delphi is Borland's answer to Visual Basic. Like Visual Basic, Delphi lets you design your user interface and then create code that makes it do something useful. The main difference between Visual Basic and Delphi is that Delphi uses the Pascal language instead of BASIC.

The Pascal language is much simpler than C++, but almost as powerful and flexible. Rather than lose the last semblance of your sanity learning the complexity of C++ programming, you might prefer to use Pascal. Pascal is slightly more powerful than BASIC but slightly less flexible than C++. (For more information about Delphi, pick up a copy of *Delphi Programming For Dummies*.)

To order Delphi, contact:

Borland International
100 Borland Way
P.O. Box 660001
Scotts Valley, CA 95067
Internet: http://www.borland.com

C++ DLL files

For the greatest flexibility and power, you can write DLL files using C++ (such as Visual C++, Borland C++, or Symantec C++). If you've never programmed in C++ before, be prepared for a long learning period. However, if you're already an experienced C++ programmer, you may find that you can create fast DLL files in C++ and then use Visual Basic to create your spiffy user interfaces.

Most programmers use Visual Basic because they specifically want to avoid the complexities of a language such as C++. So consider writing DLL files in Delphi or PowerBasic instead. But for those who can't resist the challenge of learning a programming language that virtually guarantees them employment somewhere, learning C++ is certainly a wise long-term career move.

Linking Your Program to a DLL File

After you create a DLL file, you need to make the DLL files work with your Visual Basic program. To tell your Visual Basic program to use a function (or procedure) stored in a DLL file, you need to know:

✔ The DLL file name

✔ The function (or procedure) name that you want to use, which is stored in the DLL file

✔ The number and type of arguments the DLL function (or procedure) needs

Once you know all this information, you must declare the function in a module (.BAS) file in your Visual Basic program. For example:

```
DECLARE FUNCTION FreeSpace Lib "PBDISK.DLL" (BYVAL drive As
            Integer) As Long
```

This code tells Visual Basic, "Get ready to use a function called FreeSpace located in a DLL file called PBDISK.DLL. FreeSpace, which represents a Long data type, needs an argument identified by the variable called drive."

You don't need to know how the function in the DLL file works to use it. You just need to know what type of arguments the function expects to send and receive.

You may run across problems with variables and DLL files because a DLL File might have been written using a language which may not use the exact same types of variables used by Visual Basic. For example, C++ tends to handle strings differently than Visual Basic, so a DLL file written in C++ for string processing might cause you trouble when you try to integrate with a Visual Basic program.

To shorten your function declarations, Visual Basic also lets you use cryptic symbols such as &, %, and $. These symbols are a shortcut for defining the data type that a variable represents, as shown in Table 20-1.

Table 20-1	Shortcut Symbols for Declaring Data Types	
Symbol	**Example**	**What It Means**
&	FreeSpace&	FreeSpace As Long
%	drive%	drive As Integer
$	Data$	Data As String
!	Quantity!	Quantity As Single
#	RealPrecise#	RealPrecise As Double
@	Amount@	Amount As Currency

The previous function declaration, rewritten using the symbols in Table 20-1, would look like this:

```
DECLARE FUNCTION FreeSpace& Lib "PBDISK.DLL" (BYVAL drive%)
```

To use this function in your Visual Basic program, you could use the following code:

```
Dim FreeStuff As Long
FreeStuff = FreeSpace(3) 'Check drive C:
Text1.Text = CStr(FreeStuff)
```

1. The first line declares `FreeStuff` as a variable that represents a `Long` data type.

2. The second line tells Visual Basic, "Call the function named FreeSpace and use the number 3 as the argument." In the `FreeSpace` function, the number 3 represents the drive C.

3. The third line converts the `FreeStuff` variable into a string and stuffs it in the Text property of the `Text1` text box.

Understanding the Windows API

The Windows Application Programming Interface (API) is nothing more than a toolbox of built-in routines that Microsoft kindly embedded inside every copy of Windows. These functions enable you to dig into the guts of Windows and take full control.

Of course, giving you access to the Windows API is like giving a teenager the keys to a sports car. You can do a lot, but you have to be careful. If you use the Windows API incorrectly, you can crash Windows completely, which is why Visual Basic normally shields you from accessing the Windows API.

But programmers are a curious lot by nature, so inevitably they will want to use the Windows API functions in their own Visual Basic programs. Not only are the Windows API functions fast and reliable, but they don't require you to write additional code to use them. Just declare the API function you want and then use it (but use it carefully).

Because the Windows API functions are buried in separate DLL files on your hard disk, using a Windows API function is no different than using a function stored in a DLL file. (So now you know why this chapter starts by first explaining how to use DLL files.)

Of course, how do you know which Windows API functions are available if you're just learning what the heck the Windows API is in the first place? To get a list of all available Windows API functions, you have two choices:

 ✔ Buy the Windows Software Development Kit (SDK) from Microsoft if you want to learn all the Windows API functions available along with explanations for what each Windows API function does.

 ✔ Use the Visual Basic API Text Viewer if you just want a list of all available Windows API functions (and you don't mind trying to figure out how each Windows API function works on your own).

The API Text Viewer only lists the API functions available; it does not explain what they do or how to use them. If you want to know what all the API functions do, you need the Windows SDK.

To provide some semblance of organization and give you an idea about what the Windows API functions can do for you, the Windows API functions are divided into the following categories:

 ✔ Windows manager interface
 ✔ Graphics device interface
 ✔ System services interface
 ✔ Multimedia interface

The Windows manager interface functions let you control the appearance of windows, the cursor, dialog boxes, menus, and other related user interface stuff to make your program look prettier.

The Graphics device interface functions let you change colors, lines, fonts, and printing tasks for your program.

The System services interface functions let you manage memory, program resources, operating system interrupts, and other really technical stuff that you really don't want to mess with unless you know what you're doing.

The Multimedia interface functions let you play sounds, display video, and create animation.

Using the Visual Basic API Text Viewer

The API Text Viewer lets you search through the Windows API functions and copy any constants, function declaration statements, or type definitions you need. If you're using Windows 95, you can just load the API Text Viewer directly from the Windows 95 Start button.

To use the API Text Viewer, follow these steps:

1. Click the Start button on the Windows 95 Taskbar, choose Programs⇨Visual Basic 5.0⇨API Text Viewer.

2. Choose File⇨Load Text File. The Select a Text API File dialog box appears, as shown in Figure 20-1.

3. Click Win32api and click Open. A list of API functions appears in the Available Items list box.

   Note: You can load your files faster if you convert the text files into database files. The first time you load a text file, a dialog box pops up, giving you the choice of converting your chosen text file into a database file.

4. Click the API Type list box and choose one of the following:

   • Constants

   • Declares

   • Types

5. Click an item in the Available Items list box that you want to use in your own program and then click the Add button. Your selected item appears as a function declaration in the Selected Items list box.

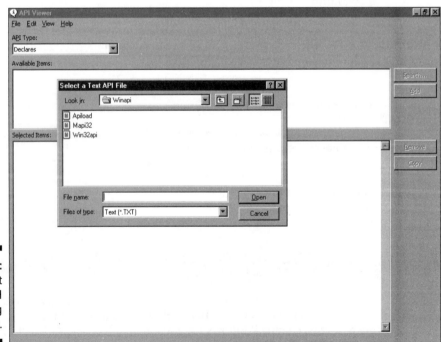

Figure 20-1:
The Select
a Text API
File dialog
box.

6. Repeat Steps 4 and 5 for every constant, type, or declaration statement necessary for the Windows API functions that you want to use in your Visual Basic program.

7. Click the Copy button.

8. Choose File⇨Exit.

9. Switch to Visual Basic and paste your copied items in a module (.BAS) file.

True to the nature of computers, the API Text Viewer is not always right. For example, if you want to use the API function called MessageBeep, the correct declaration is:

```
Declare Sub MessageBeep Lib "user32" (ByVal wType As Long)
```

However, the API Text Viewer incorrectly lists this declaration as:

```
Declare Function MessageBeep Lib "user32" Alias "BeepA"
        (ByVal wType As Long)
```

So the lesson here is that if you copy an API declaration from the API Text Viewer program and your program doesn't work, the fault could lie with an incorrect API declaration (courtesy of Microsoft). If this happens, you have to use the Windows SDK to find out the correct API declaration. (Good luck.)

By now, you are probably champing at the bit to learn how to harness the wonderful power of the Windows API. The following Visual Basic program uses Windows API functions and shows you, step-by-step, how these API functions work in a real-life program.

1. Click the Start button on the Windows 95 Taskbar, choose Programs⇨Visual Basic 5.0⇨API Text Viewer. The API Text Viewer appears.

2. Choose File⇨Load Text File. The Select a Text API File dialog box appears, as shown in Figure 20-1.

3. Click Win32api and click Open.

4. In the API Type list box, choose Types.

5. In the Available Items list box, choose SYSTEM_INFO and click Add.

6. In the API Type list box, choose Declares.

7. In the Available Items list box, choose GetSystemInfo and click Add.

8. Click Copy.

Test your newfound knowledge

1. Why would you want to use a DLL file with your Visual Basic program?

   a. To exercise your imagination, patience, and arcane knowledge of obscure technical information that 90 percent of the population couldn't care less about.

   b. So that you can use Visual Basic to create your user interface and another faster, more appropriate language (such as C++ or Pascal) for the guts.

   c. DLL files are required by law. That's why even Microsoft Windows uses DLL files.

   d. DLL files let you write an entire program, including its user interface, without using Visual Basic at all. In fact, why bother using Visual Basic when you can just hire some high school kid to do all your work for you instead?

2. What are Windows API functions and why would anyone want to use them?

   a. The Windows API is a special group of programs that make sure all non-Microsoft programs do not work properly with Windows, but that all Microsoft programs work correctly most of the time.

   b. The Windows API is a group of DLL files included with Windows that have special functions that let your Visual Basic program access the guts of Windows and do things you normally couldn't do in Visual Basic.

   c. API is an acronym that even Microsoft can't decipher.

   d. The Windows API are secret functions that let you break into the Pentagon and Kremlin computers, but only if you use Windows 95 and buy Microsoft products.

---

9. Choose File➪Exit.

10. Click the Start button on the Windows 95 Taskbar, choose Programs➪Visual Basic 5.0➪Visual Basic 5.0.

11. Double-click the Standard EXE icon in the New Project dialog box.

12. Choose Project➪Add Module. The Add Module dialog box appears.

13. Click the Module icon and click Open. The Module1 code window appears.

14. Choose Edit➪Paste, or press Ctrl+V. The SYSTEM_INFO type declaration and the GetSystemInfo procedure declarations appear in the Module1 code window, as shown in Figure 20-2.

15. Choose View➪Project Explorer, or press Ctrl+R. The Project1 window appears.

16. Click Form1 and click the View Object icon. The Form1 window appears.

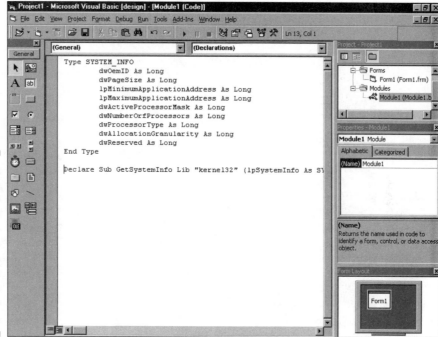

Figure 20-2:
Copying the
SYSTEM_INFO
declaration
and the Get-
SystemInfo
procedure
declaration
into the
Code
window.

17. Draw a command button on the form and press F7 to display the Code window. Visual Basic displays the `Command1_Click()` procedure.

18. Type the following:

```
Private Sub Command1_Click()
    Dim MyComputer As SYSTEM_INFO
    Call GetSystemInfo (MyComputer)
    MsgBox Str(MyComputer.dwProcessorType), 64, "Processor
        Type"
End Sub
```

19. Choose Run⇨Start, or press F5. A dialog box appears, displaying the type of processor in your computer, as shown in Figure 20-3.

20. Click OK.

21. Choose Run⇨End.

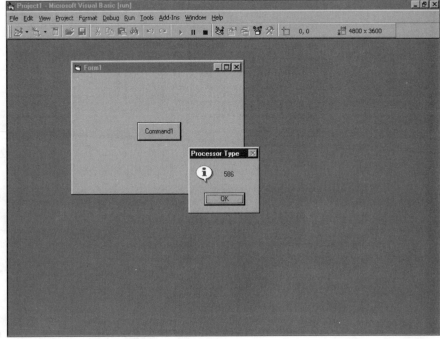

Figure 20-3:
The
processor
type as
reported
by the
Windows
API fuction.

Part VI
Polishing Your Program

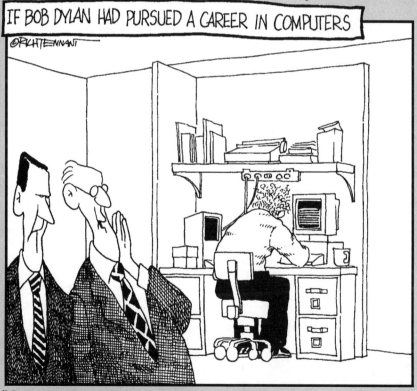

The 5th Wave   By Rich Tennant

IF BOB DYLAN HAD PURSUED A CAREER IN COMPUTERS

"PUT HIM IN FRONT OF A TERMINAL AND HE'S A GENIUS, BUT OTHER-WISE THE GUY IS SUCH A BROODING, GLOOMY GUS HE'LL NEVER BREAK INTO MANAGEMENT."

In this part . . .

Unless you enjoy writing programs for your own amusement, you may eventually want to create programs that you can sell or give away to others. To prevent your programs from fouling up another computer and crashing (like most programs from major software companies), this part of the book explains how to dig through your program for bugs. In addition, you can also find out how to compile your program and create your own installation program.

By learning the information stored in Part VI, you can take yourself out of the ranks of the programming hobbyist and move into the world of the programming professionals, selling your creations for tons of money and putting Microsoft out of business in the process.

Chapter 21

Breaking and Watching

- -

- -

*W*riting your programs is much easier than debugging them. Even major companies such as Microsoft, Borland, and IBM have trouble completely eliminating bugs from their programs, so don't feel bad when your program doesn't work 100 percent correctly the first time you run it.

When you write a program, you can't see whether your code will even work the way you hope it will. When you run the program and a bug pops up, you can't always tell where it's screwing up.

To solve this problem, Visual Basic provides a way to break into the program and temporarily stop it from running. *Breaking* into a program essentially stops it dead in its tracks so you can examine, dissect, and modify any parts of the program that seem to be messing up.

Visual Basic gives you two ways to break into a program:

✔ Press Ctrl+Break

✔ Click the Break icon in the Visual Basic Toolbar as shown in Figure 21-1

When you finish breaking into your program, you can continue the program with one of the following actions:

✔ Press F5

✔ Choose Run⇨Continue

✔ Click the Start icon in the Visual Basic Toolbar (see Figure 21-1)

Once you break into a program, you can display the Immediate window to view the guts of your program and see which parts aren't working.

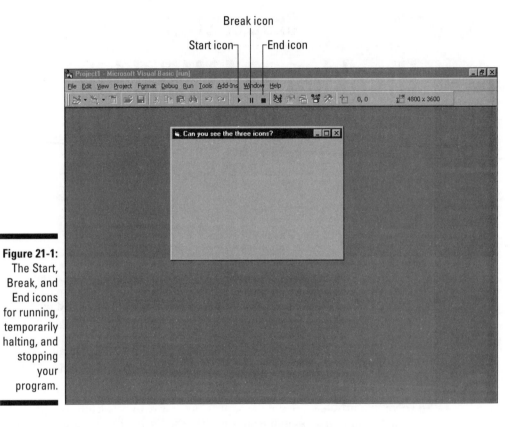

Break icon

Start icon — — End icon

Figure 21-1:
The Start,
Break, and
End icons
for running,
temporarily
halting, and
stopping
your
program.

Using the Immediate Window

Visual Basic provides two ways to open the Immediate window:

- ✓ Press Ctrl+G
- ✓ Select View⇨Immediate Window

Once you have the Immediate window displayed, you can do the following:

- ✓ Check the current values of your variables
- ✓ Assign new values to variables to see how your program reacts
- ✓ Run procedures to see whether they work properly

By checking the current values of your variables at any time, you can see whether your program is calculating a wrong value at some point. In this case, your code may be fine, but your program is feeding it the wrong information — kind of like teaching kids manners by letting them watch MTV all day. The kids will still learn something you might call "manners," but because you're feeding them the wrong type of information, they won't turn out quite the way you want.

Another cause of bugs occurs when the code in another part of your program is faulty. In this case, one part of your program might calculate values correctly but another part of your program messes those values up.

Sometimes procedures work fine 90 percent of the time. But if a procedure gets the wrong type of information just once, it screws up and drags your program to a screeching halt.

The Immediate window allows you to test for all three of these possible problems in your program.

Examining the values of variables

The Debug window lets you examine the value of any variable or property in your program while you run it. To examine the value of a variable, follow these steps:

1. Run your program by pressing F5, choosing Run⇨Start, or clicking the Run icon in the Visual Basic Toolbar.

2. Break into your program where you want to start examining the values of your variables by pressing Ctrl+Break or clicking the Break icon in the Visual Basic Toolbar, as shown in Figure 21-1.

3. Open the Immediate window by pressing Ctrl+G or choosing View⇨Immediate Window.

4. Type the following to examine each variable:

```
? VariableName
```

or:

```
Print VariableName
```

Visual Basic displays the current value of the variable identified by VariableName.

For example, to check the value of a variable called HoldMe, you type:

```
? HoldMe
```

or:

```
Print HoldMe
```

To check the value of an object's property, you type:

```
? txtName.Text
```

or:

```
Print txtName.Text
```

Figure 21-2 shows how to check the value of a variable in the Immediate window.

TIP

To make it easier to check the value of a variable at a specific location in your program, use breakpoints, explained in more detail in Chapter 22.

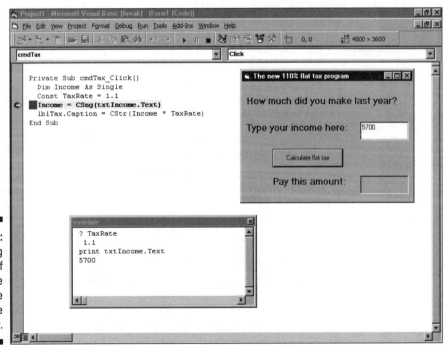

Figure 21-2:
Examining the value of a variable in the Immediate window.

Watch your variables' scope

Suppose you check the value of a variable and Visual Basic displays nothing but a blank line. The first possibility is that your variable hasn't been assigned a value. If you're positive that your program assigns a value to the particular variable, the second possibility is that you are checking outside the scope of the variable.

If you declared a variable within an event procedure, that variable contains data only in the brief moment that the event procedure is running. The moment the event procedure stops, any variables declared inside it ceases to exist.

For example, consider the following variable, called TaxRate, stored inside a command button's event procedure:

```
Private Sub Command1_Click()
  Dim TaxRate as Single
  TaxRate = 0.075
End Sub
```

Before you click the Command1 command button, the value of the TaxRate variable is undefined. When you click the Command1 command button and set the event procedure running, the value of the TaxRate variable is 0.075. However, the moment the event procedure stops running (the split second you release the mouse button), the TaxRate variable is once again undefined.

If you use the Immediate window and check the value of TaxRate after you click the Command1 command button, guess what? The Immediate window displays a blank line because the TaxRate variable is empty once the event procedure where it's stored has stopped running.

To ensure that you can check the value of a variable without worrying about its scope, declare your variables as global variables in the *(General) (Declarations)* part of the Code window.

To examine the values of an object's properties stored on another form, use this syntax:

```
? FormName!ObjectName.PropertyName
```

or:

```
Print FormName!ObjectName.PropertyName
```

If you forget to include the FormName, Visual Basic looks for the variable or object property on the current form. If it can't find the variable name or object property name, Visual Basic displays an error message.

You can examine objects stored on another form only if that form has been loaded, either as the first form that loads or by using the Load command (for example, `Load Form1`).

Changing the values of variables

Sometimes bugs can be subtle, more like gnats than tsetse flies. One time your program might work fine; another time it crashes unexpectedly. When this happens, your code is probably getting data that it doesn't know how to handle correctly.

For example, if your program asks users for their age, most of the time your program will work fine if someone types in a number between 1 to 120. But what if some joker types 248 or –9? If you don't anticipate bozos entering data like this, your program could crash.

By letting you change the values of your variables in the middle of your program, the Immediate window lets you play the role of a bozo, deliberately trying to crash your program.

To change the value of a variable or an object's property, follow these steps:

1. Run your program by pressing F5, choosing Run⇨Start, or clicking the Run icon in the Visual Basic Toolbar.

2. Break into your program where you want to start examining the values of your variables by pressing Ctrl+Break or clicking the Break icon in the Visual Basic Toolbar.

3. Open the Immediate window by pressing Ctrl+G or choosing View⇨Immediate Window.

4. Assign a new value to a variable using the following syntax, and press Enter:

```
VariableName = NewValue
```

Or assign a new value to an object property using this syntax:

```
ObjectName.PropertyName = NewValue
```

Figure 21-3 shows how to change the value of a variable within the Immediate window.

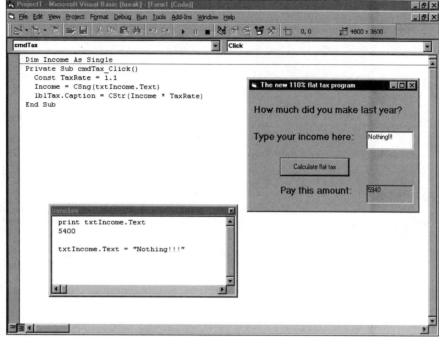

Figure 21-3:
Changing
the value of
a variable
in the
Immediate
window.

To change the value of an object's properties stored on another form, use this syntax:

```
FormName!ObjectName.PropertyName = NewValue
```

If you don't include FormName, Visual Basic looks for the variable or object property on the current form. If it can't find the variable name or object property name, Visual Basic displays an error message.

As soon as you change the value of a variable or an object property, Visual Basic immediately adjusts your program's user interface accordingly. For example, if you change the size of a text box in the Immediate window, Visual Basic would immediately change the size of the text box on the form.

Testing procedures and functions

You can test general procedures and functions by calling them directly from the Immediate window. To call a general procedure, you would type the following in the Immediate window:

```
Call ProcedureName ()
```

To test a general procedure, feed it different types of data into its argument list. For example, suppose you have a general procedure like this:

```
Private Sub Pythagoras (A, B, C)
  C = Sqr((A ^ 2) + (B ^ 2))
End Sub
```

You can call it from within the Immediate window with different arguments like this, as shown in Figure 21-4:

```
Call Pythagoras (3, 4, X)
Print X
```

You can call only general procedures from within the Immediate window. You cannot call event procedures from within the Immediate window.

Calling a function is even easier. Just use the following syntax:

```
Print FunctionName ()
```

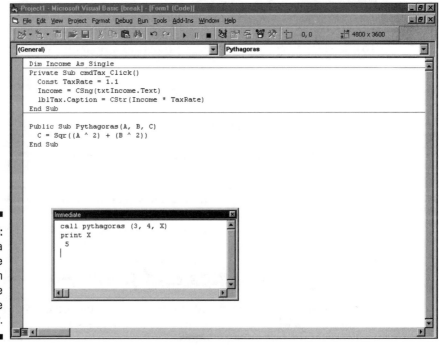

Figure 21-4:
Testing a procedure from within the Immediate window.

For example, if you have a function like this:

```
Private Function Pythagoras (A, B)
   Pythagoras = Sqr((A ^ 2) + (B ^ 2))
End Function
```

you can call it from within the Immediate window with different arguments like this:

```
Print Pythagoras (3, 4)
```

Unless you want to stay up all night working on your programs, it's pretty much impossible to test procedures and functions for every possible value in the universe. Instead, limit your tests on procedures or functions to four types of data:

- ✔ Normal data that it should be getting
- ✔ Extremely high data (huge numbers, long strings)
- ✔ Extremely low data (fractions, negative numbers)
- ✔ Zeros or empty strings

By testing a procedure with both extremely high and low numbers, string lengths, and zeros or empty strings, you can see whether the procedure still works or whether it chokes and dies on you.

Watching Your Program Work

Watching lets you specify certain variables and see how their values change as your program runs. That way, you (hopefully) can see where a variable's value may change incorrectly and (even more hopefully) find the bug that's causing the problem.

Visual Basic provides three ways to "watch" the value of a variable or an expression:

- ✔ Add a Debug.Print command directly into your code
- ✔ Use an Instant Watch after breaking into a program
- ✔ Identify a variable to watch before running the program

Test your newfound knowledge

1. What is the purpose of breaking into your Visual Basic program?

   a. When you've locked the keys inside by mistake and don't have a coat hanger handy.

   b. When a client refuses to pay you for your program.

   c. Breaking lets you stop your program and examine its variables to see where it might be messing up.

   d. Visual Basic programs are fragile by nature so it's fun to crash them every now and then by breaking them.

2. What are three ways you can use the Immediate window?

   a. You can use the Immediate window to look outside, to let in sunlight, and to let in bugs.

   b. The Immediate window can be used to hide the fact that my program doesn't really work; but at least I'm getting paid to look good and correct problems that shouldn't have been there in the first place.

   c. The Immediate window is great for covering up any games on your screen because it looks like you're really doing something important at work.

   d. You can use the Immediate window to check the current values of variables, to assign new values to variables, and to run general procedures just to see whether they work.

Using the Debug.Print command

To use the Debug.Print command, find the part of your program where you want to check the values of certain variables and then add the following command:

```
Debug.Print "VariableName = "; VariableName
```

For example:

```
Private Sub Pythagoras (A, B, C)
  C = Sqr((A ^ 2) + (B ^ 2))
  Debug.Print "C = "; C
End Sub
```

If the value of C were 5, this Debug.Print command would print

```
C = 5
```

in the Immediate window while the program is running. Note that this command doesn't open the Immediate window, although it still prints inside it. Once you open the Immediate window, you see the results inside.

To help you identify where certain Debug.Print commands are located, you might want to add a line like the third one in the following code:

```
Private Sub Pythagoras (A, B, C)
  C = Sqr((A ^ 2) + (B ^ 2))
  Debug.Print "Coming from inside the Pythagoras procedure"
  Debug.Print "C = "; C
End Sub
```

Running this procedure displays the following in the Immediate window:

```
Coming from inside the Pythagoras procedure
C = 5
```

The advantage of the Debug.Print command is that you can put it anywhere in your code (in as many places as necessary) to check the values of certain variables.

The disadvantage is that it can be time-consuming and tedious (what else is new with programming?) to put all these Debug.Print commands in your code. Even worse, before you compile your program, you have no quick way to remove all the Debug.Print commands; you have to remove them one by one yourself.

Visual Basic offers a special feature called conditional compilation, which lets you choose which code to use when you compile your program. You can use conditional compilation to place Debug.Print commands in your code while you are still testing it, and then when you're ready to compile your program for distribution, use conditional compilation to turn off the Debug.Print commands.

The syntax for using conditional compilation is as follows:

```
#If expression Then
    statements
#End If
```

So you can use conditional compilation such as:

```
Dim DebugOn As Boolean
DebugOn = True
#If DebugOn Then
    Debug.Print
#End If
```

to tell Visual Basic that if the DebugOn variable is True, then include the Debug.Print command in the program. But if the DebugOn variable is False, then don't include the Debug.Print command in the program.

Quick watches

A *quick watch* lets you examine the value of an expression, not a variable. Remember, a variable represents a single value; an expression represents an actual calculation. For example:

X   This is a variable

X + Y   This is an expression

Before you can choose the Quick Watch command, you must run your program, use the Break command, and then highlight an expression from the Code window or the Immediate window. Once you do all that, Visual Basic provides ways to choose the Quick Watch command:

- Press Shift+F9
- Select Debug⇨Quick Watch

To use a Quick Watch to check the value of an expression, follow these steps:

1. Run your program by pressing F5, selecting Run⇨Start, or clicking the Run icon in the Visual Basic Toolbar.

2. Break into your program where you want to start examining the values of your variables by pressing Ctrl+Break or clicking the Break icon in the Visual Basic Toolbar.

3. Press F7, or choose View⇨Code to display the Code window and highlight an expression to watch.

4. Press Shift+F9, or choose Debug⇨Quick Watch. The Quick Watch dialog box displays the expression you selected, its current value, and three command buttons labeled Add, Cancel, and Help as shown in Figure 21-5.

5. Click the Add button to add the expression to the watch pane portion of the Immediate window, as shown in Figure 21-6.

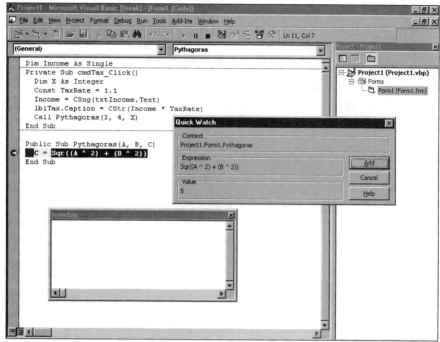

Figure 21-5:
The Quick
Watch
dialog box.

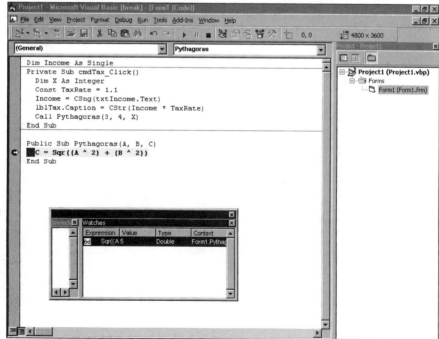

Figure 21-6:
The watch
pane
portion
of the
Immediate
window.

Watching expressions

When you select expressions to watch, they appear in the part of the Immediate window called the watch pane.

You can select an expression to watch either before you start running your program or while it's already running. To watch an expression while your program is already running, use the Quick Watch command, as explained in the preceding section.

To add an expression to watch before running your program, follow these steps:

1. Highlight the expression in the Code window.

2. Press Shift+F9, or choose Debug⇨Add Watch. Visual Basic displays an Add Watch dialog box, as shown in Figure 21-7.

3. Click the Procedure and Module list boxes to define where you want Visual Basic to watch your expression. You can tell Visual Basic to watch your expression in specific procedures, in specific forms or module files, or globally throughout your program.

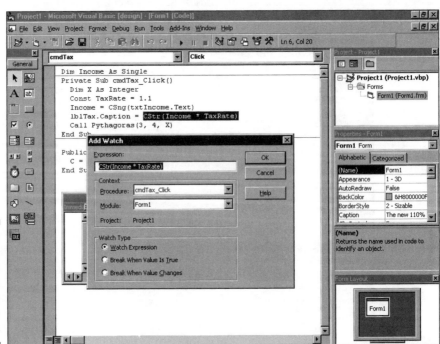

Figure 21-7: Adding an expression to watch with the Add Watch dialog box.

4. Click one of the following radio buttons in the Watch Type group:

- • Watch Expression
- • Break When Value Is True
- • Break When Value Changes

5. Click OK.

Choosing the Watch Expression option makes Visual Basic display the value of your selected expression in the Debug window at all times. To see this value, though, you have to break into your program (press Ctrl+Break) and examine it in the Immediate window.

If you want to examine your expression's value only at certain times, don't choose the Watch Expression option. If you choose the Break When Value Is True option, then each time your expression becomes True, Visual Basic automatically breaks into your program and displays the expression's value in the Immediate window.

If you choose Break When Value Changes, then each time the value of your expression changes, Visual Basic automatically breaks into your program and displays the expression's value in the Immediate window.

Depending on which Watch Type option you chose (Watch Expression, Break When Value Is True, Break When Value Changes), Visual Basic displays a different icon next to the expression to identify it in the Immediate window, as shown in Figure 21-8.

Editing and Deleting Watch Expressions in the Watch Window

Each time you add an expression to watch, Visual Basic stores it in a list. Eventually, you may want to change the expression you tell Visual Basic to watch.

To edit an expression that you already told Visual Basic to watch, follow these steps before running your program:

1. Open the Watch window by choosing View⇨Watch Window. The Immediate window appears.

2. Click the watch expression in the watch pane that you want to edit.

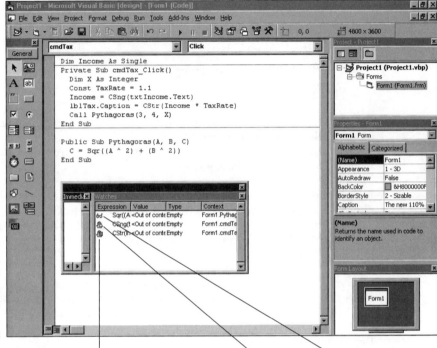

Figure 21-8:
The three
types of
icons to
identify the
watch type.

Break When Value Is True icon   Break When Value Changes icon   Watch Expression icon

3. Press Ctrl+W, choose Debug⇨Edit Watch, or click the right mouse button and choose Edit from the pop-up menu. Visual Basic displays an Edit Watch dialog box, which looks surprisingly similar to the Add Watch dialog box shown in Figure 21-7.

4. Edit your expression, choose a different Context option, or choose a different Watch Type option.

5. Click OK.

If you want to delete a watch expression and send it into oblivion, click Delete instead of OK in Step 5.

If you watch an array or structure, a plus sign appears to the left of your array or structure variable name. If you click the plus sign, the watch window displays the individual contents of your array or structure.

Chapter 22

Breaking and Tracing

● ●

In This Chapter

▶ Examining your program line by line

▶ Procedure stepping

▶ Using breakpoints

● ●

*W*hen Federal Express, the Post Office, or United Parcel Service loses a valuable package, they trace it from the shipping origin to the shipping destination to see where it might have gotten lost. Likewise, whenever your program doesn't work right, you can trace through it from beginning to end to see where it goes wrong.

Tracing means examining your program, line by line, until you find the one line that is causing the problem. After you find the offending line, you can correct it, test your program again, and more than likely, go through the whole process of tracing through your program all over again after you discover it's still buggy.

This seemingly endless test-trace-debug cycle causes most programmers to look as though their eyes are about to explode. Although debugging is probably the least fun part of writing a program, it's a necessary evil that must be handled with grace if you want to preserve your sanity.

Visual Basic provides three ways to trace through your program:

✔ Single stepping

✔ Procedure stepping

✔ Breakpoint stepping

As you step through your program, the Immediate window can display the values of your variables and expressions so that you can tell how each line may be affecting your data.

Examining Your Program Line by Line

If you have absolutely no idea where the problem may be, you must resort to single stepping. *Single stepping* enables you to examine your entire program, line by line. If you wrote a 100,000-line program, you must examine all 100,000 lines to find any bugs in it, which is why you're best off writing programs one piece at a time and then testing and checking for bugs in each piece.

Visual Basic provides two ways to single step:

- ✔ Press F8
- ✔ Choose Debug➪Step Into

Each time you choose the Step Into command, Visual Basic highlights the code in your program that is currently running, as shown in Figure 22-1. The only time Visual Basic does not highlight a line is if it is a comment, constant, or variable declaration.

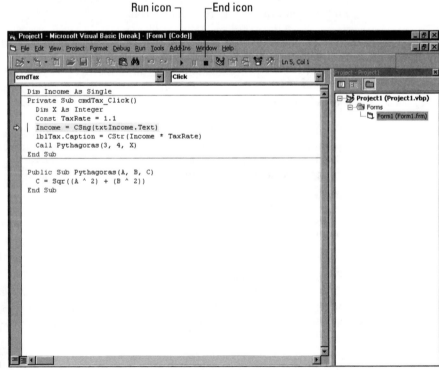

Run icon ⌐   ⌐End icon

Figure 22-1:
Visual
Basic
highlighting
a line of
code.

When the Step Into command highlights a procedure or function call, Visual Basic immediately displays that procedure or function call in the Code window and highlights the first line to run.

Single stepping continues from the very first line to the very last line of your program. If you want to stop single stepping and halt the program completely, you can choose the End command in one of two ways:

 ✔ Choose <u>R</u>un⇨<u>E</u>nd
 ✔ Click the End icon in the Visual Basic Toolbar shown in Figure 22-1

If you want to stop single stepping but want to run the rest of the program, choose the Run command in one of two ways:

 ✔ Choose <u>R</u>un⇨<u>C</u>ontinue
 ✔ Press F5

Procedure Stepping

The problem with using the Step Into command is that each time you reach a call to a procedure or function, you get sucked into viewing that particular procedure or function line by line. Although the Step Into command can be useful for debugging procedures and functions, it's not so useful if you already know that a procedure or function works just fine.

If you're absolutely positive that a particular procedure or function is bug-free, you can skip over its code by using procedure stepping.

Procedure stepping works the same as single stepping, with one exception. As soon as you reach a procedure or function call, procedure stepping runs all the lines stored inside the procedure or function call without forcing you to step through it line by line.

Visual Basic provides two ways to procedure step:

 ✔ Press Shift+F8
 ✔ Choose <u>D</u>ebug⇨Step <u>O</u>ver

You can switch from procedure stepping to single stepping and vice versa at any time just by choosing the appropriate command. For example, you may want to use procedure stepping first to skip procedures that you know already work. But if you come across other procedures that you aren't sure of, you can switch to single stepping. Then, when you want to skip a procedure, choose procedure stepping again.

To run the rest of the commands in a procedure without having to step through every command line by line, use one of the following two commands:

- ✔ Press Ctrl+Shift+F8
- ✔ Choose Debug⇨Step Out

Using Breakpoints

Whether you choose single stepping (Step Into) or procedure stepping (Step Over), you must still start from the beginning of your program and exhaustively examine each line until you get to the end or until you choose the End command and stop prematurely.

To fully test your program, you must step through every part of your program. In larger programs, many procedures (such as event procedures for command buttons) may only occasionally run during the normal course of using your program, but when they do, they need to be bug-free just like everything else. So be sure to test every part of your program for possible bugs.

Unfortunately, single or procedure stepping can make you intimately familiar with the beginning of your program (having traced through it, line by line, searching for bugs), but what if you just want to examine the middle or end of your program? In that case, you can use breakpoints.

A *breakpoint* is a way to tell Visual Basic, "See that line right there? Let's start single or procedure stepping from this point on." Breakpoints enable you to specify the exact location in your code to stop and examine. By using a breakpoint, you can quickly examine code anywhere in your program without starting from the beginning each time.

Setting breakpoints

To set a breakpoint in your code, follow these steps:

1. Move the cursor on the line of code in the Code window where you want to start single or procedure stepping.

2. Press F9 or choose Debug⇨Toggle Breakpoint. Visual Basic displays breakpoints by highlighting the entire line as shown in Figure 22-2.

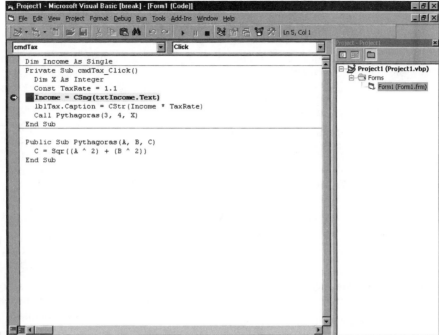

Figure 22-2:
Visual Basic highlighting a breakpoint.

3. Press F5, choose Run⇨Start, or click the Run icon in the Visual Basic Toolbar, shown in Figure 22-1. This causes Visual Basic to run your program from the beginning until it reaches your breakpoint, and then stop.

4. Select the Step Into or Step Over command to examine the rest of your program line by line.

You can place as many breakpoints in your program as you want. Ideally, you should put a breakpoint at the start of any code that you think may be causing a problem. For example, you could use single stepping to check for bugs in your program. The moment you find a bug and fix it, place a breakpoint. Then run your program right up to the breakpoint before you start single or procedure stepping once again.

If you'd rather not litter your program with breakpoints, just move the cursor to any line in the Code window and press Ctrl+F8 or choose Debug⇨Run To Cursor. This runs your program and stops on the line where the cursor appears.

Test your newfound knowledge

1. What are the three ways to trace through your Visual Basic program?

   a. Using tracing paper, a strong light underneath, and a lead pencil.

   b. Single stepping, procedure stepping, and breakpoint stepping.

   c. There is only one way to trace through a Visual Basic program, but I'm not going to tell you what it is.

   d. Visual Basic refuses to let anyone trace anything. That's what makes the language so easy to use and abuse.

2. What are the advantages of procedure stepping (Step Over) and using breakpoints?

   a. Procedure stepping enables you to skip over procedures or functions that you already know work. Breakpoints enable you to start examining your program, line by line, starting from the middle of your program.

   b. Procedure stepping crashes your computer every time and breakpoints tell you how much stress your program withstood before falling apart at the seams.

   c. There is no advantage to using procedure stepping or breakpoints. It's always easier to examine your program, line by line, from the beginning to the end — even if your program is 100,000 lines long.

   d. The only way breakpoints and procedure stepping are useful is when your program has already failed miserably but the government has paid you millions for it anyway.

Deleting breakpoints

After you're through using your breakpoints, you must get rid of them. Visual Basic provides two ways to remove a breakpoint:

- ✔ Move the cursor on the breakpoint and press F9 or choose Debug⇨ Toggle Breakpoint
- ✔ Press Ctrl+Shift+F9 or choose Debug⇨Clear All Breakpoints

If you have a lot of breakpoints you want to remove and don't feel like exerting yourself to look for all of them, choose Debug⇨Clear All Breakpoints. This command wipes out every breakpoint you ever set in your entire program.

If you want to selectively remove breakpoints, you're best off finding each breakpoint and removing it by pressing F9 or choosing Debug⇨Toggle Breakpoint.

Whenever you exit Visual Basic, it automatically removes any breakpoints buried in your program.

Chapter 23

Error Trapping

*T*he three types of errors (bugs) that can keep your program from working right are syntax, logic, and run-time errors. A *syntax error* occurs if you type a word wrong, such as Sbu instead of Sub or Ennd instead of End.

Logic errors occur if you screw up and give the computer the wrong commands to follow — the commands may make sense syntactically, but they are giving instructions to your program that you didn't intend. In this case, your program works perfectly (from the computer's point of view) but is really screwing up (from your point of view). Because logic errors are your fault, you need to use stepping, breakpoints, and watches to see where the problem lies.

Run-time errors are the most troublesome because they are usually caused by the user typing in data that your program doesn't know how to handle correctly. Instead of notifying the user that something went wrong, the program just crashes and dies.

To prevent your program from crashing, use error trapping. Essentially, error trapping does two things when a run-time error occurs:

✔ Display an error message to your users so that they know what went wrong

✔ Avoid crashing and either give users another chance to enter acceptable data, or exit the program gracefully

Programs are especially error-prone when performing input and output functions, such as modifying and saving a file to the hard disk, displaying graphics on the screen, or sending and receiving data through a parallel port or modem. So always be on the lookout for errors in the input/output portions of your program.

How Error Traps Work

Setting an error trap can be as interesting or as disgusting as setting a mouse trap and waiting for it to kill something. You can set error traps only inside procedures or functions.

A typical error trap looks like this:

```
Private Sub TypicalProcedure ()
  ' Constant and variable declarations go here
On Error GoTo ErrorTrap
  ' Code to make your procedure do something
  Exit Sub
ErrorTrap:
  ' Code to handle error trapping
End Sub
```

In this example procedure, the line `On Error GoTo ErrorTrap` tells Visual Basic, "Any time a run-time error occurs, find a label called ErrorTrap and follow the instructions listed below it."

The next part of this procedure would normally contain code that makes your procedure do whatever it is supposed to do (such as calculate tax results, display graphics on the screen, or erase a file from your hard disk). At the end of this chunk of code, you need to put

```
Exit Sub
```

to exit the procedure and keep Visual Basic from wandering into the error trap by mistake.

The error trap appears last in the procedure, and provides code for handling any type of possible errors that may occur.

So what happens if an error occurs in a procedure or function that doesn't have an error trap? The error gets trapped in the first procedure or function with an error trap it runs into. If you don't have any error traps, Visual Basic itself tries to take care of the error, and usually notifies you by just displaying an error message dialog box.

For example, suppose you have two procedures, such as:

```
Private Sub Command1_Click()
  On Error GoTo ErrorTrap
    DisplayText
  ErrorTrap:
    MsgBox "Error trapped here, 64, "Error message"
End Sub

Public Sub DisplayText()
   ' Error occurs here
End Sub
```

If an error occurs inside the Command1_Click procedure, the error gets trapped by the ErrorTrap code. If an error occurs inside the DisplayText procedure, the error also gets trapped by the ErrorTrap code stored in the Command1_Click procedure.

Setting an error trap

You need only one error trap per procedure or function — that one error trap can handle any number of possible errors.

To set an error trap, use the following syntax at the beginning of your procedures or functions:

```
On Error GoTo ErrorCodeLabel
```

You can substitute any valid name for ErrorCodeLabel, such as:

```
ErrorTrap
BugMotel
HandleStupidUsers
```

You can only use a label name once in your program.

For particularly large procedures or functions, you may want to include the procedure name in your error code label, such as:

```
On Error GoTo Command1_Click_ErrorTrap
```

By including the procedure name as part of your error code label, you can easily identify the procedure or function where the error trap is located.

Writing error trap code

First, you need to define the beginning of your error trapping code. If you set your error trap like this:

```
On Error GoTo Utopia
```

you would define the start of your error trapping code like this:

```
Utopia:
```

In this case, the error-trapping label is called `Utopia`.

To help you figure out which error occurred, Visual Basic is kind enough to identify the error with a number, called its *error code*. Visual Basic stores this error code in a variable called `Err`. Table 23-1 lists some common error codes.

Table 23-1	Common Error Codes
Value of Err (error code)	*What It Means*
5	You tried calling a function that doesn't exist. (Shame on you!)
7	Your computer ran out of memory. Stop being so cheap and buy more RAM.
11	Division by zero. Not only is this mathematically impossible but computers don't like it either.
53	File not found. Are you sure you know what you're looking for?
61	Disk full. Get another disk.
71	Disk not ready. Either the disk drive is open or the disk drive is busted.

To handle different types of errors, use an If-Then statement or a Select-Case statement. For example:

```
If Err = 61 Then
    MsgBox "Disk is full. Get another disk."
ElseIf Err = 71 Then
    MsgBox "Something's wrong with your disk."
End If
```

This error trapping code checks for two possible errors: The user tried saving a file to a disk that ran out of room, or the disk drive may be open or broken.

As an alternative, you could use a Select-Case statement, such as:

```
Select Case Err
   Case 61
      MsgBox "Disk is full. Get another disk."
   Case 71
      MsgBox "Something's wrong with your disk."
End Select
```

Exiting your error trapping code

After your error trap responds to a particular error, you have several choices for the code which follows:

- ✔ Stop the program completely
- ✔ Run the command that caused the error
- ✔ Skip to the next command
- ✔ Exit the procedure
- ✔ Jump to another part of the procedure

Stopping your program completely

Many times, you want your program to stop immediately upon finding an error. That way, you can go back and correct it right away. To stop your program completely the moment an error occurs, use this command:

```
Stop
```

The Stop command immediately breaks into your program and so you can use the Immediate window to start poking around your program's variables and expressions and see what may have gone wrong.

For example:

```
Select Case Err
   Case 61
     MsgBox "Disk is full. Get another disk."
     Stop
   Case 71
     MsgBox "Something's wrong with your disk."
     Stop
End Select
```

Whenever a disk full or disk drive error occurs, this example displays an error message in a dialog box on the screen and then stops the program from running. To make the program start running again, do one of the following:

- ✔ Choose Run⇨Continue
- ✔ Press F5
- ✔ Click the Start icon in the Visual Basic Toolbar

After you finish testing your program, delete all the Stop commands from your program before compiling it. If a compiled version of your program runs into a Stop command, the program exits immediately and the poor user won't have a clue as to what went wrong.

Running the same command over again

Sometimes you may not want your program to stop. Instead, you may want it to wait for the user to correct the problem (such as by inserting a floppy disk in the disk drive) before trying to run the same command again.

To make your program run the same command that caused the error in the first place, use this command:

```
Resume (0)
```

For example:

```
Select Case Err
   Case 61
      MsgBox "Disk is full. Get another disk."
      Resume (0)
   Case 71
      MsgBox "Something's wrong with your disk."
      Resume (0)
End Select
```

Whenever a disk full or disk drive error occurs, this example displays an error message in a dialog box and then goes right back to the command that caused the error in the first place.

Skipping to the next command

If you know your program has a bug in it but you don't want to halt everything to examine it, you can tell your error code to ignore the error and skip to the next command.

To make your program run the command immediately following the one that caused the error in the first place, use this command:

```
Resume Next
```

For example:

```
Select Case Err
  Case 61
    MsgBox "Disk is full. Get another disk."
    Resume Next
  Case 71
    MsgBox "Something's wrong with your disk."
    Resume Next
End Select
```

Whenever a disk full or disk drive error occurs, this example displays an error message in a dialog box and then goes to the next command following the one that caused the error in the first place.

This method essentially ignores the error and blindly goes working anyway.

If you want special code to run when a particular error occurs, you can use this command:

```
Resume "Line"
```

where `"Line"` represents a label identifying the code that you want to run next. For example:

```
Select Case Err
  Case 61
    MsgBox "Disk is full. Get another disk."
    Resume SecondChance
  Case 71
    MsgBox "Something's wrong with your disk."
    Resume SecondChance
End Select
SecondChance:
  MsgBox "Don't you wish you had a Macintosh instead?"
```

Whenever a disk full or disk drive error occurs, this example displays an error message in a dialog box and then jumps to the commands identified by the label called `SecondChance`. In this case, it immediately displays a new dialog box with the message, `Don't you wish you had a Macintosh instead?`

By using the Resume statement as part of your error trap, you can write specific code to certain errors you might want to address, and then jump to more general code to work with all other types of errors.

The only restriction to the Resume "Label" command is that you can only jump to code stored within the same procedure. You can't have an error-trapping routine jump to code stored in another procedure.

Testing Your Error Trapping Code

After you write error trapping code, you need to test it so that your error trapping code doesn't contain its own errors. You can test your error trapping code two ways:

- ✔ Erase files, wreck your disks, disconnect your printer, and so on
- ✔ Simulate errors by using the Error command

Unless you like physically ruining your computer just to test whether your error trapping code works, you're best off just simulating errors.

To simulate any error, use this syntax:

```
Err.Raise ErrorNumber
```

where ErrorNumber is the Err value that represents a specific error. Look in Table 23-1 or in the Microsoft Language Reference manual for the exact Err values for each error.

To test your error trapping code, just shove a simulated error directly in your code, like in the first line in the next code:

```
Err.Raise 61
If Err = 61 Then
  MsgBox "Disk is full. Get another disk."
ElseIf Err = 71 Then
  MsgBox "Something's wrong with your disk."
End If
```

This example simulates a disk full error (see Table 23-1 for a list of some errors) so that you can see whether your error trapping code for this particular error actually works.

Of course, after you test your error trapping code, you need to remove all the simulated errors before compiling your program. Otherwise, the simulated errors keep working, making your program look buggy, unreliable, and exactly like commercial packages sold by name brand software publishers.

Delaying Error Handling

If an error occurs, you want your finished program to handle it immediately. But while you're still writing and debugging your code, you may want to temporarily ignore errors and keep your program running.

This is the equivalent of driving cross-country and having your kids complain that they have to go to the bathroom. Because you can't stop on the side of the highway, you just ignore their cries (error messages) until you can find the nearest rest area, gas station, or Denny's restaurant.

To temporarily ignore errors, use the following commands:

```
On Error Resume Next
ErrorNumber = Err
```

This essentially tells Visual Basic to make a note that an error occurred, but keep going anyway. To find out which error occurred at the time, the value of `Err` gets stuffed into a global variable called `ErrorNumber` so that you can examine it later to find out what error actually occurred.

Turning Off Error Handling

If you want to disable your error trapping code temporarily, use this command:

```
On Error GoTo 0
```

Put this anywhere in front of your error trapping code to tell Visual Basic to detect any errors, but to ignore your error trapping code.

To turn error trapping back on, use this command:

```
On Error GoTo "Label"
```

where `"Label"` represents a label that identifies the code you want to run next.

You can turn error trapping off and on as many times as you like, although it's pretty silly to turn it off and on again for no apparent reason.

Test your newfound knowledge

1. What are the three types of bugs, and how can error trapping help you find them in your program?

    a. There are no errors in software. Computers are perfect in every way and if anything goes wrong, it's the user's fault.

    b. The three types of program bugs are officially designated endangered species under the environmental protection act, and thus it's illegal to use error trapping to catch and kill them.

    c. Error trapping can help you figure out why so many people keep buying software when everyone knows that it rarely works as advertised.

    d. The three types of program bugs are syntax, logic, and run-time errors. Error trapping can help you locate run-time errors in your program.

2. If an error trap catches a bug, what can it do next?

    a. Shut down your program immediately, rerun the command that caused the error in the first place, run the command immediately following the one that caused the error, or run commands identified by a label.

    b. Flush it down the toilet.

    c. Squash it with a big crunching noise.

    d. If an error trap catches a bug, it not only shuts down your computer but also crashes every other computer in the world running Windows 95. So be careful when using error traps.

Try It Yourself

To experiment with different error numbers and see what they really mean, create the following program, as shown in Figure 23-1.

Object	Property	Setting
Form	Caption	Pick an error message
	Height	3255
	Left	2625
	Top	1575
	Width	5880
Label1	Caption	Error number
	Height	255
	Left	360
	Top	480
	Width	1095

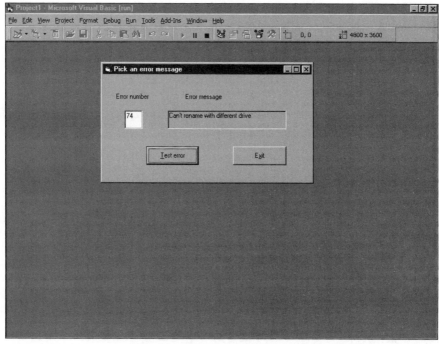

Object	Property	Setting
Label2	Caption	Error message
	Height	255
	Left	2280
	Top	480
	Width	1575
Text1	Height	495
	Left	600
	Text	(Empty)
	Top	960
	Width	495
Label3	BorderStyle	1 – Fixed Single
	Caption	(Empty)
	Height	495
	Left	1800

Object	Property	Setting
	Top	960
	Width	3255
Command1	Caption	&Test error
	Height	495
	Left	1200
	Top	1920
	Width	1455
Command2	Caption	E&xit
	Height	495
	Left	3600
	Top	1920
	Width	1455

Type the following in the Code window:

```
Private Sub Command1_Click()
  Dim ErrorNumber As Integer
  On Error Resume Next
  ErrorNumber = Int(CSng(Text1.Text))
  Err.Clear
  Err.Raise ErrorNumber
  If Err.Number <> 0 Then
    Label3.Caption = Err.Description
  End If
End Sub

Private Sub Command2_Click()
  Unload Me
End Sub
```

Chapter 24

Compiling and
Using the Setup Wizard

. . . .

In This Chapter

▶ Getting your program ready for market

▶ Compiling your code

▶ Using the Setup Wizard

. . . .

*A*fter you test and debug your program to the best of your ability (or the limits of your patience), you eventually want to distribute your program for others to use. To distribute your program, you need to compile it into an executable file, which is also known as an *.EXE* file because it ends with the .EXE file extension.

Getting Your Program Ready for Market

Before compiling your program, you need to decide:

> ✔ The name of your program
>
> ✔ The icon to represent your program on the Windows desktop
>
> ✔ How to compile your program (P-code vs. Native code)

Defining the name of your program

Unless you specify otherwise, the name of your compiled Visual Basic .EXE program is the same as the name of your Visual Basic project file (*.VBP file). So if you compile a project called HELLO.VBP, Visual Basic stores the compiled program in a HELLO.EXE file.

If you want change the name of your program, follow these steps:

1. Choose Project⇨Properties. The Project Properties dialog box appears.

2. Click the General tab as shown in Figure 24-1.

3. Type a new project name (as a single word; no spaces) in the Project Name box and click OK.

You can also change the name of your compiled .EXE program by choosing File⇨Make. When a Make Project dialog box appears, type a new name for your program in the File name box and click OK.

Defining an icon for your program

More important than the name of your program is the icon (*.ICO file) used to represent it. You can use any of the icons included with Visual Basic, or you can create your own using any drawing or painting program that can create *.ICO files.

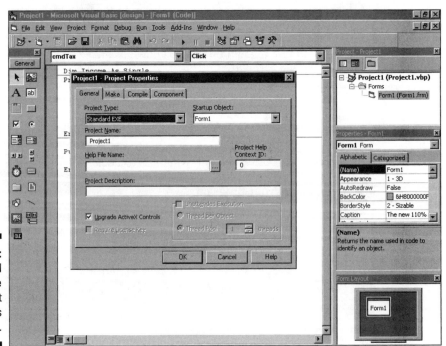

Figure 24-1:
The General tab in the Project Properties dialog box.

The icon that represents the first form in your program is the default icon that Visual Basic uses to represent your entire program. To determine the first form that loads and defines an icon for your program, follow these steps:

1. Choose Project⇨Properties. The Project Properties dialog box appears.

2. Click the Make tab, as shown in Figure 24-2. The form name that appears in the Icon list box is the first form that loads in your program and its icon appears to the right of the Icon list box.

3. Click OK. The Project Properties dialog box disappears.

4. Choose View⇨Project Explorer, or press Ctrl+R. The Project Explorer window appears.

5. In the Project window, click the form name that was listed in the Icon list box in Step 2, and then click the View Object icon.

6. Open the Properties window (by pressing F4, choosing View⇨Properties Window, or clicking the Properties window icon on the toolbar).

7. Double-click the Icon property. A Load Icon dialog box appears.

8. Click the icon that you want to use, and click Open. Your chosen icon is now the one used to represent both the entire program and its first form.

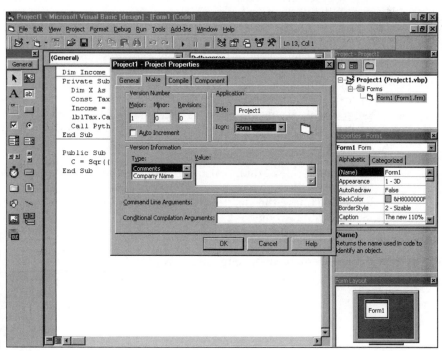

Figure 24-2:
The Make tab in the Project Properties dialog box.

Choosing P-code or Native code

Visual Basic provides two ways to compile your program:

- ✔ As P-Code
- ✔ As Native Code

The Learning Edition of Visual Basic 5.0 does not have a native code compiler.

P-code (also called pseudo-code) converts your BASIC commands into a pseudo programming language that your computer doesn't know how to use. The advantage of P-code is that you can run your program without having a copy of Visual Basic installed. The disadvantage is that P-Code requires a special run-time file called MSVBVM50.DLL, and P-code compiled programs don't run as fast as programs compiled into Native code.

Native code is a fancy term that means Visual Basic converts your BASIC commands into 0's and 1's, which is the native language of your computer. It's not much of a conversational language, but computers can understand this language. Compiling a program into Native code is like speaking English to a native English speaker. Compiling a program into P-code is like speaking Arabic to a native English speaker through an English-Arabic translator. You can do it, but the result is much slower and clumsier.

So now that you have a choice, how should you compile your program? Unlike cults and pseudo-religions, there are no simple answers.

When you compile a program to P-code, the file is much smaller in size than the exact same file compiled to Native code. The reason is that P-code programs always need to use the MSVBVM50.DLL file, so the P-code program contains only the bare minimum of instructions it needs to run on your computer.

As a general rule of thumb, if speed is important, compile your program to Native code. If small file size is important, compile your program to P-code. If you don't have the slightest idea what any of this means, you probably picked up the wrong book to read. Put it down now and get a teenage kid to help you with your computer.

For some odd reason, compiling a program to Native code creates a slightly larger file that still needs the accompanying MSVBVM50.DLL file.

To choose either P-code or Native code, follow these steps:

1. Choose Project➪Properties. The Project Properties dialog box appears.

2. Click the Compile tab as shown in Figure 24-3.

3. Click one of the following radio buttons:

    • Compile to P-Code

    • Compile to Native Code

4. Click OK.

If you choose to compile to Native code, Visual Basic bombards you with five other options.

Optimize for Fast Code — As the name implies, this option helps create the fastest running program possible. The disadvantage is that your program's file size may be larger than if you compiled it without this option.

Optimize for Small Code — This tells Visual Basic to try and create the smallest possible file size for your program. The disadvantage is that your program may run slower than if you ignored this option.

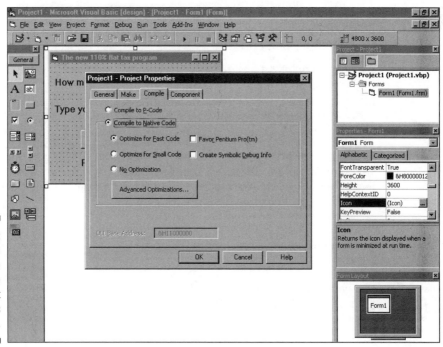

Figure 24-3:
The Compile tab in the Project Properties dialog box.

No Optimization — Just as the option implies, no optimization for speed or size is included in the compiled program.

Favor Pentium Pro — This option tells Visual Basic to create a program especially suited for running on Pentium Pro computers. The program can still run on older processors, such as the Pentium or 80486, but it may run slow on these processors.

Create Symbolic Debug Info — Creates special debugging information that you can use to root out any lingering bugs in your program. You should not choose this option when compiling your final program for distribution since this extra debugging information requires additional disk space (and you hope your users will not run into bugs anyway).

Compiling Your Code

After choosing your project name, the icon to represent it, and whether to compile to P-code or Native code, you're ready to compile your program into an .EXE file. When you compile your program, Visual Basic gives you several options to define the following:

- ✔ Version number
- ✔ Company name
- ✔ File description
- ✔ Legal copyright
- ✔ Legal trademarks
- ✔ Product name

The version number consists of three parts: Major, Minor, and Revision. For example, your first program can be called version 1.00. If you revise it, the version can be 1.01. Then, ten minor revisions later, the version number would be 1.11. Then if you make a major change to it, the version number can be 2.11, and so on.

The company name, file description, legal copyright, legal trademarks, and product name appear only when the user views the properties of your program, as shown in Figure 24-4.

You can modify the Version number, Company name, File description, etc. of your program by choosing Project➪Properties and clicking the Make tab. Or you can follow the instructions listed next.

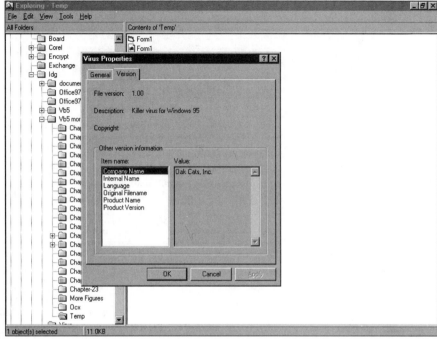

Figure 24-4:
Viewing the
properties
of a
compiled
.EXE
program.

To compile your program, follow these steps:

1. Choose File⇨Make. Visual Basic displays the name of your project in the menu, such as Make VIRUS.EXE. The Make Project dialog box appears.

2. Click Options. The Project Properties dialog box appears, as shown in Figure 24-5.

3. Type the Major, Minor, and Revision numbers of your program in the appropriate boxes.

4. Click the Auto Increment check box if you want Visual Basic to automatically increment the Revision number by one each time you compile your program.

5. Click Comments, Company Name, File Description, Legal Copyright, Legal Trademarks, or Product Name in the Type list box, and type the information in the Value box.

6. Click OK. The Make Project dialog box appears again.

7. Click the Save in list box and choose the drive and directory where you want to save your .EXE file.

8. Click OK.

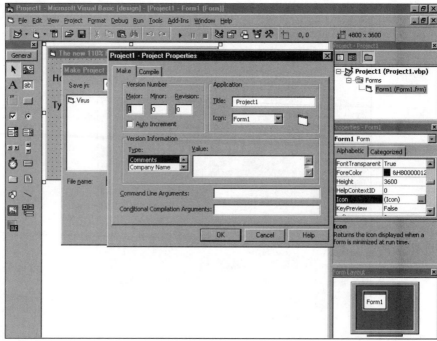

Figure 24-5:
The Project
Properties
dialog box.

Using the Setup Wizard

After you compile your Visual Basic program into an .EXE file, you can distribute it to others. However, for maximum convenience (for both you and your technical support staff), you should create a separate installation program. By running this installation program, users can install your Visual Basic .EXE file on their own computer with minimal fuss and trouble.

To help you create an installation program, Microsoft has generously provided an installation program called the Application Setup Wizard.

Every ActiveX control that appears in the Visual Basic Toolbox when you compile your program gets included with your installation program as well. For example, you might have added an ActiveX control to the Visual Basic Toolbox but never actually used it in your program. Rather than remove ActiveX controls yourself, you can have Visual Basic do it for you automatically by pressing Ctrl+T to open the Components dialog box, holding down the Shift key, and clicking OK.

To use the Application Setup Wizard, follow these steps:

1. Click the Start button in the Windows 95 taskbar, choose Programs⇨ Visual Basic 5.0⇨Application Setup Wizard. The initial Application Setup Wizard dialog box appears as shown in Figure 24-6.

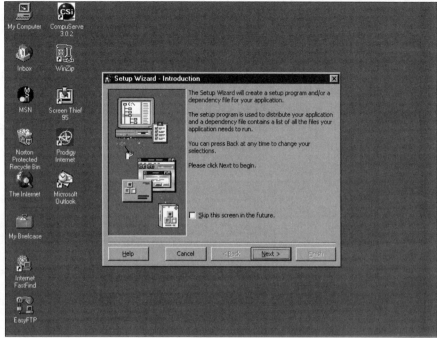

Figure 24-6:
The initial
Application
Setup
Wizard
dialog box.

2. Click <u>N</u>ext. The Setup Wizard – Select Project and Options dialog box appears.

3. If you changed your Visual Basic program since the last time you compiled it, click <u>R</u>ebuild the Project check box.

4. Click the Bro<u>w</u>se button. A Locate VB application's .VBP file dialog box appears.

5. Click the Look <u>i</u>n list box and choose the drive and directory containing the .VBP project file that you want to use. Then click <u>O</u>pen.

6. Click <u>N</u>ext. The Setup Wizard – Distribution Method dialog box appears.

7. Click one of the following radio buttons:

    • F<u>l</u>oppy disk – stores your installation program on a floppy disk

    • <u>S</u>ingle Directory – stores your installation program on a directory on your hard disk

    • <u>D</u>isk directories (\Disk1, \Disk2, etc.) – stores your installation program in separate directories on your hard disk so you can copy them to floppy disks later

8. Click <u>N</u>ext. Depending on what option you chose in Step 7, another Setup Wizard dialog box appears.

9. Choose the directory or type of floppy disk you want to use and click <u>N</u>ext. The Setup Wizard – ActiveX Server Components dialog box appears as shown in Figure 24-7.

10. Click <u>N</u>ext. The Setup Wizard – File Summary dialog box appears. This dialog box lists all the files you need to include with your Visual Basic program.

11. Click <u>N</u>ext. The Setup Wizard – Finished! Dialog box appears as shown in Figure 24-8.

12. Click <u>F</u>inish. A final Setup Wizard dialog box appears.

13. Click OK.

After the Setup Wizard has created your installation program for you, you can start passing out your program on disk to other people. To install your program, your users need to run the SETUP.EXE file just like any other software.

For greater flexibility, you may want to avoid the Setup Wizard and buy a separate installation program such as InstallShield Express, PC-Install, or WISE Install. These separate installation programs let you customize the background of your installation screen (to display your company logo, registration information, pleas to the user not to copy the software illegally, jokes about your boss, etc.) or add sound or video to accompany your installation.

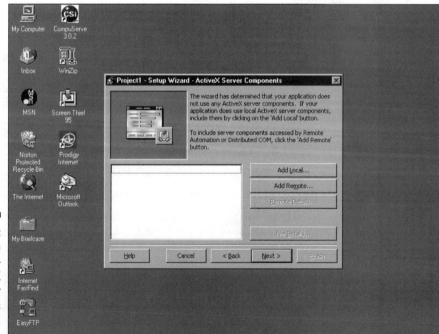

Figure 24-7:
The Setup
Wizard –
ActiveX
Server
Components
dialog box.

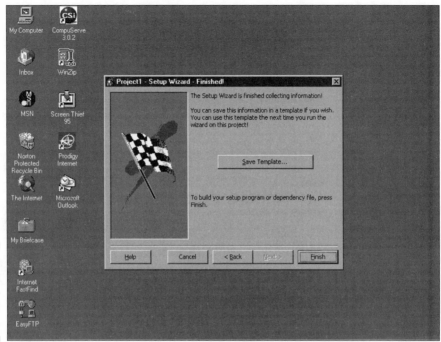

Naturally, the separate installation programs cost money, but if you want to give your program a custom, professional appearance, buying and using a separate installation program may be preferable than using the generic Setup Wizard that comes with Visual Basic.

Test your newfound knowledge

1. What is the difference between P-code and Native code?

   a. P-code only runs under OS/2 and other operating systems that Microsoft can't make money selling. Native code can only be used by people who were born in this country.

   b. P-code is a nickname for Native code and therefore there is absolutely no difference between the two of them.

   c. P-code converts a program into pseudocode. Native code converts a program into 0's and 1's, which is the native language of your computer.

   d. P-code programs are inherently superior to Native code programs. Or is it the other way around?

2. What is the purpose of the Setup Wizard?

   a. The Setup Wizard helps you create an installation program and stores it on one or more floppy disks that you can sell or give away to others.

   b. The Setup Wizard is a demonic creation that goes against everything that organized religion stands for.

   c. The Setup Wizard helps you erase Visual Basic from your hard disk so that you can put more games on it instead.

   d. There is no purpose for the Setup Wizard because Microsoft didn't know what they were doing when they created Visual Basic in the first place.

Part VII
Shortcuts
and Tips Galore

The 5th Wave   By Rich Tennant

PORTRAIT OF A
CYBERHOLIC

SO, HOW'S DAD?

CYBERHOLICS DON'T WRITE LETTERS.
IF YOU DON'T HAVE A MODEM THEY
DON'T WANT TO TALK TO YOU.

In this part . . .

This part of the book provides tips for customizing Visual Basic, along with sample programs that can create special effects that you may want to plug into your own programs.

Although this is the end of the book, it doesn't mean you have to end your Visual Basic education. So keep up your Visual Basic programming skills and crank out those useful, interesting programs that lots of people really need but no one else is selling — except maybe you.

Chapter 25

Tips for Using Visual Basic

• •

• •

*T*o help you write the best Visual Basic programs possible, you can customize the way Visual Basic works. That way, no matter what peculiar programming habits you may have, Visual Basic cheerfully accommodates you so that you can spend more time writing programs and less time wrestling with the Visual Basic user interface.

So browse through the following tips. You may not need all of them, but you're likely to find one or two that can make Visual Basic easier to use and help you write better programs faster than before.

Customizing the Code Window

The Visual Basic Code window enables you to write and modify your BASIC code to make your program do something. Because you spend a lot of time staring at the Code window, you may as well learn how to change its appearance so that it looks nice to you.

Colors and fonts

To help identify certain parts of a program such as comments or keywords, Visual Basic can display them in different colors, fonts, or type sizes. To change the way Visual Basic displays certain text in the Code window, follow these steps:

1. Choose Tools⇨Options. The Options dialog box appears.

2. Click the Editor Format tab as shown in Figure 25-1.

3. In the Code Colors list box, click the type of text you want to modify (such as Comment Text or Keyword Text).

4. Click one or both of the following list boxes to change their values:

    • Foreground list box

    • Background list box

5. Click the Font list box and choose a font for the text you chose in Step 3.

6. Click the Size list box and choose a size for the text you chose in Step 3.

7. Repeat Steps 3 through 6 for each type of text you want to modify.

8. Click OK.

Displaying pop-up hints

Unless you care to memorize the Visual Basic manuals, you may occasionally need help when typing specific Visual Basic commands such as MsgBox or If-Then statements. To help you write code faster than ever before, Visual

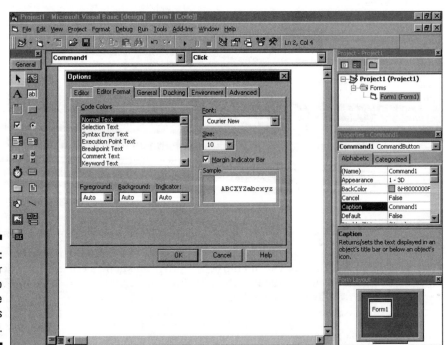

Figure 25-1:
The Editor
Format tab
in the
Options
dialog box.

Basic can pop-up friendly hints on, or even fill in the syntax required by a specific command (such as MsgBox). Visual Basic can also offer pop-up hints on the properties associated with an object on your user interface.

Letting Visual Basic type commands for you automatically

To have Visual Basic help you type a command, follow these steps:

1. Start typing as much of the specific command as you can remember, such as `ms` to type the MsgBox command.

2. Press Ctrl+Space, or choose Edit⇨Complete Word. If you type enough of a particular command, Visual Basic automatically finishes typing the rest of it for you. If you only type one or two letters of a particular command, Visual Basic displays a helpful pop-up menu of commands you can choose from, as shown in Figure 25-2.

Getting syntax information for using Visual Basic commands

Many Visual Basic command can accept a variety of parameters. For example, the MsgBox command can be used in the following ways:

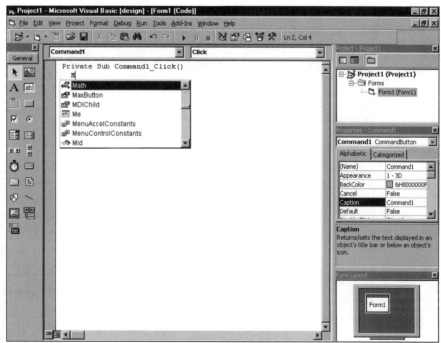

Figure 25-2:
Visual Basic offers a pop-up menu of commands that begin with the letter M.

```
MsgBox "Hello, world!"
MsgBox "Stop!", , "Warning message"
MsgBox "Do you really want to erase your hard disk?",
        vbWarning, "Warning"
```

From the previous example, you can see that the MsgBox command can accept a variety of different parameters that define the appearance of a displayed message box. So how do you know how many parameters a particular Visual Basic command can accept?

As you type a Visual Basic command, Visual Basic normally displays syntax information for a command. But just in case you want to see this information after you've already typed a Visual Basic command, follow these steps:

1. Move the cursor to the end of the line containing the Visual Basic command for which you want to display a parameter list, such as MsgBox.

2. Type part of the parameters you want to include and press Ctrl+Shift+I, or choose Edit➪Parameter Info. Visual Basic displays a pop-up window, listing the particular command's parameters, as shown in Figure 25-3.

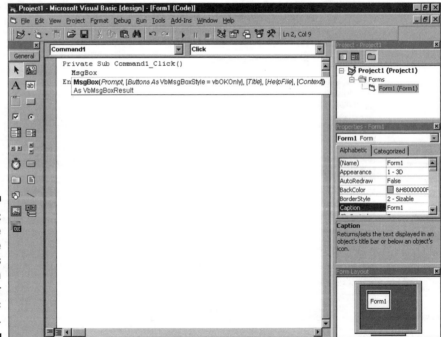

Figure 25-3: List of the acceptable parameters for a particular Visual Basic command.

Examining the properties of an object

To make your user interface do something, you need to draw objects such as command buttons or check boxes on a form. To modify the appearance of an object, you need to change that object's properties.

To find the specific property name for a particular object, you could open the Properties window, click the list box that appears at the top of the Properties window, and then scroll down the long list of displayed properties until you find the one you want.

As an alternative way to get the properties information on a particular object, you can type an object's name followed by a period. Visual Basic then displays a pop-up menu, as shown in Figure 25-4. You can also get properties information by following these steps:

1. Move the cursor in the object's property. For example, to examine the available properties for a command button named cmdExit, move the cursor after the period that appears to the right of cmdExit.

2. Press Ctrl+J, or choose Edit⇨List Properties/Methods. A pop-up list appears, as shown in Figure 25-4.

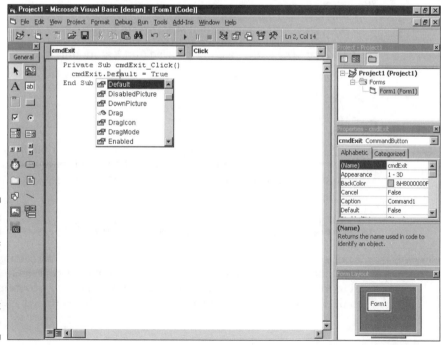

Figure 25-4: A pop-up list of available properties for the cmdExit object.

Writing Better Programs

After you customize the Code window so that it works the way you like, take a look at the way you write your programs. You are perfectly free to write the same program a million different ways, but you may find one way convoluted and confusing and another simple and clear.

To help make your programming easier, you are best off writing the simplest and most understandable programs possible. Then, if you (or another programmer) need to modify the program at a later date, you won't find the process like trying to decipher the Rosetta Stone.

Comment liberally

If you think you can remember how your program works six months after you write it, try to remember what you ate for breakfast this morning. If that stumps you, you probably won't remember how your program works either.

To make sure that you can understand how your program works, write plenty of comments throughout it. Some suggestions for comments include the following:

- Who wrote the code (so you know who to blame)
- The date the code was first created and last modified
- What your code is supposed to do
- What variables the code uses
- How your code modifies any data

When Visual Basic compiles your code, it ignores all your comments. So feel free to write as many comments as you like because the number or size of your comments doesn't affect the size or speed of your program in any way.

Use descriptive variable names

In a perfect world, reading a program should be as easy as reading a book. Unfortunately, this is not a perfect world, which means that most programs tend to look as cryptic as a CIA cipher. To help make your programs as easy to understand as possible, use descriptive names for variables and objects.

For example, look at the following code:

```
X = Y * 0.075
Text1.Text = CStr(X)
```

If you think you can tell what this code does, you're probably lying to yourself. What do X and Y really represent and what does the number 0.075 mean? To make this code a little easier to understand without actually running it, consider the following rewritten code:

```
Const SALESTAX = 0.075
Total = SalesAmount * SALESTAX
txtDisplayTotal.Text = CStr(Total)
```

By using more descriptive names, you can quickly understand what the code does without having to run it, guess, or ask the original programmer for help.

Some people like using a mixture of uppercase and lowercase letters, such as:

```
SalesAmount = 1500
```

Others prefer using the underscore character, such as:

```
Sales_amount = 1500
```

Whatever method you like, use it consistently so that you or other programmers can easily adapt to your style and understand your program easier.

Keep procedures short and simple

What's easier to read and understand, a one-page letter or a five-hundred-page tax form? Unless you're really weird, you probably find that a one-page letter is much easier to read than a five-hundred-page document. So when you write a procedure, keep it short and simple.

Ideally, your procedure should accomplish one task and fit in the Code window without forcing you to scroll up or down to see the whole procedure. The shorter and simpler your procedures, the easier it is to understand exactly how they work so that you can track and kill any bugs that may be lurking in them.

Separate your program into modules

A large Visual Basic program can consist of event procedures and general procedures. Event procedures tell Visual Basic what to do when the user does something with your program's user interface. General procedures usually calculate a result based on data stored in a file or collected from the user interface.

Although you don't ever need to use module files, they can help you divide your program into two distinct parts:

- ✔ The user interface
- ✔ The code that makes your program do something

Your form (.FRM) files contain the user interface, whereas your module (.BAS) files contain the code to make your program work. By separating your program into these two distinct parts, you can easily modify your user interface without risking the possibility of messing up the code that makes your program calculate something important.

Even better, if you create enough useful module files, you can easily plug them into other Visual Basic programs so that you don't need to rewrite the same code.

Use .RC resource files

If you write programs for different languages (that is, spoken languages such as English and French), you might have to create one version of your user interface in English and a second in French. Naturally, this means you might introduce bugs into either program version. As a simpler alternative, you can use something called .RC resource files instead.

A resource file is nothing more than a separate file that contains the text that appears on your user interface. By creating different resource files (one for each language), you can simply swap in a new resource file to create a different language version of your program, rather than messing around with changing your user interface.

While the exact way to use resource files isn't covered in this book, be aware that they exist so in case you need to write foreign language versions of your program, you can save a lot of time and grief.

Force yourself to use classes (object-oriented programming)

Most people resist change, which explains why social progress in the human race takes centuries to spread. If you aren't convinced that classes (object-oriented programming) are worth learning, think again. (For more information on using class modules, pick up a copy of *Visual Basic 5 For Dummies.*)

Like module files, class modules can help you further isolate your code so that modifying your program at a future date will be easier and more reliable. Although you could timidly add classes sporadically throughout your programs, try to force yourself to design your next Visual Basic program completely using class modules.

This new way of thinking may slow you down and make you feel like a clumsy beginner again, but classes can help organize your programs into distinct building blocks. The quicker you learn and use class modules now, the more likely you'll be able to write reliable and easy-to-maintain programs later. And best of all, claiming that you have object-oriented programming skills on your resume is a sure way to get noticed and land yourself a new job.

Verify that your code works correctly

Every time you add new code to your program, test it immediately. That way, if your program suddenly acts weird when it was working perfectly fine before you modified it, you can isolate the problem in your new code.

If you don't test your newly added code right away and just keep modifying your program, guess what? When you finally decide to test it and it doesn't work right, you must dig through all of your newly added code to find the bug.

Using Data Types

Visual Basic allows you to create variables in two ways:

- By creating them as you need them
- By declaring them by using the Dim keyword

For example, you may create a procedure such as the following:

```
Private Sub Command1_Click ()
   Quantity = 36
   Price = 45.95
   Total = Quantity * Price
End Sub
```

In this example, the three variables Quantity, Price, and Total are created when they're needed. Although this is perfectly fine, it's frowned upon by the programming community because it encourages sloppy programming. If this were a really long program, you could be creating variables all over the place and it would be nearly impossible for anyone to know the exact number of variables your program uses.

As an alternative to creating variables when you need them, serious programmers like to declare variables at the top of each program or procedure. For example:

```
Private Sub Command1_Click ()
   Dim Quantity
   Dim Price
   Dim Total
   Quantity = 36
   Price = 45.95
   Total = Quantity * Price
End Sub
```

In this example, you can quickly see how many variables this procedure uses. In really small programs, declaring your variables isn't necessary. But in extremely large programs or procedures, declaring the number and names of your variables ahead of time can help you remember how your code works.

Besides declaring your variables ahead of time, it's also a good idea to define a data type for each variable such as:

```
Private Sub Command1_Click ()
   Dim Quantity As Integer
   Dim Price As Currency
   Dim Total As Double
   Quantity = 36
   Price = 45.95
   Total = Quantity * Price
End Sub
```

Force yourself to declare variables

Visual Basic lets you create variables whenever you need them. However, if you want to pick up a good programming habit and force yourself to declare variables ahead of time, you have two ways to do this:

- ✔ Add the Option Explicit statement
- ✔ Customize Visual Basic so that it forces you to declare your variables

So which method should you choose? If you just want to force yourself to declare variables in a single form (.FRM) or module (.BAS) file, use the Option Explicit statement. If you want to force yourself to always declare variables every time you program in Visual Basic, customize Visual Basic to force you to declare variables.

To add the Option Explicit statement in your form or module file, follow these steps:

1. Press F7 to open the code window.

2. Choose *(General)* in the Object list box.

3. Type **Option Explicit** in the Code window.

If you use Option Explicit, Visual Basic forces you to declare variables only in the .FRM or .BAS file where you typed Option Explicit. So, if you declare Option Explicit only in a Form1.FRM file, you still don't have to declare variables in any other file that goes into your program.

To customize Visual Basic so that it always makes you declare variables in every program you write, follow these steps:

1. Choose Tools➪Options. An Options dialog box appears.

2. Click the Editor tab as shown in Figure 25-5.

3. Click the Require Variable Declaration check box so that a check mark appears.

4. Click OK.

Create default variable declarations

If you're really particular about your variable names and the type of data they represent, you can declare all variables that begin with the letter *S* to be strings, all variables that begin with *I* to be integers, all variables that begin with *B* to be Boolean data types, and so on.

To create these default variable declarations, you must place one of the statements listed in the following table in a form (.FRM) file or a module (.BAS) file.

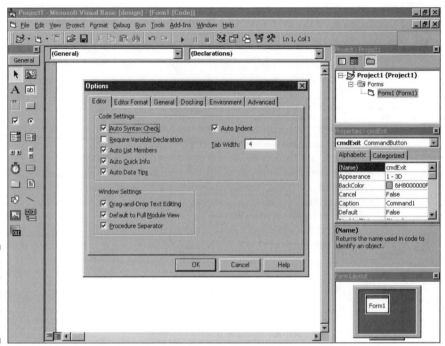

Figure 25-5:
The Editor
tab in the
Options
dialog box.

Statement	Default Data Type	Typical Values
DefBool	Boolean	True or False
DefByte	Byte	0 to 255
DefInt	Integer	−32,768 to 32,767
DefLng	Long	−2,147,483,648 to 2,147,483,647
DefCur	Currency	−922,337,203,685,477.5808 to 922,337,203,685,477.5807
DefSng	Single	−3.402823E38 to −1.401298E45 (negative values); 1.401298E−45 to 3.402823E38 (positive values)
DefDbl	Double	−1.79769313486232E308 to −4.94065645841247E−324 (negative values); 4.94065645841247E−324 to 1.79769313486232E308 (positive values)
DefDate	Date	January 1, 100 to December 31, 9999
DefStr	String	0 to 2 billion characters
DefVar	Variant	Any numeric or text value

For example, if you want to declare all variables beginning with the letters *A* through *F* as integers, you could use the following:

```
DefInt A-F
```

To declare all variables that begin with *S* as a string, use the following:

```
DefStr S
```

When you declare default variable declarations, they only work within the file you declare them in. For example, if you declare default variable definitions in a .BAS module file, those default variable definitions are valid only within that same .BAS module file — not in another .BAS module file.

If you declare all variables that begin with the letter *S* to represent strings, you can still create a variable that begins with the letter *S* to represent a different data type. For example:

```
DefStr S
Dim Summary As Integer
```

1. The first line tells Visual Basic, "Anytime you see a variable that begins with the letter S, assume it represents a string value."

2. The second line tells Visual Basic, "The Summary variable represents an integer."

Automatically Saving Your Files

Suppose you modify your program and run it, and suddenly it crashes. What went wrong? If you didn't save your program right before running it, any modifications you made to it are lost, which means that you may have no idea what went wrong.

To prevent this problem, you can do one of the following:

✔ Trust that you always save your files before running your program

✔ Have Visual Basic automatically save your files for you before running your program

If you can trust yourself implicitly and completely, simply save your files before running your program. However, it's much easier to have Visual Basic save the files for you automatically. To customize Visual Basic to save your files right before you run your program, follow these steps:

1. Choose Tools⇨Options. The Options dialog box appears.

2. Click the Environment tab as shown in Figure 25-6.

3. Click one of the following radio buttons in the When a program starts group:

   - Save Changes – saves your valuable Visual Basic program before running it

   - Prompt to Save Changes – politely asks if you would like to do the smart thing and save your program before running it

   - Don't Save Changes – lets you live dangerously and run your program without saving any changes, possibly crashing your computer and losing your changes as well

4. Click OK.

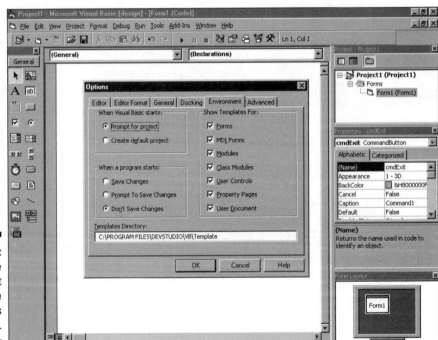

Figure 25-6:
The Environment tab in the Options dialog box.

Chapter 26
Unique Visual Basic Effects

● ●

In This Chapter

▶ Making a scrolling marquee

▶ Creating a splash screen

▶ Displaying the Tip of the Day

▶ Hiding (and displaying) Easter Eggs

● ●

Some people learn best by watching. Others learn best by listening. Still others learn best by experimenting on their own, or spending long hours memorizing and studying. But no matter which method you prefer, one of the easiest ways to learn anything is by copying someone else's work.

In the business world this might be known as copyright infringement, and in the programming world it can also be known as copyright infringement if you're not careful. Fortunately, many programmers create simple programs that they generously donate to the public domain for others to study and learn from.

By studying code that you know already works, you can pick up tricks from other programmers. Even better, you can see how another programmer accomplished a task and experiment with doing it faster or more simply.

So to give you a head start creating your own programs, here are some unique programming tips and samples for you to examine and plug into your own Visual Basic programs. Feel free to copy, modify, or include any of the following code in your own programs.

Making a Scrolling Marquee

Scrolling marquees simply spice up the appearance of text. Rather than display a dull message on the screen, a scrolling marquee scrolls text across the screen from left to right as shown in Figure 26-1. Such a display is guaranteed to catch the eye of even the most bored computer user, at least for a moment.

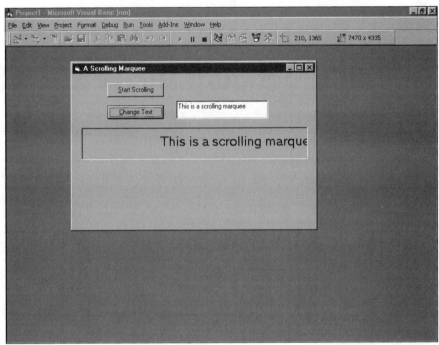

Figure 26-1:
A scrolling
marquee.

To create a scrolling marquee, follow these steps:

1. Click the PictureBox icon in the Visual Basic Toolbox and draw a picture box on the form.

2. Click the Label icon in the Visual Basic Toolbox and draw the label inside the picture box.

3. Open the Properties window (by pressing F4, choosing View⇨Properties Window, or clicking on the Properties window icon on the toolbar).

4. Click the AutoSize property and set its value to True.

5. Click the Visible property and set its value to False.

6. Click the Caption property and type the text that you want to appear in the scrolling marquee.

7. Double-click the Font property to display the Font dialog box.

8. Change the font, font style, or size if you want, and then click OK.

9. Click the Timer icon in the Visual Basic Toolbox and draw the timer anywhere on the form.

10. Press F7 or choose View⇨Code.

11. Add the following code inside the `Timer1_Timer` event procedure:

```
Private Sub Timer1_Timer()
   Label1.Move (Label1.Left) - 50
   If (Label1.Left + Label1.Width) < 0 Then
      Label1.Left = Picture1.Width + 10
   End If
End Sub
```

Note: To make the scrolling marquee faster, choose a number higher than 50 in the second line. To make the scrolling marquee slower, choose a number lower than 50 in the second line.

12. Click the Object list box in the Code window and choose Form to display the `Form_Load` event procedure.

13. Add the following code inside the `Form_Load` event procedure:

```
Private Sub Form_Load()
   Timer1.Interval = 50
   Timer1.Enabled = True
   Label1.Left = Picture1.Width + 10
   Label1.Visible = True
End Sub
```

Note: To make the scrolling marquee move faster, choose a number lower than 50 in the second line. To make the scrolling marquee slower, choose a number higher than 50 in the second line.

If you don't want to start the scrolling marquee right away, move the four lines in the `Form_Load` event procedure into a command button event procedure. That way, you can start the scrolling marquee by clicking a command button.

Creating a Splash Screen

Load any program and the first thing you see is a splash screen. Splash screens usually display the program's name along with a graphic such as the software company logo. Although splash screens are never necessary, they do provide users with that all-important first impression of your program. Because splash screens are so prevalent in programs today, you may want to create a splash screen for your own programs as well.

Creating splash screens in Visual Basic is surprisingly simple because Visual Basic has already created a generic splash screen that you can add to your programs. To add a splash screen to your program, follow these steps:

1. Choose Project⇨Add Form. The Add Form dialog box appears.

2. Click the Splash Screen icon and click Open. Visual Basic displays a generic splash screen as shown in Figure 26-2.

3. Choose Project⇨Properties to display the Project Properties dialog box.

4. Click the Startup Object list box and choose frmSplash to make the splash screen form the first form that loads when your program runs.

5. Click OK.

6. Click the Timer icon in the Toolbox and draw the Timer control anywhere on the frmSplash form.

7. Open the Properties window (by pressing F4, choosing View⇨Properties Window, or clicking the Properties window icon on the toolbar).

8. Click the Interval property and type a number such as 1000. (An interval of 1000 equals 1 second; an interval of 65,535 is approximately 1 minute. You may have to experiment with the proper interval to display for your splash screen.)

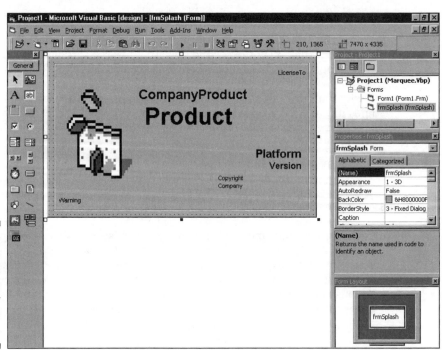

Figure 26-2: A generic splash screen ready for your evil bidding.

9. Choose View⇨Code, or press F7.

10. Type the following in the `Timer1` event procedure:

```
Private Sub Timer1_Timer ()
   Load frmMain      ' frmMain is the first form of your
   Unload frmSplash ' program
   frmMain.Show
End Sub
```

The previous code tells Visual Basic that after the Timer control waits for the time specified by the Interval property, it should load frmMain (assuming that frmMain is the name of the first form of your program), unload frmSplash (your splash screen), and then display frmMain.

By adding the Timer control to your splash screen, your users have a choice of either waiting for the Timer control to make the splash screen go away, or clicking the mouse or pressing a key to make the splash screen disappear.

Unless you want your program to display the generic Visual Basic splash screen, you probably want to modify the splash screen to display your company name, message, logo, and so on. Experiment with creating splash screens for all your programs. Splash screens are a simple yet effective way to make your programs more acceptable to the average user.

Displaying a Tip of the Day

To help guide users, many programs now offer a Tip of the Day dialog box as soon as the program loads. This Tip of the Day dialog box displays a hint that can explain shortcuts or obscure facts that your users might find handy (or just plain amusing) as shown in Figure 26-3.

Typically a Tip of the Day dialog box appears first (or second if you have a splash screen appear first). To create a Tip of the Day dialog box, follow these steps:

1. Choose Project⇨Add Form. The Add Form dialog box appears.

2. Click the Tip of the Day icon and click Open. Visual Basic displays a generic Tip of the Day dialog box as shown in Figure 26-4.

3. Choose View⇨Code, or press F7.

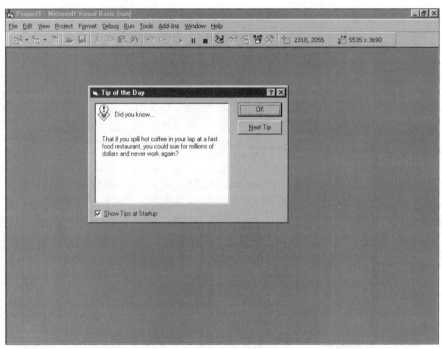

Figure 26-3:
A typical
Tip of
the Day
dialog box.

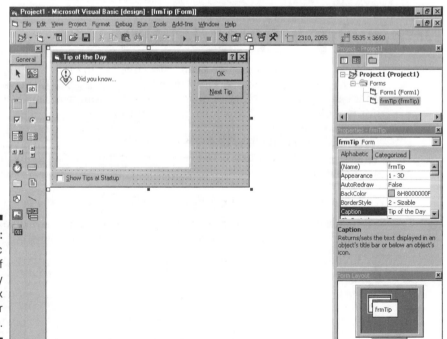

Figure 26-4:
A generic
Tip of
the Day
dialog box
ready for
modifying.

4. Change the Private Sub cmdOK_Click() event procedure as follows:

```
Private Sub cmdOK_Click()
    Unload frmTip    ' Unload the Tip of the Day screen
    Load frmMain     ' Load frmMain (assuming that this
    frmMain.Show     ' is the first form of your
End Sub              ' program
```

Before you can make your Tip of the Day dialog box work, you need to create a text file called TIPOFDAY.TXT to store your tips for your program to use, with each tip on a separate, single line.

Hiding (And Displaying) Easter Eggs

Easter Eggs are messages or pictures that programmers like to hide in their programs. Because many companies frown upon giving individual programmers credit, programmers often hide their names in the program's About window. By pressing the right keys, a user can see a list of the programmers who wrote the program.

Because many programs have Easter Eggs buried in them, why should you leave your program out of the fun? Easter Eggs serve no functional purpose, but they do give programmers something to play around with and they upset their superiors to no end.

Displaying the Windows 95 Easter Egg

In case you want to view the Windows 95 Easter Egg on your own computer, follow these steps:

1. Right click the Windows 95 Desktop.

2. Choose New⇨Folder.

3. Name the folder "and now, the moment you've all been waiting for"

4. Right click on the folder and rename it to "we proudly present for your viewing pleasure"

5. Right click the folder and rename it again to "The Microsoft Windows 95 Product Team!"

6. Open the folder and the Windows 95 credits will appear. The folder will remain so anytime you want to view the credits again, all you have to do is re-open the folder.

In the following example, the Easter Egg is a simple list of names that magically appears out of a boring About dialog box if the user presses the correct keystrokes. To define a secret keystroke to display your program's Easter Egg, first determine which keys you want to use.

For this example, the Easter Egg appears if the user types any keystroke combination that adds up to 19. In Visual Basic, the number 5 is represented by the Ctrl+E keystroke, and the number 7 is represented by the Ctrl+G keystroke. Ctrl+E (5) plus Ctrl+G (7) plus Ctrl+G (7) equals 19. (The number 1 is represented by Ctrl+A, the number 2 is represented by Ctrl+B, and so on up to the number 26, which is represented by Ctrl+Z.) So the Easter Egg appears if the user holds down the Ctrl key and types **EGG**.

Note: Any keystrokes that add up to 19 will trigger the Easter Egg, but at least EGG is something that users can remember easily.

You want the secret keystrokes that reveal your Easter Egg to be easy to remember, but not so common that the user might press them by mistake while using your program.

To create an Easter Egg that appears when the user presses Ctrl+E, Ctrl+G, and Ctrl+G, create a form with a picture box, two labels inside the picture box, and a timer control as shown in Figure 26-5.

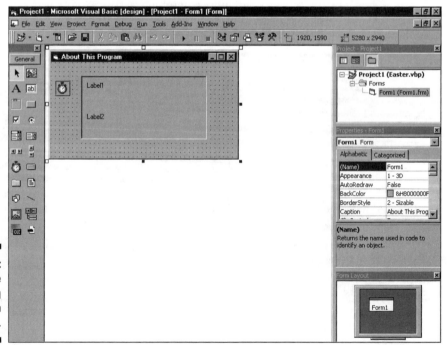

Figure 26-5:
What the Easter Egg program looks like.

Modify the properties as follows:

Object	Property	Setting
Form	Caption	About This Program
	Left	1920
	Height	2940
	Top	1590
	Width	5280
Picture1	Left	840
	Height	1695
	Top	360
	Width	3495

Make sure you draw Label1 and Label2 inside the Picture1 picture box.

Object	Property	Setting
Label1	AutoSize	True
	Height	195
	Left	120
	Top	120
	Width	3135
	WordWrap	True
Label2	AutoSize	True
	Height	195
	Left	120
	Top	960
	Visible	False
	Width	3135
	WordWrap	True
Timer1	Left	120
	Top	480

Type the following in the *(General) (declarations)* part of the Code window:

```
Dim Secret, MoveMe As Integer

Dim NL As String
```

(continued)

(continued)

```
Public Sub EasterEgg()
  Timer1.Interval = 50
  Timer1.Enabled = True
  NL = Chr(13) & Chr(10)
  Label1.Visible = False
  Label2.Visible = True
  Label2.Caption = "Program created by" & NL & NL
           "BotheCat"& NL & "Looney Tunes" & NL & "Scraps
           the Cat"
End Sub
Type the following in the Code window:
Private Sub Form_Load()
  MoveMe = 50
  NL = Chr(13) & Chr(10)
  Label1.Caption = "Microsoft Visual Basic" & NL
     & "Version 5.0" & NL & "Copyright (C) 1996"
     & NL & NL & "Serial number: 123-456-789"
  Label1.Top = 120
  Label2.Top = Picture1.Height
End Sub

Private Sub Picture1_KeyPress(KeyAscii As Integer)
  Secret = Secret + KeyAscii
  If Secret = 19 Then
    EasterEgg
  End If
End Sub

Private Sub Timer1_Timer()
  Label2.Move Label2.Left, Label2.Top - MoveMe
  If Label2.Top < 0 Then
    MoveMe = -MoveMe
  End If
  If Label2.Top > Picture1.Height Then
    MoveMe = -MoveMe
    Timer1.Enabled = False
    Label2.Visible = False
    Label2.Top = Picture1.Height
    Label1.Visible = True
    Secret = 0
  End If
End Sub
```

Index

• *Q* •

• *R* •

The Fun & Easy Way™ to learn about computers and more!

7/29/96

Windows® 3.11 For Dummies,® 3rd Edition
by Andy Rathbone

ISBN: 1-56884-370-4
$16.95 USA/
$22.95 Canada

SUPER STAR

Mutual Funds For Dummies™
by Eric Tyson

ISBN: 1-56884-226-0
$16.99 USA/
$22.99 Canada

SUPER STAR

DOS For Dummies,® 2nd Edition
by Dan Gookin

ISBN: 1-878058-75-4
$16.95 USA/
$22.95 Canada

SUPER STAR

The Internet For Dummies,® 2nd Edition
by John Levine & Carol Baroudi

ISBN: 1-56884-222-8
$19.99 USA/
$26.99 Canada

Personal Finance For Dummies™
by Eric Tyson

ISBN: 1-56884-150-7
$16.95 USA/
$22.95 Canada

SUPER STAR

PCs For Dummies,® 3rd Edition
by Dan Gookin & Andy Rathbone

ISBN: 1-56884-904-4
$16.99 USA/
$22.99 Canada

Macs® For Dummies,® 3rd Edition
by David Pogue

ISBN: 1-56884-239-2
$19.99 USA/
$26.99 Canada

SUPER STAR

The SAT® I For Dummies™
by Suzee Vlk

ISBN: 1-56884-213-9
$14.99 USA/
$20.99 Canada

SUPER STAR

Here's a complete listing of IDG Books' ...For Dummies® titles

Title	Author	ISBN	Price
DATABASE			
Access 2 For Dummies®	by Scott Palmer	ISBN: 1-56884-090-X	$19.95 USA/$26.95 Canada
Access Programming For Dummies®	by Rob Krumm	ISBN: 1-56884-091-8	$19.95 USA/$26.95 Canada
Approach 3 For Windows® For Dummies®	by Doug Lowe	ISBN: 1-56884-233-3	$19.99 USA/$26.99 Canada
dBASE For DOS For Dummies®	by Scott Palmer & Michael Stabler	ISBN: 1-56884-188-4	$19.95 USA/$26.95 Canada
dBASE For Windows® For Dummies®	by Scott Palmer	ISBN: 1-56884-179-5	$19.95 USA/$26.95 Canada
dBASE 5 For Windows® Programming For Dummies®	by Ted Coombs & Jason Coombs	ISBN: 1-56884-215-5	$19.99 USA/$26.99 Canada
FoxPro 2.6 For Windows® For Dummies®	by John Kaufeld	ISBN: 1-56884-187-6	$19.95 USA/$26.95 Canada
Paradox 5 For Windows® For Dummies®	by John Kaufeld	ISBN: 1-56884-185-X	$19.95 USA/$26.95 Canada
DESKTOP PUBLISHING/ILLUSTRATION/GRAPHICS			
CorelDRAW! 5 For Dummies®	by Deke McClelland	ISBN: 1-56884-157-4	$19.95 USA/$26.95 Canada
CorelDRAW! For Dummies®	by Deke McClelland	ISBN: 1-56884-042-X	$19.95 USA/$26.95 Canada
Desktop Publishing & Design For Dummies®	by Roger C. Parker	ISBN: 1-56884-234-1	$19.99 USA/$26.99 Canada
Harvard Graphics 2 For Windows® For Dummies®	by Roger C. Parker	ISBN: 1-56884-092-6	$19.95 USA/$26.95 Canada
PageMaker 5 For Macs® For Dummies®	by Galen Gruman & Deke McClelland	ISBN: 1-56884-178-7	$19.95 USA/$26.95 Canada
PageMaker 5 For Windows® For Dummies®	by Deke McClelland & Galen Gruman	ISBN: 1-56884-160-4	$19.95 USA/$26.95 Canada
Photoshop 3 For Macs® For Dummies®	by Deke McClelland	ISBN: 1-56884-208-2	$19.99 USA/$26.99 Canada
QuarkXPress 3.3 For Dummies®	by Galen Gruman & Barbara Assadi	ISBN: 1-56884-217-1	$19.99 USA/$26.99 Canada
FINANCE/PERSONAL FINANCE/TEST TAKING REFERENCE			
Everyday Math For Dummies™	by Charles Seiter	ISBN: 1-56884-248-1	$14.99 USA/$22.99 Canada
Personal Finance For Dummies™ For Canadians	by Eric Tyson & Tony Martin	ISBN: 1-56884-378-X	$18.99 USA/$24.99 Canada
QuickBooks 3 For Dummies®	by Stephen L. Nelson	ISBN: 1-56884-227-9	$19.99 USA/$26.99 Canada
Quicken 8 For DOS For Dummies,® 2nd Edition	by Stephen L. Nelson	ISBN: 1-56884-210-4	$19.95 USA/$26.95 Canada
Quicken 5 For Macs® For Dummies®	by Stephen L. Nelson	ISBN: 1-56884-211-2	$19.95 USA/$26.95 Canada
Quicken 4 For Windows® For Dummies,® 2nd Edition	by Stephen L. Nelson	ISBN: 1-56884-209-0	$19.95 USA/$26.95 Canada
Taxes For Dummies,™ 1995 Edition	by Eric Tyson & David J. Silverman	ISBN: 1-56884-220-1	$14.99 USA/$20.99 Canada
The GMAT® For Dummies™	by Suzee Vlk, Series Editor	ISBN: 1-56884-376-3	$14.99 USA/$20.99 Canada
The GRE® For Dummies™	by Suzee Vlk, Series Editor	ISBN: 1-56884-375-5	$14.99 USA/$20.99 Canada
Time Management For Dummies™	by Jeffrey J. Mayer	ISBN: 1-56884-360-7	$16.99 USA/$22.99 Canada
TurboTax For Windows® For Dummies®	by Gail A. Helsel, CPA	ISBN: 1-56884-228-7	$19.99 USA/$26.99 Canada
GROUPWARE/INTEGRATED			
ClarisWorks For Macs® For Dummies®	by Frank Higgins	ISBN: 1-56884-363-1	$19.99 USA/$26.99 Canada
Lotus Notes For Dummies®	by Pat Freeland & Stephen Londergan	ISBN: 1-56884-212-0	$19.95 USA/$26.95 Canada
Microsoft® Office 4 For Windows® For Dummies®	by Roger C. Parker	ISBN: 1-56884-183-3	$19.95 USA/$26.95 Canada
Microsoft® Works 3 For Windows® For Dummies®	by David C. Kay	ISBN: 1-56884-214-7	$19.99 USA/$26.99 Canada
SmartSuite 3 For Dummies®	by Jan Weingarten & John Weingarten	ISBN: 1-56884-367-4	$19.99 USA/$26.99 Canada
INTERNET/COMMUNICATIONS/NETWORKING			
America Online® For Dummies,® 2nd Edition	by John Kaufeld	ISBN: 1-56884-933-8	$19.99 USA/$26.99 Canada
CompuServe For Dummies,® 2nd Edition	by Wallace Wang	ISBN: 1-56884-937-0	$19.99 USA/$26.99 Canada
Modems For Dummies,® 2nd Edition	by Tina Rathbone	ISBN: 1-56884-223-6	$19.99 USA/$26.99 Canada
MORE Internet For Dummies®	by John R. Levine & Margaret Levine Young	ISBN: 1-56884-164-7	$19.95 USA/$26.95 Canada
MORE Modems & On-line Services For Dummies®	by Tina Rathbone	ISBN: 1-56884-365-8	$19.99 USA/$26.99 Canada
Mosaic For Dummies,® Windows Edition	by David Angell & Brent Heslop	ISBN: 1-56884-242-2	$19.99 USA/$26.99 Canada
NetWare For Dummies,® 2nd Edition	by Ed Tittel, Deni Connor & Earl Follis	ISBN: 1-56884-369-0	$19.99 USA/$26.99 Canada
Networking For Dummies®	by Doug Lowe	ISBN: 1-56884-079-9	$19.95 USA/$26.95 Canada
PROCOMM PLUS 2 For Windows® For Dummies®	by Wallace Wang	ISBN: 1-56884-219-8	$19.99 USA/$26.99 Canada
TCP/IP For Dummies®	by Marshall Wilensky & Candace Leiden	ISBN: 1-56884-241-4	$19.99 USA/$26.99 Canada

Microsoft and Windows are registered trademarks of Microsoft Corporation. Mac is a registered trademark of Apple Computer. SAT is a registered trademark of the College Entrance Examination Board. GMAT is a registered trademark of the Graduate Management Admission Council. GRE is a registered trademark of the Educational Testing Service. America Online is a registered trademark of America Online, Inc. The "...For Dummies Book Series" logo, the IDG Books Worldwide logos, Dummies Press, and The Fun & Easy Way are trademarks, and ---- For Dummies and ... For Dummies are registered trademarks under exclusive license to IDG Books Worldwide, Inc., from International Data Group, Inc.

For scholastic requests & educational orders please call Educational Sales at 1. 800. 434. 2086

FOR MORE INFO OR TO ORDER, PLEASE CALL ▶ 800. 762. 2974

For volume discounts & special orders please call Corporate Sales, at 415. 655. 3000

Windows is a registered trademark of Microsoft Corporation. Mac is a registered trademark of Apple Computer. OS/2 is a registered trademark of IBM. UNIX is a registered trademark of AT&T. WordPerfect is a registered trademark of Novell. The "...For Dummies Book Series" logo, the IDG Books Worldwide logos, Dummies Press, and The Fun & Easy Way are trademarks, and ---- For Dummies and ... For Dummies are registered trademarks under exclusive license to IDG Books Worldwide, Inc., from International Data Group, Inc.

7/29/96

For scholastic requests & educational orders please call Educational Sales at 1. 800. 434. 2086

FOR MORE INFO OR TO ORDER, PLEASE CALL ▶ 800. 762. 2974

For volume discounts & special orders please call Corporate Sales, at 415. 655. 3000

Order Center: **(800) 762-2974** *(8 a.m.–6 p.m., EST, weekdays)*

Quantity	ISBN	Title	Price	Total

Shipping & Handling Charges

	Description	First book	Each additional book	Total
Domestic	Normal	$4.50	$1.50	$
	Two Day Air	$8.50	$2.50	$
	Overnight	$18.00	$3.00	$
International	Surface	$8.00	$8.00	$
	Airmail	$16.00	$16.00	$
	DHL Air	$17.00	$17.00	$

*For large quantities call for shipping & handling charges.
**Prices are subject to change without notice.

Ship to:

Name _____

Company _____

Address _____

City/State/Zip _____

Daytime Phone _____

Payment: ☐ Check to IDG Books Worldwide (US Funds Only)

☐ VISA ☐ MasterCard ☐ American Express

Card # _____ Expires _____

Signature _____

Subtotal _____

CA residents add
applicable sales tax _____

IN, MA, and MD
residents add
5% sales tax _____

IL residents add
6.25% sales tax _____

RI residents add
7% sales tax _____

TX residents add
8.25% sales tax _____

Shipping _____

Total _____

Please send this order form to:

**IDG Books Worldwide, Inc.
Attn: Order Entry Dept.
7260 Shadeland Station, Suite 100
Indianapolis, IN 46256**

*Allow up to 3 weeks for delivery.
Thank you!*

IDG BOOKS WORLDWIDE, INC. END-USER LICENSE AGREEMENT

Read This. You should carefully read these terms and conditions before opening the software packet(s) included with this book ("Book"). This is a license agreement ("Agreement") between you and IDG Books Worldwide, Inc. ("IDGB"). By opening the accompanying software packet(s), you acknowledge that you have read and accept the following terms and conditions. If you do not agree and do not want to be bound by such terms and conditions, promptly return the Book and the unopened software packet(s) to the place you obtained them for a full refund.

1. **License Grant**. IDGB grants to you (either an individual or entity) a nonexclusive license to use one copy of the enclosed software program(s) (collectively, the "Software") solely for your own personal or business purposes on a single computer (whether a standard computer or a workstation component of a multiuser network). The Software is in use on a computer when it is loaded into temporary memory (i.e., RAM) or installed into permanent memory (e.g., hard disk, CD-ROM, or other storage device). IDGB reserves all rights not expressly granted herein.

2. **Ownership**. IDGB is the owner of all right, title, and interest, including copyright, in and to the compilation of the Software recorded on the disk(s)/CD-ROM. Copyright to the individual programs on the disk(s)/CD-ROM is owned by the author or other authorized copyright owner of each program. Ownership of the Software and all proprietary rights relating thereto remain with IDGB and its licensors.

3. **Restrictions on Use and Transfer**.

   (a) You may only (i) make one copy of the Software for backup or archival purposes, or (ii) transfer the Software to a single hard disk, provided that you keep the original for backup or archival purposes. You may not (i) rent or lease the Software, (ii) copy or reproduce the Software through a LAN or other network system or through any computer subscriber system or bulletin-board system, or (iii) modify, adapt, or create derivative works based on the Software.

   (b) You may not reverse engineer, decompile, or disassemble the Software. You may transfer the Software and user documentation on a permanent basis, provided that the transferee agrees to accept the terms and conditions of this Agreement and you retain no copies. If the Software is an update or has been updated, any transfer must include the most recent update and all prior versions.

4. **Restrictions on Use of Individual Programs**. You must follow the individual requirements and restrictions detailed for each individual program in the "What's on the Disk?" section at the back of this Book. These limitations are contained in the individual license agreements recorded on the disk(s)/CD-ROM. These restrictions may include a requirement that after using the program for the period of time specified in its text, the user must pay a registration fee or discontinue use. By opening the Software packet(s), you will be agreeing to abide by the licenses and restrictions for these individual programs. None of the material on this disk(s) or listed in this Book may ever be distributed, in original or modified form, for commercial purposes.

5. Limited Warranty.

(a) IDGB warrants that the Software and disk(s)/CD-ROM are free from defects in materials and workmanship under normal use for a period of sixty (60) days from the date of purchase of this Book. If IDGB receives notification within the warranty period of defects in materials or workmanship, IDGB will replace the defective disk(s)/CD-ROM.

(b) IDGB AND THE AUTHOR OF THE BOOK DISCLAIM ALL OTHER WARRANTIES, EXPRESS OR IMPLIED, INCLUDING WITHOUT LIMITATION IMPLIED WARRANTIES OF MERCHANTABILITY AND FITNESS FOR A PARTICULAR PURPOSE, WITH RESPECT TO THE SOFTWARE, THE PROGRAMS, THE SOURCE CODE CONTAINED THEREIN, AND/OR THE TECHNIQUES DESCRIBED IN THIS BOOK. IDGB DOES NOT WARRANT THAT THE FUNCTIONS CONTAINED IN THE SOFTWARE WILL MEET YOUR REQUIREMENTS OR THAT THE OPERATION OF THE SOFTWARE WILL BE ERROR FREE.

(c) This limited warranty gives you specific legal rights, and you may have other rights which vary from jurisdiction to jurisdiction.

6. Remedies.

(a) IDGB's entire liability and your exclusive remedy for defects in materials and workmanship shall be limited to replacement of the Software, which may be returned to IDGB with a copy of your receipt at the following address: Disk Fulfillment Department, Attn: More Visual Basic 5 For Windows For Dummies, IDG Books Worldwide, Inc., 7260 Shadeland Station, Ste. 100, Indianapolis, IN 46256, or call 1-800-762-2974. Please allow 3–4 weeks for delivery. This Limited Warranty is void if failure of the Software has resulted from accident, abuse, or misapplication. Any replacement Software will be warranted for the remainder of the original warranty period or thirty (30) days, whichever is longer.

(b) In no event shall IDGB or the author be liable for any damages whatsoever (including without limitation damages for loss of business profits, business interruption, loss of business information, or any other pecuniary loss) arising from the use of or inability to use the Book or the Software, even if IDGB has been advised of the possibility of such damages.

(c) Because some jurisdictions do not allow the exclusion or limitation of liability for consequential or incidental damages, the above limitation or exclusion may not apply to you.

7. U.S. Government Restricted Rights.
Use, duplication, or disclosure of the Software by the U.S. Government is subject to restrictions stated in paragraph (c) (1) (ii) of the Rights in Technical Data and Computer Software clause of DFARS 252.227-7013, and in subparagraphs (a) through (d) of the Commercial Computer — Restricted Rights clause at FAR 52.227-19, and in similar clauses in the NASA FAR supplement, when applicable.

8. General.
This Agreement constitutes the entire understanding of the parties and revokes and supersedes all prior agreements, oral or written, between them and may not be modified or amended except in a writing signed by both parties hereto which specifically refers to this Agreement. This Agreement shall take precedence over any other documents that may be in conflict herewith. If any one or more provisions contained in this Agreement are held by any court or tribunal to be invalid, illegal, or otherwise unenforceable, each and every other provision shall remain in full force and effect.

What's on the Disk?

As long as somebody hasn't taken a razor blade and sliced open the plastic envelope in the back of this book, you should have a single 3.5-inch floppy disk that contains various sample programs from different chapters of the book.

To help you find a particular sample program, just look in the appropriate directory. For example, if you want to find the sample program for Chapter 13, look in the directory named Chapter-13 on the floppy disk. For example, look at the following table:

What's on the Disk

Directory Name	Program Name
Chapter-13	
Area chart	AreaChart
Bar chart	BarChart
Line chart	LineChart
Pie chart	PieChart

While you can run the sample programs directly off the floppy disk, you should copy the files onto your hard disk. Not only will the programs run faster from your hard disk, but then you also protect the floppy disk from any modifications you may make.